ESCAPE FROM THE
GOLDEN CAGE

ESCAPE FROM THE GOLDEN CAGE

An insight for working women who believe in themselves and
urge to balance their professional and family life successfully

ARTI KOTAK TRIKLANI

PARTRIDGE

ISBN: Softcover   978-1-5437-0545-4
               eBook   978-1-5437-0546-1

Print information available on the last page.

To order additional copies of this book, contact
Partridge India
000 800 10062 62
orders.india@partridgepublishing.com

www.partridgepublishing.com/india

CONTENTS

This book is dedicated with
deepest love and respect to
those women who play the vital role
of funambulist for their professional and family life.

ACKNOWLEDGMENT

First and foremost, thank you God, the All-knowing and the All-wise who has given me the great opportunity and the great blessings to accomplish this work.

I thank my husband, Kapil Triklani, for his invaluable support and assistance for the completion of this book.

I thank my two years old son, Jashvardhan Triklani who constantly supported me without disturbance.

Huge thanks to my entire family, my parents - Devidas Kotak and Sushila Kotak; my in-laws - Chandrakant Triklani and Mangla Triklani for their constant support for my progress.

I thank my maid servants - Millicent, Mercy and my friends of neighbourhood who helped me rigorously to take care of my child which motivated me to accomplish the work successfully.

Publishers and editors of Partridge Publication, who helped me wholeheartedly to fulfil my dream of publishing a book.

My professors and my college friends who gave me critical comments on my manuscript.

Huge thanks to women around me who helped me for my research in this particular area. I am grateful to them for contributing their time for filling up my questionnaire to go forward in my research which helped me to write effective dialogues; and also helped to portray the characters in an authentic way.The research assisted me to give a realistic touch to my fictional characters.

PROLOGUE

'Good morning ma'am! Should I bring you a cup of coffee? asked Saroj (maid servant)

'No, thanks dear.' responded I.

Saroj: 'Ma'am, if you don't mind can I ask you a question?'

'Sure dear.' responded I by keeping my specs on the table.

Saroj: 'I have always found you reading books, don't you get bored?'

'No dear, I love to be with books, it's my passion or I can say books are my best friends.' replied I with a gentle smile.

Saroj: 'You are down in the dumps, what are you reading ma'am?'

'I am reading 'I am Malala by Malala Yousafzai', these kinds of books make me upset and make me ponder on the women who still are not free and not permitted to fulfil their dreams and goals of life. Even today in this century, they are forced to fight for accomplishing their ambitions.' replied I by flipping the pages of book.

Saroj: 'Ma'am, you were also writing a story of a girl who struggled for her dreams and ambitions, is it completed?'

'Yes, it was my story, dear.' replied I

Saroj: 'Yours? But you are independent and successful working lady, how can it be your story?'

'I have walked through the fire for this, dear. ' replied I by looking at her and giving a gentle smile.

Saroj: 'Can I read your book, please'

'Sure dear, here it is.' I handed over the book to her.

Saroj: 'May I start reading it now?'

'Sure.'

She starts reading………..

This book throws light on the social issues which take place within four walls of house, especially with women. These kinds of issues might not be brought to light as women themselves are found at the drop of a hat to divulge them outside the home due to discouragement but these minor issues take the mode of major ones sometimes. These are not the apparent problems like terrorism, religious rebels, pollution issues, racisms, global warming, etc. These are the hidden issues which suppress and destroy the whole life of women silently, especially those women who have their own wings to fly.

This book is for women by a woman. I am a woman who want to fulfill her dreams, goals and ambitions. But I have born in a small town of India and I am a daughter of a middle class family. I am hardworking and sincere about my education and want to achieve my goals by crossing various difficulties. I want to help my father financially with the help of my work. I want the society to expel the belief that only a son can be the pillar of the family. Somehow I struggled and managed to accomplish my dreams before marriage but now I am a married woman; so do I need to give up on my career? Should I stop dreaming of my career success as I am a daughter-in-law and mother of a child? Marriage and motherhood are considered to be god gifts. Is our God that much cruel that He would love to snatch away our rights to dream as successful women in our career? If God is supportive, then who puts the barrier on a woman to have her freedom, independence and education? We blame this male dominated society but we never think about women. Does a woman support a woman for her progress in life?

It is story of a girl who struggles and fights with the narrow-minded society to be a working woman and also combats to help her father financially.

Thank you for reading my story.

Here, I have given my rash efforts to share my views on the protocols whipped up for working women by the Indian society by giving them the metaphor of gold. In all most the cases, women have played a vital role to agitate these protocols for women.

Gold. Such a tempting word! When we hear this word, mind gets a kick to have a lot of thoughts. It is said, 'Gold dust blinds all eyes.' Especially women's eyes. It attracts women more. When a woman hears this word, she starts thinking about buying it for wearing or for investment. They might not have any problem to buy the golden bungalows or palace. They might also love to buy all decorative things of gold. Just imagine if today's girl gets a golden bungalow with all golden furniture in it, and she is considered the queen of that bungalow but she will have to follow one condition that she won't be allowed to go out of that bungalow and she will be required to spend her entire life inside that bungalow. Will this gold be able to make her life happy or satisfactory or she will find that Golden Bungalow as a Golden Cage? Is Gold that much important for today's girl? Here, gold is the metaphor of our society's customs, beliefs and rules agitated for a girl who wants to fulfil her dreams. Why is an Indian girl always required to be the queen of a golden bungalow and kitchen only where she must be found in Salwar – Kurta making chapattis on stove and must be found with spatula and spoon in her hand cooking for her father, brother, husband and in-laws? Does today's girl really need that much gold? Will she be able to carry that much burden of it? Weight of that much gold will destroy all her thoughts, dreams and happiness. Of course, she can wear little bit of light weighted gold in this century, but that much gold will suffocate her and she won't be able to even breathe out properly. It is very difficult for her to take place of a free bird which has all the freedom of life but at least, she can demand a little bit of freedom from this society for her thoughts and for her own life.

CHAPTER 1

It was 5:30 in the morning, the weather was pretty hot. The sun had got up like a baby and was about to start painting the dark black sky into a deep blue and golden yellow. The bright looking milky clouds were about to get up from sleep and pop out from the sky to travel around it. Fresh, cool and calm air started whistling like a silent ghost. Colorful birds woke up and started twitting their morning melody. The little colorful cute butterflies were dancing and going from tress to plants, from plants to bunches. The green and brown countless leaves whispered to each other about their morning plans. The streets of Morbi (a small town in Gujarat) were silent and calm. All of a sudden, in that silence, a scream of a lady was heard from one house. The lady was screaming due to labor pain. All the members of the family woke up and took her to the hospital. Within an hour, a cute - little girl was born with fair completion and chubby cheeks. It was me - Aditi. I was born with few qualities gifted by God. They were purity, innocence, ignorance, curiosity, joy-fullness, trust-fullness and love. But today, I have grown up with other qualities like understanding, knowledge, discrimination, expectations, comparisons and many more which I have achieved from this society and people around me.

I am Aditi, an Indian girl who hails from a small town of Gujarat. I was born to my parents after three years of their marriage. After worshiping intensely, my parents got me. They felt to be in seventh heaven and spark of joy in their eyes made happy to everyone in the family. But Yamuna aunty (a normal looking woman with jealous nature), my eldest aunt, was happier even than my parents as Sarita, my mother, gave birth to a daughter and she had a son so my mother could not be the winner in the competition of high social status which was based on the gender discrimination and that kept my aunt's ego high as she was a mother of a son. She felt secure to hold her status higher in the family by being the mother of a son. Women in this kind of society feels superior due to their luck and their husband's wisdom, they are least concerned about their own thoughts and actions. I understood that phenomena by growing up in the same society. Many a times, I saw my mother getting cracked down not only by men but also by women although she was talented and full of wisdom. She carried a very nice feminine and joy full persona with good looks. Despite her dark completion, she used to carry herself very beautifully. She had very long and dark black hair. She had a very good physique. I used to find my mother being suppressed by my grandmother, Kaushalya Lakhani - a lady with short height, with red long hair and dark brown lips. She almost the time used to be busy to carry herself nicely with simple panjabi dress and long choti with green bangles and golden rings on her hands. My grand mother couldn't carry the can of wise decisions at right time as she was extremely pampered by her mother, Kamla Sunera - a very fat looking and highly dominating woman. She used to stay in the same town and always used to be with my grandmother and used to take decisions for her. But Yamuna aunt was a very difficult woman to handle as she had a great support of her sisters who also lived in the same town and her parents and brothers also lived in the nearby city of our town so she was always provided enough amount of support by each person around her and above all her husband means my uncle - Bharat Lakhani, the eldest son of the family, supported her a lot. He who was considered to be the God of the entire family. The law of the whole family was in their hands so ruling the whole family by the road of iron became their nature. It was really painful to see my parents dominated by the family members without any reason. I have seen my mother's charming persona and helping nature since my childhood. She was very active and good at everything- cooking, dancing, stitching, carrying herself in a well mannered, etc. She was always there to give respect to all family members and relatives of my grandparents. In a nutshell, my father brought a nice, well-mannered and clever maid for the family who always used to be ready for serving my grandparents, my father, my all five uncles and my two buas and all relatives and guests. So my Grandma was thrilled to bits as she got full time maid who worked for the whole family at free of cost and my grandmother's mother was happier as her daughter got full rest and time for watching TV and meeting with friends and enjoying for the whole day. After working up a sweat, she didn't get enough consideration, why? The reason of her suffering was Devang Lakhani, my father, a tall heighted person with white completion having black eyes and dark brown lips. She had to tolerate many things because of my father's calm and timid nature. He never fought for his own rights nor for his wife. Despite working hard, my father also didn't get that respect. The tragedy was my mother lost her whole life in suffering due to the timidity and discouragement of my father.

In this kind of society, almost wives are found relying on their husbands despite their intelligence and cleverness. Especially after marriage, a girl's life changes completely. Somehow they themselves accept the unwanted change. If luck bestows a girl a smart and clever husband, she also achieves the honour of smartness despite her being a dumb woman, and a clever girl might lose her whole existence if she has not got a clever and witty husband. That has been continuing to happen with many girls especially in small towns of India where the people of society possess that kind of narrow mentality. Even today our society is not exempted from various problem. Dowry system is one of them; many people still follow it rigorously.

I felt so painful when I got to know about my mother's first welcome at my dad's place. Everyone was standing outside to welcome the new bride. Some of the ladies were singing the marriage songs and some of them were dancing, few were playing the small drum at the doorsteps for the welcome.

'Oh! The procession is about to arrive.' whispered the ladies standing for welcoming the new bride.

'What you think how much gold will she bring?' asked one of the ladies to other ladies.

One of the females, 'I have heard that the girl is very fashionable, whatever she will bring, it is going to be classy.'

My mother (the second daughter-in-law of Lakhani family) entered her second home by knocking the pot filled with rice and was taken to the whole house to span her foot steps in each and every corner of the place. After few hours, she was asked to open her luggage that she got from her parents in dowry. She opened it to show everyone what she was gifted by her father means my maternal grandpa. Each female's eye became an eagle eye. They kept on staring at the bags which were about to be opened by the new bride. My mother took out all the clothes, jewellery and many other things for the family. Each and every woman started giving positive and negative comments on the things. It was sounded as if the family went for buying the things rather than wedding. My mother showed the branded make-up kit by saying that it was her favourite thing gifted by her father.

'Yes, it is branded and very nice also; better to keep it for Raksha, our sister-in-law. When she gets married, we will gift it to her. She will achieve much prestige by showing that kind of thing to her in-laws and your gold necklace is also very unique, heavy and very expensive. Keep it in the middle of everybody. It will decorate each lady of our family. I hope you don't mind.' told Yamuna aunty by snatching it from my mother's hand.

'No it is alright, that makes no difference whoever uses it.' my mother gave it without showing exclusion on her face.

As a daughter-in-law, she started working for hours and hours at home for everybody. She started taking care of each individual in the family. After few months, she got used to with the kitchen work of thirteen members of the family. She achieved good practise of cooking for all members of the family single-handedly as it was the rule in the family that only younger daughter-in-law was supposed to manage all the kitchen work. So it became very easy for all members to have a free and energetic cook as my mother was very enthusiastic and good cook from beginning. She used to cook both very well - veg and non-veg. My grandmother and other family members were very happy with my mother, as far as Yamuna aunty was consult, she was also very happy as she also got somebody to dominate on and had the luxury of having everything ready on table but it was very difficult for her to digest my mother's cleverness and smartness. She started feeling a universal problem- Female Jealousy. But my mother's life kept on going through extreme work-load of house, welcoming of numerous guests and serving them single-handedly, a lot of difficulties and other family crisis. She accepted all as gospel but she could not tolerate my father's insult in the family as it became very often in the family, my uncles and even my grand- father used to insult my father as he was not smart enough, although he was very hard-working. Instead of encouraging him, they used to demotivate him for everything.

Saroj (Maid servant) : 'Ma'am, the situation is getting worst day by day in the story. Has it really happened?'

Me : 'Yes dear.'

Saroj : 'Then why didn't your parents raise their voice for their rights?'

Me: 'That is their biggest mistake for their struggling life, I don't blame only their destiny but they themselves are more responsible for it.'

Saroj: 'Didn't even your grand parents support them?'

Me : 'Not at all. I have learnt over the period of time, if you don't stand by yourself, nobody else will stand by you in any situation of your life.'

Saroj : 'You are right, ma'am.'

Me : 'Sometimes, these kinds of situations create disrespect towards Indian joined families. But Indian woman is bound to sacrifice herself for everything. My mother wanted to do something in her life, she was very good at creative things but in the whole big family and house-hold work, she lost herself and also her all creative works. She was doing all that as she was an Indian daughter, wife and daughter-in-law. Slowly and gradually, situation went bad in the family. My mother and father became slaves in the family. Especially my father, he was a good follower and became the victim of his each brother's order. The family owned two shops of ladies saris; one in the town and the another one in the nearby town but my father was never allowed to deal with customers as my all uncles always subdued him for his less skills. He was never given opportunity to prove himself. As my elder aunt and uncle were the ruler of the family, they started dominating even my grand-parents.'

Saroj : 'But mam, it is injustice.'

Me : 'Oh dear ! *'Injustice in families'* is the common policy since the time of Ramayana and Mahabharata. Despite knowing the history of our epics, still we have not been able to stand for ourselves or fight for our rights, that is uncommon. We always cry over split milk or we are accustomed to complain about the matters rather than their solutions.'

Saroj : 'It is true ma'am, we always feel fear of society and the same fear motivates the society to go in wrong directions. Mam, I want to continue reading, May I?'

Me : 'Sure dear, you continue reading, I will finish some kitchen stuff.'

Saroj : 'Thanks ma'am.'

Bharat uncle said to my grand-father : 'Now it is time to get married of Mohan (my third uncle). All family members are happy and busy with shopping and marriage preparations. But there is a problem of small house as family members are going to be increased. There is a need to build a house upstairs but as usual financial condition is not in favour as there are many expenses of marriage and gold for new daughter-in-law.'

My grand-father said after thinking for a while : 'Why not to borrow gold from Yamuna and Sarita to build a new house upstairs? We will make gold for them as per our financial convenience.'

Bharat uncle : 'Let me first talk to Yamuna and Sarita.'
'Alright, go ahead.'

Bharat uncle went to the room in tension to take permission from Yamuna aunt. Yamuna aunt denied and said, 'How is it possible? This family is always in financial struggle, if we give our gold, I am sure we are never going to get it back and what we are going to get from this family?' But it is the suggestion or order from papa. Ask Sarita and see what she says about it.

Sarita : 'It is difficult, I am sure we get or we might not get our gold back, but it is our family so I think we should support them. God will give us better fruit in other forms.'

Yamuna aunty murmured in anger, 'Such a foolish female !'

My mother and Yamuna aunty gave the whole gold to my grandfather to construct the house. They also gave the gold which was given by their maternal parents as their marriage gift as they both were promised that they would get their gold back within few years.

My mother forgot about the given gold and she was the happiest one in the family for my uncle's marriage as she thought after ten years, somebody would come to help her in the kitchen and my mother started dreaming to have at least some relaxation from the whole kitchen work. Finally the day came, my uncle tied the knot and my new aunt, Kumud Lakhani, a short heighted and very fare lady with pink lips, entered the home in bridal wear by knocking the pot full of rice and all family members were very happy to welcome the new member of the family. According to the rule of the family, the younger daughter-in-law was supposed to do the kitchen work and elder one would help the mother-in-law in cleaning the house, chopping the vegetables and other routine works of the house. My mother followed the rule strictly for ten years and she got tired of doing that. She did it by wrapping duppata on the head even in the hot summer of March and April.

Female in our country accept this slavery very easily and they expect the same things from the coming generation. There is nothing wrong to attend upon the elders but to do slavery is wrong, if any female doesn't want to do anything excepting household work, there is no problem at all as it is her own wish but if she is forced to do nothing excepting household work especially after marriage, and she doesn't give fight against it, it is just a female's fault. Of course, to maintain house and to convert it into a home, it is her real job, she must do it. She can manage the time for household work, taking care of children and some creative stuff for herself, too. If she is allowed to fulfil her dreams, she would feel happy and satisfied and if she is happy by herself, she would be able to make everyone happy in the family. She must get that feeling that she is doing something even for herself. Whatever it can be, painting, yoga, exercise, reading, watching good movies, etc. She must have her own space to make herself happy. This happiness will make her do many good things for others.

But in our society, people don't want a human being in the form of a daughter-in-law, they want a machine which must keep on working by pressing its buttons. She must not have her own thoughts and perceptions, she can't have her own friends and if some guests come, all members of family are allowed to sit together with them, have fun but daughter-in-laws are not allowed to have all. They are ordered to just come out, bow down before the guests having dupatta on head and start their job of a servant to serve the guests. They can't have their own relations with anybody. Female have accepted by themselves that after marriage they are supposed to stop living for themselves.

In that case, my new aunt was very sharp and different; she always used to live for herself first. She started behaving very cunningly and smartly with everyone in the family.

On the third day of her marriage she came to the kitchen and said with confidence, 'Namaste everyone! I need to clarify one thing that I am not so good at cooking and I have never made chapattis.' my mother got shocked to see a new bride speaking with much confidence. My grand- mother always played the role of a blind judge. She never took any step for right things or right actions. My new aunt didn't pay any attention to house-hold work, she always used to do all works in slow motion deliberately so other members could complete the work fast and she could have relaxation.

'Mummy, it is about to be 12:00 p.m, Kumud has not yet come down. Papa and children will be back just in half an hour. When will the food be ready?' said my mother to my grandmother with little worry.

'Oh! She is still upstairs, she has not come yet.' Looking down, my grand-mother said, 'Sarita you start cooking, what difference it makes if you cook!'

My mother started preparation for lunch and whispered, 'Today it makes no difference, where had you all been before ten years? Why did nobody follow the same rule before ten years?

Even Yamuna aunty said while wiping the mirror of the room, 'No problem Sarita, you start cooking.'

My mother whispered again, 'Today no one has any problem, what about my problem of ten years?' I have been doing it since ten years without any consideration, today she got all the consideration without doing anything, why to face injustice all the time for each thing at home as well as at shop?'

My father was also facing numerous problems and injustice for each thing without any reason.

One night, 'I am disturbed a lot.' said my father keeping his hand on his head.

'Why? Is everything all right?' asked my mother keeping her dupatta on the bed and with much tiredness on the face.

'I know I am little less intelligent and smart than them but I am their elder brother, I have also my self-respect. I am the father of two daughters now. They are my younger brothers but they use abusive words for me and they also insult me all the time without any reason, especially Bharat. Being my elder brother, I respect him but he always bullies me in front of everybody, today he used so many abusive words in front of all brothers and customers. It is too much now, every day I cannot tolerate this.. I know even at home you work for the whole day in the kitchen despite being the second elder daughter-in-law of family. You have been working for my family since 13 years but I have also started observing now that you don't get the same consideration as others are getting despite their less dedication towards the family and our daughters are also suffering because of that. I am sorry, this situation has occurred because of me. But not more. We will not suffer from now onwards due to our less confidence.' said my father by changing his shirt.

'Will not suffer now-on-wards means? What do you want to say? I am not getting you', my mother asked with surprise.

'We will leave the house, we will start staying apart from the family.' replied my father showing less confidence.

'You have gone mad. We have two daughters and you are not clever enough to earn enough money even for survival.' claimed my mother with confidence. 'Above all we don't have a son, I want my both the daughters to be educated and independent so they don't face any such insulting situations or problems in their future that we have been facing since long.'

Indian women of that time always wanted to have a son but if they didn't have one, they would always use the words, 'I want my daughter to be like sons.' Ultimately they would never keep a son's value down. My mother was also one of them.

'Trust me, I will work hard and do whatever I can do, I will start a new business, we might have less facilities, we might eat less but at least, we will have a chapatti of our respect.' my father tried hard to convince my mother by wiping her tears.

'I am also tired of tortures and injustice. Despite giving various years of love, respect and hard-work to the family, no one takes it in consideration. All members in neighbourhood, other relatives and friends always respect us and love us but we don't get dignity and honour from our own family members, that hurts a lot.' said my mother.

'Each family has family issues but this is too much now, please you support me so that I can do a respectful work and can stand on my own feet.' said my father looking into my mother's eyes.

Both kept on thinking for the whole night with tearful eyes. The alarm bell rang and it was the time to go to school for me and my sister, and time to follow the routine. It was Saturday night; my father came home with the echo in his ear of one abusive word uttered by Bharat uncle which was 'You Beggar…'

Sunday morning, 'I want to be apart and want to start my own business with respect.' told my father in front of the whole family.

'Oh! The star is rising now…ha...ha...ha ' my all uncles started laughing in loud and devil form.

'Please don't laugh. I am serious. ' said my father with less confidence and keeping his eyes down.

'But what will you do? We can't do it as we don't have sufficient property that we can give you your share.' said my grandfather.

'I will do the business of raw material of saris, it is in demand nowadays, for that I need some raw-material.'

After a lot of discussion and fight, said my grandfather with little anger on his face, 'Alright, we will give you that; let us see; where you reach.'

After two days, my younger uncle, Shyam Lakhani said to Bharat uncle 'Devang is right, nowadays this business is in the demand and there is not much competition in this business, why can't we start this business instead of giving him the raw-material?'

'But father has promised to Devang to provide him the raw-material for his business.'

'We will give him something else as his share and we will keep this for us.'

'What else is there to give him?'

'We will give him a room upstairs for his residence, business he will manage by himself; he can find a job also.'

'But he is not much smart and educated, where will he work and how will he survive with wife and two daughters?'

'He might find some labour work.'

After a lot of discussion, they confirmed that they won't provide the raw-material to my father. As usual my grandfather couldn't rebel against my elder uncle.

'We will not give you the raw-material for your new business.' said my uncles to my father.

'But we discussed about it and now why are you refusing for it?' asked my father with worried face.

'As we want to start this business.'

My father looked at my grandfather but he couldn't make eye-contacts with him and looked down. My father understood everything and stop arguing with them.

'Alright, give me cash of 1 lack, I will handle everything by myself.' requested my father.

'Nope, we don't have that much money, we can't give you cash.' said my uncles bluntly.

'If I don't have shop, home, qualification, cash and raw-material for business, how will I survive? And here I don't get any opportunity to do anything. I am always disrespected without no reasons so does my wife.' said my father with grief in his eyes.

My father went out to relax his depression.

'No, I will not let you give him the house upstairs, I want to own a room there' said Yamuna aunty to her husband

'But we live in other town, we just come here once in a month, then what will you do with the room upstairs? At least we will have to give something to him for survival' said my uncle.

'I don't know anything, if they leave the house, who will handle the whole kitchen as Sarita has been doing everything since long.' said my aunt.

'Let them go, if they leave, there will be only four brothers for sharing the property.' said my uncle being clever and practical.

Next morning, in the sitting room, all family members got together including kids.

'Sorry, we won't be able to give you anything.' said Bharat uncle.

'You don't have even respect to give, so what else can be expected from you' said my father. 'Alright. We will leave without anything.' said my father with frighten eyes and tension of survival on his head.

Inside the room, my mother said, 'No, we can't leave the house without any share, we have two daughters and don't have a son, how will you manage everything?' she always used to pity on themselves for not having a son. At that time, she was behaving as if a son would do all the miracles at a very early age.

'Trust me; I will keep you happy and will give you a respectful life' said my father. 'No, I don't trust you.' said my mother with anger.

After a lot of fights and discussions, my father convinced her for the same.

It is said answers of all questions regarding the problems of life have been hidden in the Bhagavad Geeta.

It has been said in chapter - 1 shloka – 38

यद्यप्येते न पश्यन्ति लोभोपहतचेतस:।
कुलक्षयकृतं दोषं मित्रद्रोहे च पातकम्॥३८॥

**Even if these people, immersed in greed, do not see
the sin involved in the destruction of their families
and in opposing their friends and relatives.**

Greed makes a person go beyond any limitation in life.
Greed can be for many things. In Bhagavad Geeta, we are
asked to keep ourselves away from greed but is it possible
in this century? Today's psychology has given a different
theory of greed. Somehow, that theory gives positive signs
for greedy people as without greed, a person, community,
or society may lack the motivation to build or achieve, move
or change—and may also be rendered more vulnerable to
the greed of others. Greed, though an imperfect force, is the
only consistent human motivation, and produces preferable
economic and social outcomes most of the time and under
most conditions. Like it or not, our society mostly operates
on greed. Indeed, greed seems to be the driving force behind
all successful societies. There is nothing wrong to follow
the greed but it should not meet the jealousy as jealousy is
the cousin of greed and that ruins a person completely in
any century. Our Modern Geeta might follow the positive
aspects of greed for one's success and survival but can
never favour jealousy. As fulfillment of greed might provide
satisfaction of life but jealousy can never. Modern Geeta
manifests to be happy in life despite carrying the symptom
of greed but also manifests not to convert it into jealousy
which might destroy your family, friends and yourself, too.

CHAPTER 2

Next Morning, it front of everybody, my father announced his decision, 'I want to leave the house with the family.' Everybody seemed so sad, especially my mother as she was extremely family oriented lady, she never thought of leaving the family. She spent thirteen years of her life with the same family. Despite many tyrannies, she used to face everything and used to work silently but didn't want to be apart from the family. Despite bountiful problems in the family, she used to find the ways to be happy and to keep everybody united. So it was very difficult for her to fall apart from the big family.

They left the house or it can be said that they were forced to leave the house in 1995, since then they got their self respect but with a very struggling life. It is said true respect and love are not easy and free to achieve, my parents realized that. They paid price for it and the price was misery in life for each and everything.

In the beginning, my father found a house on rent in a very normal area. The house was very old and big. It consisted of eight rooms and five kitchens. It was giving the look of a haunted house. Many people were living there on rent. In that big house, my father could find one room and a very small kitchen with a common toilet-bathroom among twenty-nine members living around. The room that we got was with broken walls and window shutters couldn't be locked and they kept on ratting outside. The ceiling had big halls. It was very difficult to survive there in the monsoon and above all, the backside view of the house was extremely unhygienic and was sounded as a mega dustbin where people of the whole society used to throw the garbage so after 7 o'clock, lots of mosquitoes used to come to visit our room. It was so difficult to survive there and above all outside of the place, there was a Pan-Shop which was a place of smoking and drinking for various kinds of people. In that case, that area also caused safety issues. That situation made my mother think about her gold that she gave to build the house of her brother-in-laws and she didn't even get the right of owning a single room in that house. What kind of injustice it was!

My father didn't have any source of income so it was the only affordable place to live in. In the first month after separation, he needed to pay for house-rent, shop-rent, gas-bill, light-bill, food, school-fees, etc. How could a person manage this without any source of income? My father started a new business of dress-material, but price of raw-material and shop-rent were too high to pick up the pieces in one month. But he showed his courage and also took help from some good people and provided us with all the needed things of routine life. We kept on spending all the difficult days happily with the hope to see the light at the end of the tunnel soon. Now I and my sister grew up so we required a bigger house. We found another place and shifted to another rented house which had two rooms and one kitchen although that area was also very junky as there was an iron factory nearby the house, people used to work there till late night and used to smoke and drink. But that was the only afforded place that we could afford and above all it was near to my grandfather's house so my mother wanted to be there. We stayed there for many years. Meanwhile we kept on growing up and always saw my parents' struggling life for paying rent for house, shop and our school fees.

One day my grand-mother said to my mother, 'Sarita, I want you to conceive and want to see you as a mother of one son as my all sons are bestowed with sons excepting you.'

'But now it might be crucial and painful as Aditi is ten years old and Harsha is eight years old, as per my age, it would be difficult to conceive and if that happens, it is going to be very difficult for me to bring up a child as I am also working. My stitching work, batches of beauty-parlour classes and household responsibilities, you can understand.' said my mother with tension on her face.

'I can understand but after two-three years, the baby will grow up, then you will again be fine and you will also get a scion.' said my grandmother. My grand-mother always showed worries for my parents and for us. There was a good friendship between my mother and my grand-mother as my mother always remained obedient to my grand-mother despite various problems in the family. After few years of my parents' leaving home, my grand-parents realized the value of my parents as my other uncles and aunties started treating them very badly. So each and every moment, my grand-parents used to remember my parents and recall the injustice happened to them. They also repented for their deeds.

One morning, 'I think we should try.' said my mother to my father.

'For what?' my father asked wrapping dress material in a polythene for shop.

'For a baby boy.' replied my mother with shy on her face.

'But we are fine with two daughters, aren't we?' asked my father with little confidence.

'In our society, sisters need at least one brother for their better future, don't you know? Otherwise I love my daughters and also bring them up like sons. We have not kept any difference between sons and daughters.' said my mother again showing the importance of a son in the society indirectly.

After five minutes, 'Alright, if you insist we will try.' replied my father.

After three months, 'One good news, I am pregnant' said my mother with shyness on her face.

'After a long time, god has again gifted you this, please take a lot of care of yourself.' advised my grand-mother.

It is really easy to give advice to anybody for anything but it is really difficult to help somebody when time comes. Everybody is very fine with goody-goody advises and talks, I have been observing this since my childhood.

After a month, my mother complained to my father, 'I am feeling under the weather.'

'Lets us go to a doctor.' said my father.

'Is it your first child?'' asked the doctor, seeing the age of my mother.

'No, third one.' said my mother.

'At this age, third child? Despite having two daughters, why?' asked the doctor with a surprise.

'As I want a son now. I am in the kind of society where to have a son is very prestigious' said my mother.

'You are also the part of society, you yourself make the society, so I think you want a son rather than the society.' said the doctor rigorously.

My mother kept her eyes down with shame. We are always ready to blame the society. I might have started blaming somebody else for the same but as she is my mother, I stop going ahead in the discussion. Finally my mother continued her pregnancy but unfortunately she got her miscarriage after three months. Again after six months, she became pregnant and again the same thing happened due to her age or some other physical issues. That happened to my mother six times in four years, and then also she couldn't stop herself to get rid of the belief of having a son. Already my father was facing a struggling period; he had to face medical bills. After six miss deliveries, finally she conceived at the age of forty-one. My mother passed nine months with some or other difficulties and many responsibilities of house-hold work and other work that she used to do apart from house-hold one.

Finally on one night, at 11:00 p.m. my mother screamed : 'Aditi…Aditi..please call your father, I will have to rush to the hospital.'

'Ok mummy.' I rushed to the terrace as my father was sleeping on the terrace to have fresh air in the hot summer of May.

My father came down rapidly and called for an auto-rickshaw to take my mother to the hospital. My father took her to the hospital and called my grand-parents. They reached there and I and my sister were doing the experience in the kitchen to make healthy food for my mother.

'I hope the baby to be healthy as Sarita's age is above forty so…' some of the relatives and well wishers of my parents expressing their worries to one another.

'Stop talking nonsense, everything will be fine.' said my grand-mother.

The doctor came out and informed, 'she has given birth to a baby boy and it is a normal delivery.'

I and my sister rushed to the hospital with food for my mother. I blessed with a little brother, we gave him a name - Tushar, a baby with sparkling eyes, wheat completion and having chubby cheeks with good height. There was a gap of sixteen years between me and my brother. In the beginning, I used to feel embarrassed when someone used to ask me about my siblings. Well, our well-wishers became very happy as everyone was sympathizer of my father. They considered Tushar as a jewel found from the sea by my parents.

Bhanu aunty, our neighbour congratulated me while coming back from the hospital and said, 'you leave the dreams for your education, now your parents won't make you study.'

'Why?' asked I with bitter and irritable expressions.

'As now they have got the right person to make him educated, if they give education to your brother, he will bring him money, so definitely they will invest their money in him, what will you do after your education? You will study and will go to the place of your in-laws and in our society, normally daughter-in-laws are not allowed to work so what's the use of that kind of education. It is very difficult to bring up a child, now your mother will remain busy in bringing up your little brother and house-hold work, she will not be able to give you enough time for your studies and your extra activities. Now you both sisters start making chapattis by leaving the books and dreams aside.'

At that early age, I realized that a female is the best enemy of another female in our society. A female doesn't want another female to go ahead in her career or in any good thing. But my parents were different. They never differentiated among us. My father brought us every needed thing which we wanted even in critical financial condition. My parents sent me to the classes of almost extra activities. They supported me for dancing, singing, spoken English Classes and for various participations in school and family functions. Slowly and gradually, I started being noticed by the people around me as if a fish became visible in the sea. Day by day, I started becoming so active that I left sitting free for a single moment. I used to go to school, tuition-class, drawing-class, dancing –class and also used to help my mother in house-hold work. I was so much fond of carrying myself in a well manner, wearing good clothes, caring myself in a unique way. My parents always supported me in each and every thing. They allowed me to be independent and they allowed me to wear what I wanted to wear and the way I wanted to carry myself. Actually in our caste, when the girls become young, they are not allowed to wear jeans or skirts, they are forced to wear only Salwar –Kurta with dupatta. But my parents never minded about my dressing.

One day in a marriage function, I and my sister wore skirt and t-shirt with open hair and some make-up on the face, one of the relatives started talking among themselves 'Sarita has given much freedom to her daughters, don't you think that Mrs. Motvani?'

'I agree, in a small town, girls should not be allowed to wear this kind of stylish cloths.' replied mrs. Motwani by staring at us rudely.

On that day I observed and understood the narrow mindset of our society.

'A small town girl can't have right to live the way she wants or to wear what she wants to wear. Shorts are far away but they are not even allowed to wear jeans and top, for that she is supposed to born in a mega city. How ridiculous!' – I whispered.

'Mom, everyone says that you have given us a lot of freedom and people in our neighbourhood also say that now you will not provide us sufficient education as we are the girls, they say, you will educate only Tushar as he will bring money to you in return, we will not.' asked I with agitation.

'Let people talk what they understand, you don't take tension and focus on your goals and studies, we are always with you.' my mother gave me confidence.

After my mother's confidence, I got satisfaction but I realized when you grow up in this kind of society and culture, you start making yourself feminist and you always start proving yourself better than males and your mind goes in the search of equality between males and females.

One hand I was building the confidence to do something, all of a sudden, we came to know that the area we were living became quite unsafe and risky, many a times thieves used to intrude. So again black cloud started hovering on my father's head, again he was forced to find a new house on rent. At the same time, problems also took place in the business as the shop owner wanted to start his business so he asked my father to vacant the shop. Now my father was in need of finding both- a rented house and a shop.

'I have severe headache, please give me a cup of ginger-tea' my father entered home, wiping his perseverance from the head.

'You found any shop or house? We have just seventeen days, this month is about to end.' said my mother with tension.

'I am trying Sarita, I have shortlisted some places but we can't afford rent for some good places, nowadays rent for good shops has been increased and market is very down so business is also not going on well. If it goes on like this, I will be forced to start even a new business for our bread and butter.' said my father.

'Harsha, papa is so disturbed, I want to do something for him.' I said to my younger sister, making my little brother sleep in my lap.

'I also want to do something for mom and papa but we are so little, what can we do? Di, why are we so miserable among all our cousins? Why papa has not been given his share of property? Papa is also the son of our grandparents like other uncles, why did they do it with him?' my sister continued asking questions.

'Because papa and mummy don't have fighting spirit, I suppose. They are facing all these problems due to their over tolerant and merciful nature.' I could say that much only with anger on my face.

Finally after a lot of search, my father could find a house and a shop on rent. We founded the house exact in front of my grandparent's house. Despite that much injustice, we always wanted to be with them or nearby them as my mother had good attachment with my grandmother and both her sister-in-laws, means my buas. But somehow my aunties were seemed to be unhappy due to our arrival nearby their place as they knew my grandmother was more attached with us. We people can never escape ourselves from all these fake possessiveness.

'Today it is a good day, I got a house as well as a shop, of course it is on rent but at least we have got safe areas.' said my father with calmness on his face.

'So now which business are you planning to start?' asked my mother.

'Dress material only but I will try to increase the range in this as I don't have enough money to invest in some other business, rent of both house and shop eat the 70% of monthly income.' said my father.

I have been listening to the same topic of discussion – house, shop, business and rent since thirteen years. But slowly and gradually my father got little upgrades in his business and saved some money. My mother also saved some money from her parlour batches and stitching work, she gave it to my father for the development of his business. My maternal grandpa also helped my father financially. Finally, my father owned a small shop but it was not in the main area, it was quite inside the road so it was difficult to start any business in that shop but he invested money in it. Then he realized that the shop was not earning him bread and butter as it was not on the main road of the market, customers were not able to find the shop so he decide to sell the shop and from that money he wanted to buy a small house which was suggested by one of his friends.

'We are supposed to shift in Ajmera Society, I am planning to buy a house there.' said my father in front of us.

'But what about money? And that area is too far and not even developed yet, how can we survive there? Our parents are here so we should buy a place here only.' said my mother without knowing the market situation.

'First of all, it is not possible to buy a place here as this area is too costly and I will have to sell the shop to buy the house.' said my father.

'Then how will you earn and pay the rent and school fees of children?' asked my mother.

'This shop is a complete wastage as it is not recognized by the customers due to its location.' said my father.

'I warned you even before, I told you not to buy this shop as it is going to be a big loss but you never consider me or listen to me.' said my mom in anger.

'Yes, you are God, you know everything.' said my father in little anger.

They always used to have small or big fights due to rent and business. At that time, I realized money is not everything but money can buy many things, sometimes it can buy also happiness and satisfaction. Of course money doesn't speak but money makes speak. I also observed at an early age that money brings the family members near as there is sympathy in everybody's heart for one another. I remember those days, despite tough financial condition; my parents never let us face any problem, especially they gave their best efforts to make us independent. My mother never differentiated among my brother and us. She suffered a lot but provided us enough time to make us stand on our own feet.

Finally, we purchased a very small house in an average area and my father also started developing his business. Of course, initially we felt much uncomfortable with the new small house and new neighbourhood. Me and my mother almost the time used to cry in the remembrance of our grandparents and old neighbourhood and my little sister used to console us, compare to us, she was little practical. But after few months, we started enjoying in the new neighbourhood and the area also started developing. After a long time, it was a happy time in the family. I and my sister got good grips with education and other activities, my brother also started growing up. Of course my mother and father both spreaded themselves too thin for their work as my father used to handle everything alone at shop, and mom always used to get much tired due to bringing up a small baby and both of us. Many a times, it was not possible for both of us to help mom in the household work due to school, tutions, classes for other activities, etc. So she had to manage both single handedly- to take care of a small baby who occupied her for the whole day and on the top of it she had to do whole house hold work and kitchen work of all five members. Due to a lot of miscarriages, her physical strength became weak so she used to get extremely tired by night but she managed it anyhow.

One day seeing my mother's tired face, few female in the neighbourhood asked her, 'why do you manage all the things alone? Why don't you ask your daughters to help you in your household work? Why do you give them much time for their education? They are girls, if they are studying; nothing is going to come to you as they are going to go somebody else's house where they will have to do only household work. In our society, who will make them work outside? If they work, they are not going to bring you money and you are wasting a lot of money behind them despite weak financial condition, nobody will understand that in future. Better you save money for educating your son and take care of your health, don't push yourself to do the household work alone. We are your friends so warning you.'

'If we female continue getting hold on this kind of mentality, how will our society change? We need to initiate for better future of girls, after all they are also our blood. Generation is changing nowadays, we should not differentiate between girls and boys, our parents did it so we suffered a lot, we should not repeat the history. I do understand, it is not easy to make a girl educated and independent in this kind of society but change is always difficult and challenging. When our daughters are independent and happy, we would also feel happy and satisfied wherever they would be in future. I insist, you should also encourage your daughters to have further education or encourage them to involve in any activities which would keep them active and happy. It will also increase their self-confidence.' said my mother with confidence.

After few days my mother said to my father, 'Finally our daughters have got admission in good government high-school, they got good percentage and got it easily otherwise private schools are too costly, let them study till 10th std, then we will think ahead for their education. Let us see their performance and area of their subject interest which will help them to decide their stream ahead.'

It gave me immense pleasure, satisfaction, courage and confidence to do something in my life when I found my parents with me, especially when the whole society was against their mentality and actions. It pushed me to work ahead and also to do something for them. When almost relatives and neighbors possessed the thoughts of binding the girls only for household work, when they considered the girls only to be the machine of kitchen work, at that time, my parents gave me freedom to fulfil my dreams and supported me in each and every step, this freedom prevented me to have freedom of doing any negative work in my life.

When I found my parents keenly interested in our education, I made up my mind on the same day that I would never take any wrong step in my life, I deter-minded never to make them feel ashamed of any of my work. From that day, I started working hard for my studies and became very serious about my career at an early age. I wanted to do something for my parents; especially I wanted to help my father financially.

It has been said,

न चरहारयं न च राजहारयं
न भरातृभाजयं न च भारकारी ।
वयये कते वरधते एव नतियं
विदियाधनं सरवधन परधानम् ॥

Cant be stolen by a thief, cant be snatched by kings, Cant be partitioned by brothers, Nor is it heavy. The more you expend, the more it grows; The wealth of knowledge is the supreme of all wealths.

After facing financial struggle, I realized after few years that the real wealth is knowledge not money only. Of course, we need money for survival but it cannot buy satisfaction but experience of knowledge can lead towards content life.

CHAPTER 3

Now I am a big girl. I completed my primary education and it was time to join the high-school. It was the first day of girls' high-school, Saraswati Kanya Vidyalaya - the best girls' high school in the town, Morbi. It was very difficult to take admission in that school as the girls of only Patel caste could take admission in it. I was not a Patel girl so it was very difficult for me to take admission. My best friend since my Primary education – Garima was a Patel girl. She took admission very easily, well she was a very clever and rich girl, her parents were well-known gynecologists and had a very big hospital in the town. There was a great influence of hers and her family on me and my mother as we were in touch of each other from the first day of Primary School. Garima's parents always used to appreciate my mother's upbringing of both the daughters despite having a narrow-minded family and weak financial condition. Finally God kept me and Garima together even in high-school. I got good percentage and luckily got admission on the basis of merit list.

'Dear, the time of school is little fluky, from 10:00 a.m. to 5:00 p.m., so what will you take breakfast or lunch? I think you should have your lunch otherwise it will be difficult for you to study till 5:00 o'clock.' said my mother.

'Mom, but how will you manage the whole work single handedly as we would be busy with tutions and school from early morning to evening, better you give some breakfast, it will do.' said I to prevent my mother from harsh work.

'You don't worry about anything, I will manage.'

'Thanks mom, you are the best mom.' said I with a smile.

'I will take my new bicycle to the school that papa bought me last week' said I with happy mood.

'Sure dear.' said my mother packing snacks in the lunchbox for recess time.

I entered the school, it was the first day. All the new students assembled in the assembly hall. It was a very exciting day as I was in new pink uniform – punjabi salwar kurta with dupatta wrapped in 'V' shape on both the shoulders with safety-pins. We were supposed to tie a pony tail with a black ribbon and supposed to wear black shoes with white socks. As I was thin and had wheat complexion, the uniform gave me a charming and sophisticated look. Papa got me a new school bag before a week so I was observing everybody's bag to check whose bag was better and comfortable than mine.

Everybody was looking at each other and were trying to find friends and make groups as this is girls' common therapy to make group and then start groupism. Well I was never interested in this kind of girlish stuff. I always wanted to keep good terms with each and everybody around me. But I was very possessive about my best friend Garima from beginning. But slowly and gradually, I started realizing that she was an independent and practical girl genetically. I observed that I used to follow her blindly almost the time but she never did it. Well she was right at her end, I realized it afterwards. Although we were best friends and used to share a lot of things with each other, always used to be together, used to participate in all the activities and cultural programmes, used to go to each other's place. Of course, she was cleverer and smarter than me.

On Wednesday, one of my classmates said, 'Hey Aditi, looking nice in this skirt.'

'Oh! Thanks! She made my day as I was the kind of girl who literally worshipped the praising but I also wanted praising for my friend Garima as I never left her alone in any situation so I added, 'Yes, me and my best friend both are looking nice, ya ! Again I added, 'I think our school should add one more day for free-dress code, not only Wednesdays so we can take opportunity to look pretty two days in a week.'

From that Wednesday, Garima started dressing up very nicely and kept on getting lots of compliments for her dresses, shoes and accessories as she never used to repeat the dress on any Wednesday as her father was very rich so it was very easy for her to afford various cloths and ornaments. She never took me beside when she was praised, infect she started insulting me when I used to repeat the dress on Wednesday.

After two months of school, there was an election for 'the head girl of class'. At that age, it was found so interesting to monitor the class and to take the responsibility of it, go to the staff-rooms and to get the attention of all classmates. I also wanted to be the part of it; I also participated in the election. It lasted for the whole day and when the result was about to come, one of our P.T. teachers came and said, 'put the results aside, I, myself, will select the monitor.' Everyone shouted Aditi-Aditi-Aditi as I had good terms with all most the classmates but she neglected the sound and said, 'Garima is the monitor of this class.' The teacher had good terms with her parents and everybody was aware of her richness.

At that time, I realized, in this world contacts and money play a vital role. Well I congratulated her with wholeheartedly with smile on my face. I kept one clue in my mind that my best friend has been elected so some of my mischiefs and waggeries would be neglected by her. Days passed and I realized it was just my guess as she treated me and the whole class equally. She was completely right practically but it was little difficult and hurting to understand for an emotional fool like me.

Bit by bit, I realized that despite being hard-working and smart, I used to be identified by the name of my friend. Everyone used to call me, 'You are Garima's friend, right? You both look nice together. Your friend's parents are doctors, recently she has bought black – dashing scootypep, now your bicycle days are over, she will always be there to give you a lift.'

She never offered me a lift, infect to let me down; at the time of leaving the school, she used to wait for me with her scooty –pep. I used to ask her to go as I had a bicycle so was not possible to go side by side, I could not go by her speed. But she used to insist me to go with her, she would keep the scooty's speed less as she did not like to go alone on road and excepting me, there was not any other fool to agree on that. So I used to go with her, but I was on bicycle and she on scooty, which really used to embarrass me sometimes as all the friends on the road used to look at me and laugh. I used to think, 'why can't I say 'No' for anything to anybody?' I cursed myself for my behaviour. 'Till what age will I feel myself to be a caged bird of all these golden cages?'

'Dear, you seem to be so tired from school, tutions and homework; you spend your whole day in all this.' asked my father one day at night when I was reading with a tired face.

'Yes papa, school and tutions time are too much so...' said I.

'I am planning to buy you a scooty for your convenience.' said my father.

'Oh! Papa, how you understand all that?' said I with tears in my eyes.

'We are always there to support you for everything, you keep it up for your goals.' said my mother by supporting my father.

'But how will you afford it as it would be costly and nobody has it in our whole big family, what would people say about our financial condition, you don't have enough money but I would have forced you to buy it for me.' I questioned to my father by keeping my books in the bag.

'Oh! Don't think much at this age, just focus on your work.' said my mother.

After few days, my father bought me a second-hand green color scooty for my convenience; I was on the top of the sky on that day. I used to wash it every day and used to take a lot of care, even more than myself. Many rich people in our family never bought their daughter scooty as they used to think that once a girl would start driving a vehicle, she would find her own wings and would fly with them, then they couldn't be controlled but my parents never thought all that and they kept on going ahead for our happiness. I didn't know to drive a scooty but with my passion; I learnt it just in one day. On one Sunday, I and my father went to a big ground from 5:00 am to 1:00 am at night, I continued learning my driving and learnt it. I learnt it very fast as I did not have patience and couldn't stop myself to take the scooty to school on Monday. I reached the school and was waiting for Garima to come so that I could show her my scooty. How stupid I was! I always used to compare myself with her to go ahead in life and for my progress.

It is said, a happiest person in the world is the one who has found his work. I realized that I was the kind of person who needed work to be happy and did not want to waste a single minute of life. I realized it when I joined an English Classes named – Mehta Classes. I must admit that it was a turning point of my life. I was a student of vernacular medium so a student like me always would want to have good command over English. Mehta Classes was very famous in the town for its proper and accurate teaching and Kartik Mehtasir, owner of the Classes, was also well known for his discipline and strictness. He was tall heighted with white beard and always used to keep himself in a simple dress. People used to say those who really wanted to learn and bear his strict behaviour, only those could survive there. I by nature was much disciplined girl and had good tolerance power so I found my heaven there. In 9th std, I joined that Classes and he used to teach us not only English subject but he focused a lot on English language. He never made us memorize the grammar but he made us speak the grammar fluently. He used to give too much home-work, due to that I started keeping myself extremely busy, even in school, in my free lectures, I used to complete my home-work which gave me the confidence of speaking English fluently. Kartiksir also used to teach us morals of life and he was so well read person that he used to teach us the lessons of life by telling the stories of history, the Geeta, the Bible and the Quran. An hour spent in his class used to make my day, I used to feel supremely motivated for doing something in life. He made us write essays by our own without taking any reference from any book or any other sources. I do remember, my essays always used to be selected as the best ones and used to be stuck on the notice board of the main office of the Classes. All the students used to read my all essays while passing by the notice board. It gave me immense pleasure and satisfaction. I used to show it to my parents and also used to bring them to the Classes to see those pages of my essays on the notice board. My parents felt extremely proud to see my hard work and dedication for my studies.

I became busy as a beaver in enhancing the command over English language and to make my English speech better and better. I used to win all most the debates and competitions held to enrich English language. The certificate of winner used to give me the confidence to take part in more competitions. That busy phase of life kept me away from all the negative thoughts of life. Even my best friend started chasing me but I was not free for any comparisons now. I got busy in developing myself. I realized that now I also started being identified in the school on the basis of my own capabilities. I made my own identity as 'a busy bee'. But I was very happy as I found my work which provided me enough amount of enjoyment and satisfaction. I used to write essays of 20-25 pages every week, although I used to make grammatical mistakes but little by little, I overcame them and started writing correct English and aesthetic writing.

It was the end of 9th std, suddenly my friend Garima informed me that she was leaving the school, infect she was leaving the town for the good as her brother was going to opt for the science stream so they were shifting to a city for further education. When I got to know about it, it was a big shock for me as I realized that somehow I was dependent on her, emotionally and psychologically. Although she was very practical and strong due to her rich

and educated background but some or other way she and
her family left a very positive impact on me and my family
especially for fulfilling our goals. Otherwise our social
background was very conservative for girls' development
and their freedom but when her father came to home to
pick her up or drop her, he always used to talk about a girl
child's education. His talks played a vital role to increase
my parents' motivation for our education and freedom.
When I used to go to her home, I used to get attracted by
their disciplined and calm and systematic lifestyle. I used
to share that with my parents and they tried to provide us
that kind of lifestyle. Garima and her parents might not
know about their influence on us but I and my mother do
confess about their contribution. As we almost the time
followed her, this time the same thing happened. I also
wanted to shift to a city for further education. But when
it became difficult to pay the petrol bill for the short root
of a small town, it was out of imagination to dream for
the high fees for higher education. Of course, since my
childhood, I wanted to be a doctor but I put full stop on my
thoughts and dreams at least for some time. I thought to
complete my 10th std with good percentage, then I decided
to convince my father to let me go in science field.

Coaching of 10th std. started in the vacation period of
9th std. What a great conspiracy of these Tuition Classes
to trap the students or to bind the students!

'Mom, when are you planning to go to mama's place
(place of my maternal uncle – Chiman Sahi)?' asked I by
feeling the admission form of tuition classes.

'I think I should not go this year as your tuition classes
are going to start so you will have to work hard for your
10th std. If I go, who will take care of you and home?' said
my mother making chapattis in the kitchen.

'Oh! really ! How sweet, mom. It is so nice of you.' said I.

It was felt like the whole family was supposed to give the exam of 10th not only me. The atmosphere of entire house turned to be studious; everybody started talking about my 10th std seriously which motivated me to study well and to go forward for my dreams.

'Mom, I want to get my hair cut.' said I.

'Why?' asked my mother. 'As I don't want to waste my single moment in my S.S.C. board, and you know how much time it takes me to wash and oil my hair.' I said with little worry on my face.

'Are you sure, just look at the length of your hair, it is up to your waist.' warned my mother.

'I am sure mom, please come with me to the beauty parlour.'

'Alright.'supported my mother.

I went and got my hair cut in the beginning of my 10th std. When I came back from parlour with hair up to shoulders, my all friends in neighbourhood shouted with surprise.

'Bloody stupid studious !' one of my friends murmured. I didn't react much on the comment and came inside the house. Finally my S.S.C board started and I worked days and nights for scoring good marks in exams. I skipped attending many functions due to my tests, even my family, especially my mother avoided going to many social functions to give me the whole time for my studies as I was not able to help her in household work or to bring up my one year old brother.

'She is working so hard.' said a school teacher to my mother in parents' meeting. My father heard the same words from the tuition teacher when he came to pay the annual fees.

'I want to score rank in board.' I showed my desire to my parents.

'You keep it up, we are always with you.' motivated my parents.

I do remember I used to score above 90 plus marks in science, Maths, English and Social Studies. I was a bookworm and hardworking so used to mug up the books like anything, I also remembered the page numbers of all most the questions but somehow I could not manage well with grammar of Sanskrit and Gujarati Language which always kept my result down.

'Mom, due to Gujarati and Sanskrit grammar, I stand behind in my result, else I score very well in all subjects, it is just one month remaining for the final exam, I am worried.' I shared my worries.

I always used to share my worries, problems and happiness with my mother, my best friend.

'Let me think something in this matter.' supported my mother.

After two days said my mother, 'I have found a teacher who teaches Sanskrit and Gujarati grammar, he stays in the next street of our house. You can go every Saturday and Sunday for two hours.'

'Oh thank you mom, you do so much for my career.' I felt less tension.

Finally, the date of final exams arrived. All the students tightened up their belt. All the teachers of schools and tutions were ready to print the photos of their talented students to represent their classes and schools as best ones in the town, precious marketing time arrived for them.

Before a day of exam, 'All the best beta', 'All the best dear', 'All the best di, give your best.' I continued receiving calls.

'Thank you for your best wishes.' I kept on replying to my friends and relatives on my landline in the middle of my studies.

Telephone rang for twelfth time. 'Aditi, it would be for you, please receive fast, else Tushar will get up.' my mom summoned me.

'Yes mom,' I rushed towards the phone with book in my hand and my eyes were stuck up to the last sentence of the paragraph.

'Aditi, receive my hands are occupied in flour ' shouted my mom. 'Yes mom, just finished my paragraph.' I received with smiling face again to say 'Thank you'.

'Uff, this book-worm.' my one ear received this message of my mother and another ear got shocked with a terrible news on phone. The news was my cousin sister Rita's husband met with an accident and he passed away. My heartbeats raised and I started shivering after listening that. We all loved that person a lot and before few days he came to our house to wish me good luck for my exams and after few days I came to know that he was not in the world. Instead of my exam paper, his face was flashing in my sleep and dreams. Such a terrible night and in the morning I needed to give my first paper of my final exams. My mother controlled me, motivated me and asked me to have courage for exams. She gave me a spiritual lecture and made me mentally prepared for the exams.

'Dear, now I will have to go there for few days for his funeral, it is compulsory so you will have to face your exam without me. I will ask your grand-mother to be here with you and I and your dad will have to go.' said my mother.

'Oh no! mom, how will I appear for my exams without you. I can't do anything without you. Please don't go.' I started crying.

'Nothing stops without anything or anybody in life. This is only your book exams, you will also have to face exams of your life without me, I think this is the beginning, be strong. I supported you for the whole year without going anywhere but now God wants you to face your first important exam independently, without me.' motivated my mother.

In the morning, she left for the funeral and I left for my first paper. It was the first day of S.S.C. exam so my heart was full of fear and nervousness; I carried my compass-box and receipt which I packed at night. I was feeling little drowsy as I was not able to sleep for the whole night. It was strange feelings- Fear with Excitement. My father had to catch the bus so my uncle came to drop me to the school where I got my seat number for exams. On the way, lot of thoughts were wavering in my mind. I was thinking about my paper, atmosphere of the school, benches of the school, supervisors, student next to me, about my parents, their bus, my cousin who became widow at an early age, about the death body. Along with all those thoughts, I was checking my compass box again and again to conform that I did not forget anything required for the exam. So restless I was!

I reached to the ground of school. Parents, students, friends and relatives were standing outside waiting for the entry bell to be rung. Excitement and fear was visible on everyone's face. Finally the bell rang; the students were allowed to enter the ground and were made to stand in the queue for entering the classrooms. We were checked from head to toe and our compass-boxes were also checked to prevent us from cheating. It gives you proud and confidence when you have nothing to hide.

I reached near the door of the class and looked behind to say 'buy-buy' to my uncle; he wished me good luck with the thumps-up sign. I was badly missing my parents, was imagining them to be there to wish me good luck. I found my seat number on the first bench of the class, although I had nothing to hide, I was feeling little uncomfortable in the first raw. The bell rang to inform all the supervisors about remaining last ten minutes for distributing the paper. Everyone was looking at each other and worshiping their god. Finally the bell rang and we were distributed the exam papers. First paper was of Gujarati. I first skimmed the whole paper in just a minute and got confidence that I would be able to attempt all the questions and grammar, too. Three hours flew like anything. All students came out with a smile on their face as the paper was easy comparatively. It seemed like the fear of Board Exam got reduced a bit. Outside the classroom, some students were discussing the question paper, some were laughing loudly, some were drinking water, some were wishing best luck for next day's paper and some were biding 'bye-bye' to go back home. My uncle came to receive me and on the way to home, I started thinking about next paper. Four papers went fast, now it was time for fifth paper - Mathematics.

Next day, papers were distributed. After three hours asked my uncle, 'So how was the paper, dear?'

'Oh god ! This paper can never be forgotten as the sums were out of the syllabus. 40% paper was out of the syllabus. Three hours passed like a nightmare.' replied I by wiping sweat from my head.

My Uncle, 'What about others?'

'Coming out, all sincere students were looking at each other with much worries on their faces and were asking each other about the paper and were trying to solve the queries, I was one of them. Some were bombarding by saying that it was very easy.' I replied. Despite knowing about those students' lies and fake laughter, I felt little uneasy. Sometimes other's fake and over confidence could down your real confidence. I realized it on that day, well I didn't tell uncle about my those feelings.

Anyways, it was time to cover the stuff in the next paper which was science. That paper was also tough but at least better than Maths. It was Saturday. Monday was the last day of exam, end of the year. On Sunday, to console myself, I called one of my cousins and few of my friends about their Maths and Science papers to compare my fear with them regarding those papers. Finally, I finished with my exams and my parents also returned from the funeral ceremony.

'How was your exam, beta?' asked my parents.

'It was good, I am feeling that some heavy load has been reduced from my head.' said I while making chapatis and serving them to my parents.

I was starring at my parents and was recalling the day of my cousin's husband's death and felt down in the dump, then I realized, it was better to accept the reality of life and go on. I called my-widow cousin and consoled her. My parents also advised me to go back to work.

Next morning, I got up late in the morning without any burden of exams or test-papers and said, 'Mom result might come after two months.'

'So?' asked my mother.

'So what will I do during the whole vacation? You know I can't sit at home without doing anything.' said I while brushing my teeth.

'Dear, one day of your vacation has not passed yet and you have started getting bored, learn to relax also.' said my mother with a little scolding.

'To do new things is relaxation for me.' said I by wiping my face with the napkin.

'I will provide you a lot of new things to learn during the whole vacation, don't worry.' said my mother sharply.

'Which new things will you teach me?' asked I with surprise.

My mother took my hand and drew me towards the kitchen and gave me utensils and some vegetables to cook.

'Mom, what is this?' asked I with surprise.

'This is your new course that you need to finish in this vacation, from today you are going to prepare lunch and dinner for all of us, and even breakfast otherwise when you get married, your husband and in-laws would blame us for giving you only qualification and certificates of studies excepting cooking and other house-hold work. So from today your training of a house girl is going to start under my leadership and I also believe it is the moral duty of each female.' said my mother.

'First of all, I don't want to get married, I want to do something in my life.' said I rigorously.

'Calm down dear, every ambitious girl says that in the beginning but when time comes, she finds the groom for herself and tells the parents that she wants to get married.' said my mother.

'Don't dream like that, nothing will happen like that in my case as I want to be the son of my father, I will never leave him and definitely will do something for him.' said

I bluntly. Today I also gave importance to son's gender indirectly. After all, I was my mother's daughter.

'Alright, alright. Don't go anywhere but go in the kitchen now, go..go...go...' my mother pushed me inside the kitchen.

'Mom, don't you think that I need some relaxation, it's the first day of my vacation.' I said by collecting the vegetables from my mother's hand with a cunning smile.

So finally I started learning cooking and some other household work every day. It was such a relaxing period. To get up early in the morning with no burden of exams, have fresh air, do some jogging and exercise while listening melodious songs, then to help mother in household and kitchen work, play with siblings, watch T.V, have ice-cream at night with family, talk unlimited on unnecessary things, no time limit for any work. How wonderful the life was!

Living that life, I asked my mother, 'I am a female, if I don't study or don't focus on career, nobody will force me for anything, in fact our society wants that kinds of girls, then why am I struggling and running after tough things? Am I right or wrong, mom?'

'Don't think much, you live this life for the whole vacation, ask me about it at the end of your vacation.' said my mother.

Ten days passed of my vacation and I literally started feeling bored.

I told my mother that I was feeling very bored I wanted to join Spoken English Classes; it would help me in my career too.

My mother asked me, 'your peaceful life over? Before few days you were asking me few questions about your struggling and career.'

'I got my all answers mom. A girl like me is not born only to do household work. Of course I love to be at home, to take care of everybody, be with everybody, cooking, and have fun with all. But this is not sufficient for my satisfaction and I know my satisfaction is not free and easy; I need to do struggle for that. I will have to juggle with various things at a time. I want to join Spoken Class in the same Classes – Mehta Classes. In the evening for two hours, it will really give me satisfaction and happiness, I will also help you in cooking and household work along with that, please.' I requested my mother.

'You don't need to request, I will ask your father to pay the fees tomorrow, so you join from tomorrow, it will keep you active and happy, too.' supported my mother.

Finally I started my Spoken English Classes in the evening. It was such a wonderful experience of the class – it gave me opportunity to participate in all debates, elocution competitions, and vocabulary contest. I wrote various essays on multiple topics and also got good grips on English language. I realized that speaking in English became my passion, I started loving writing, even in vacation, I used to wake up till midnight and used to write and think in English for practice, also used to read a lot of books suggested by Kartiksir for improving English language. Gradually, I realized that I started speaking English very nicely and stood in the queue of the English Medium students. I enjoyed my vacation a lot.

'Mom, just eight days to go for the result. I am worried.' said I by flipping the pages of essays written by me.

'Worry? Worry for what? You have given your best efforts, so you will defiantly get what you deserve.' said my mom.

That is true but you know my nature, right. I am a little worried and conscious person as far as my hard-work and honesty for any work is concerned.' said I.

'You are just fifteen years old, you don't need to be that much serious about life, afterwards many situations might come to make you much serious and conscious in life, so now just chill alright?' explained my mother while feeding my little brother.

Count down started, it is said you can never change a person's nature; I couldn't stop thinking about my result all the time. I do remember, we were at Chimanmama's (my maternal uncle) place for the vacation. Manish, my cousin (mama's son) was also in 10th std, we both appeared for exams in the same year but he was more confident about his result despite not working hard for the whole year. It was the day of result, I got up at 5 o'clock in the morning, had my bath and worshipped God and had a glass of milk given by Krishnamami (maternal aunt). After that I settled myself near the telephone as my father was going to go to school and collect my result. At that time, everyone didn't have internet facility, as such I was an insecure person so might not have trusted on internet result as I wanted my father to read the marks from the hard copy of the result. On that day, I was not feeling to go away from the telephone and received all the calls till 11 o'clock at noon. Finally I got my father's call at 11:08 a.m and he informed that I got 82% in S.S.C board. I felt happy as it was not a bad result but I was not satisfied. The result was not up to my hard-work. But my mother became so happy, she was in the bathroom and was taking bath, but when she heard in the bathroom that I was taking to my father on phone, she came out in wrapped towel. She hold my cousin sister's hand and started spinning with her.

All got surprised to see my mother's excitement about her daughter's education as none of her siblings had that kind of consciousness for their children's education or career.

I smiled at everyone and then went inside the room. Seeing my dissatisfaction, my mother came to me and asked by wearing her remaining cloths, 'what happened, dear?'

'Mom don't you think my hard-work was harder than this result?' asked I.

'You worked hard so you got that much, you are supposed to do too much to get little in this word, that is the universal rule of life. Every-time luck doesn't favor up to the mark. Those who would have got 90 plus percentage might have worked harder than you and might be provided better facilities and tutions by their parents, somewhere we might have also lacked in some things, somewhere you too. So it is fine, you have not got that less, just enjoy and think for further studies.' consoled my mother.

'Manish has also gone to take result, well he was very confident about his papers, so he would definitely get better marks.' said I comparing my result with him.

'He always talks much and does less, not like you who does a lot and says nothing. You lack your confidence about your work that is why your hard-work is never seen.' interrupted my sister while feeding a banana to my brother.

'Oh! Manish is here. He is back from the school.' said I.

'Hey what is your percentage?' asked I with curiosity.

'It is 69%.' he said that and went to his room and lied down on the bed.

My sister directly looked at me and I recalled her words about Manish. I went to see him and we talked, he said the result had gone very down due to the difficult papers of Maths and Science. 'Yes, papa said the same thing on phone. My maths teacher informed it to my father.' said I.

'Anyways, so what are you planning for further studies.' asked I.

'I have not given a thought to it as you know we have a very big shop so I don't need money, we have that much money that nobody would mind if I don't even study further, our next three generation can enjoy my father's and my grandfather's earning so I don't need to get much worried about my education and career like you. By the way, why are you also so worried about your studies? What will you do after achieving qualification, you will get married, will have kids and will handle kitchen work, only. Why you always seem to talk about career, job and education, after all you are a girl, after few years, time would arrive to think about your marriage, not a career opportunity.' He started laughing loudly. He continued again by pouring water in the glass from the jug, 'females are just born for that. To take care of house, husband and children. Nobody will like a girl like you who always talk about doing something in life, it is better to involve yourself much in household and kitchen work like your other cousin sisters.'

He told me all those words to decrease the value of my higher percentage than his. He showed me that there was no value of my percentage as I was a girl. By showing my weak financial background, he showed his less worries about his career and education.

It hurt me a lot but I gave him a cold shoulder. I got busy in receiving calls from my classmates about the result. I got to know that my best friend Garima also got 87 % despite being much intelligent and clever. I got more confidence to do something again and also trusted on my father's talk that the result went really down in that year due to tough papers. I also realized one thing on that day, we should keep on working without sharing and discussing much about our progress as even our own family members and friends might not able to digest it and would definitely try to demotivate us. I also felt, comparison for good things is not wrong but we just need to take care, it should not be harmful to anyone, especially the person whom we are comparing ourselves. If good comparison makes us go in positive direction, we can always have a role model.

At the night of result, my mama and my nana (maternal grandpa) entered home from the shop, my nana wished me congratulation for scoring 80 plus percentage and wished me best luck for further studies. Pinakmama, my younger mama, demanded party from me for having good percentage which really made me happy but my elder mama, Chimanmama, full of narrow thinking, came and said, 'Hey Aditi – good – very good, congrats but when will you start achieving good marks in household work which is really required for you as a girl? You are not going to study for the whole life in schools and universities.' He kept on taunting as his son didn't score well and he also believed that girls should not study much.

He insulted me in front of everybody which really scraped me and my mother but we didn't say anything. My few cousins sisters who were just 10th passed out and didn't study further became happy on mama's comment but other cousin sisters who were my well wishers asked me to ignore the stuff. My mother had four sisters so I was blessed with nine cousin sisters who had different opinions about girl's education and career.

I realized on that day, every time society is not responsible for girl child's education but girls themselves also don't support themselves for their progress. In that case, I found my mother quite different from all her siblings and thanked God to give me such a wonderful mother.

Next day it was Sunday, so the whole family was at home. My nana, both mamas and all cousins, we sat for breakfast, there were many varieties in breakfast - jalebi gathiya, kachori, poha, many types of chattnis, dry fruits and many more. All were having fun of vacation. I wanted it to be continued and didn't want anybody to talk on the topic of result and education in that enjoyment, but that was the prime thing happened in vacation so everywhere children, parents and relatives were busy in the hot discussion of 10th std result and which stream should be selected for further education. Everywhere Science and Commerce fields were seemed to be on the top of selection. But I didn't want to discuss anything there, just wanted to complete the vacation happily and wanted to go back to my town, to my papa, where I could share anything freely about my education and career. My mother also supported me for the same.

I asked my mother silently, 'how come that you are so different from your siblings?'

She gave me a smart answer, 'I have already become a victim of this kind of society despite having smartness as my parents couldn't take any step for their daughters, I don't want to repeat the history, distinguishing my courage, God has given me daughters like you, I suppose.'

It is said those who want to taunt will defiantly find any way to do it.

'Oh! The laddu is not broken, it is so strong like Aditi.' said Chimanmama with a loud laugh and putting the laddu between his teeth.

'So Aditi, what have you decided for further studies. Do you want to study or is it enough?' asked my mama.

'Of course I will study further and that is also with hard work and patience.' said I confidently.

My mother pinched me and gave me a sign by using her eyes for keeping my mouth shut and not to speak much in front of everyone. But I was young blood so I couldn't stop myself.

'Mama, you are much worried about my education and career even than me, so you suggest which field should I opt for?' asked I looking in front of everybody.

'I think you should select the stream of stitching, cooking, beauty parlour, mehandi course and knitting the things – all household work which will make your in-laws and husband feel proud of you.' suggested he in the pin drop silence of the drawing-room.

'Mami never knew all these things, she learnt even her cooking here so didn't she satisfy you and my grand - parents? And who knows my husband and in-laws might need a lady who takes care of house and also would be involved in some profession like a doctor or a teacher.' said I by eating Jalebi.

'In our society, girls are just bound to do house hold work, they are not allowed to work outside, dear. Don't waste time and energy in this, and above all save your father's money who is already struggling, don't make him sink in debt due to a daughter like you. He is the only earning member of the family, how much will he be able to do for your education or for your marriage? Stop dreaming much and be at home and help your mom.' he told it with a scold in front of everybody.

I felt so hurt and tears were about to roll down my cheeks but somehow I just controlled them and my mother was also asking me not to speak anything by giving signs and with the help of her constant pinches.

I just asked one question to my mama, 'alright you don't have a daughter so you won't be able to understand. Leave girls' education aside and tell me what are you thinking for Manish, he is a boy so he has all the rights to have higher education and to do anything in his life. What are you thinking to make him in his life?'

'Yes, absolutely. He is my king, he can do anything but he does not require to study further. He can earn ten times better in the business that we have already set up rather than doing a job under any boss. He will be the boss of himself.' My mama said it with much proud by patting his son's back and offering one kachori to him to give him respect for being a son.

'It is true.' I just said it with a mild smile.

Going inside the room, 'Mom I just want to leave now and want to go to my papa, I don't want to be in this kind of suffocated atmosphere. Why our own people always blame us for being a girl and my father to be a father of a girl? Don't we have any right to see dreams? When will we get freedom from this kind of thoughts, what is the benefit of that much gold that we girls are gifted from parents and in-laws?' complained I with tears in my eyes.

'Mom, since childhood we have been spending very good and exciting time with everyone here, now all of a sudden why have they become against me without any reason? I have been playing with them since my childhood and they love me a lot, when we go back from here, we cry in their remembrance for so many days, where has that love gone today?' asked I.

'It is always like that, when you are found to climb the ladder of success, people around you will start having problems with you as people love to use the adjectives 'oh so poor', 'so helpless', till you are sympathized and follow them, you are loved and pampered more by your loved ones but when you decide to chose your own path, you come to know who actually loves you by heart and who wants to see your progress. That is the universal truth of life.' explained my mother. 'Don't worry, we are just leaving after two days, our tickets have been booked.' said my mother folding the cloths.

'Thanks mom for being my mother.' said I folding my clothes for packing.

Finally we got the bus for my home-town – Morbi. Everyone came to say buy to us as we might meet after one or two years in the next vacation due to long geographical distance. When I sat on bus, I felt fit as a fiddle. It felt like a bird had been kept out from the cage and it got freedom again to fly in the sky. While travelling, I and my mother discussed a lot for the whole night regarding all that stuff and reached home early in the morning. Directly I went to my father and just looked at him. I wanted to say so many things to him, wanted to appreciate but I got a lump in my throat and couldn't speak a single word due to my emotions.

I realized our own hut can give extreme calmness than anybody else's palace. I started loving my small home more and more as it was the home of freedom. Although it was a small one but used to allow us to see big dreams.

It is said in chapter-2 shloka – 24

अच्छेद्योऽयमदाह्योऽयमक्लेद्योऽशोष्य एव च।
नित्यः सर्वगतः स्थाणुरचलोऽयं सनातनः॥२४॥

The self is uncleavable. The self is incombustible.
The self cannot be wetted nor the self can be dried.
The self is eternal, all-pervading, unchanging
and immovable. The self is everlasting.

The realization of self is the most important aspect in
Bhagavad Geeta. But in this rapid world, it becomes little
difficult to culminate the realization of self in very short
journey of life. But it can be achieved with the help of
meditation or believing in yourself and keeping yourself
away from negative energies like jealousy, ego, hatred, etc.
I tried to achieve my self by involving myself in positive
activities and by keeping myself busy in progressive
works.

CHAPTER 4

It was a Sunday morning. We got up little late and were fresh due to enough rest. We sat for having break-fast. Bred-butter was the fix variety for Sunday's breakfast. My little brother was playing with butter like a little Krishna. We were also playing with him and my mother was making him eat.While putting a piece of bread in my mouth, I requested 'Papa, I want to opt for science stream and want to become a doctor.'

My father looked up while taking a sip of tea from his cup and said after thinking for seventeen seconds 'Why not? I will ask for the good schools and fees.'

After two days, when my father came to home for lunch, he said 'there is not any good school in our town for Science Stream; you will have to go to Rajkot for further studies. Rajkot is one of the best cities for Science education, there are various private schools in this city.'

I called some of my friends for some information and they said the same thing, some of them informed that they already filled the form for the same. We went to Meera's place, one of my good friends, for the information as she was also interested in the same field. She said they went to fill the form to one of the best schools of Rajkot. Her parents and my parents had a discussion about fees, courses, pg places, tiffins, etc. Meera's parents were teachers by profession and it was also a middle class family having limited salary but somehow they could manage fees for her daughter and Meera had an elder brother who also earned and used to send some money for his sister's education. Meera, with whom I spent my two years, also finalized to go to Rajkot for further studies.

We came back home and discussed each and everything.

'Papa, for one year you will have to pay minimum 1.5 lack for fees, tiffins, pg rent, books and some other things. Will you be able to afford it? My friends informed that if we have minimum 3 lacks in our pocket, then only we should take admission in these schools, and that is also for two years only, not for all years of education. They also informed that if I score good percentage, we will have to pay more and more lacks for further education.' clarified I.

'Dear, you don't worry about it; I will arrange that for you. You just select the school.' said my father.

I went to the kitchen and expressed my tension, 'mom, papa wants me to go ahead but now I want to leg behind in my decisions, as I think we won't be able to manage it financially, it is not the matter of only two years of school but afterwards if I score good, more money will be required. I am not the only child. After me, Harsha and Tushar are also supposed to be provided equal education, right?'

'If you want to study, we are with you. Don't think much and focus on selecting the good school for your field.' advised my mother while chopping the potatoes.

I didn't speak a single word and constantly thought for two days. Many thoughts covered my mind. I started asking multiple questions to myself. Should I select science field? Should I harass my father financially? If I get good percentage, will my father be able to arrange more lacks for my further education? If my father is not able to arrange money, will I have to leave my study in between? Will I be called just 12th science passed out with good percentage? What if I don't get good percentage in

12th science or what if I fail? Will I ever be able to forgive myself?

Lots of thoughts came and went. My mind went into the ocean where waves were not planing to stop even for a second. Finally my mind reached to a seaboard and decided not to be a science student. I thought, I will do something else which my father can also afford easily. If I do anything by heart, I will be able to do the best in any field.

'Mom and Dad, I have decided that I am not going to opt for Science field.' said I with tears in my eyes.

'But why? We have started arranging money. You won't believe but when Chimanmama came to know that you are that much sincere about your study, he became ready to pay your fees.' said my mother.

'Oh! that is very sweet of him but I don't want papa to be the debtor of anybody due to me and my ambition and if I am not able to perform well in my 12th std, all this money will be in vain. It would be better to opt for something else.' said I with sad tone.

'No dear, you want to be a doctor, you will go for Science stream only.' forced my parents.

'Then? After being doctor, will you allow me to open my clinic here or will you force me to get married? Then what about your money? Will I ever be able to return this? When I complete my education, you will have to prepare for my dowry, fees for other siblings, how will you manage all this?' asked I with anger.

'Alright, we will not give you dowry, we will give you degrees.' smiled my parents and looked at each other and said, 'our daughter has really grown up and has become quite mature at a very young age. She thinks too much for everyone, how lucky we are!'.

'No parents demand anything from their daughter, as they are also equal to sons, you have the same right of education, we want to educate you without any expectations. You just be happy, you will make us proud when you will be valued as an educated daughter and daughter-in-law, that is going to be our precious reward.' said my parents.

'No.no.no. I will not opt for this as I know it is easy to say but difficult to do.' I went to the room, slammed the door and kept on crying, sitting on the bed with folded hands. I came to know that my all friends who were with me in 10th std, opted for Science field and shifted to Rajkot for further studies. In my whole group, I remained all alone. I cried a lot for my friends, for new city, new school and especially for my dream and goal. But somehow I observed that my decision removed the cloud of tension from my father's head. Although he didn't say a single word but I found him free from debt of fees. My Science field filled the house full of tension but my final decision of not selecting the field brought peace at home. Bit by bit, I also changed my mind completely for not selecting that stream, I thought for long term and I found myself right in my decision. Now it was the time for thinking – if not Science, then what? Commerce or Arts?

It is said in Bhagavad Geeta chapter-2, shloka -47

कर्मण्येवाधिकारस्ते मा फलेषु कदाचन।
मा कर्मफलहेतुर्भूर्मा ते संगोऽस्त्वकर्मणि।।४७।।

**Your right is only to perform action
and not to its fruits.
Do not be attached to inaction,
nor act only for the fruit.**

I was struggling for selecting streams as I was more interested in fruit rather than performing my duty. I was craving for fruits (status and salary) but Bhagavad Geeta showed me the path of my performance in any stream which can lead towards happiness and satisfaction. It motivated me to keep on working without expecting the fruits.

CHAPTER 5

I asked few of my friends about Arts and Commerce stream. I and my mother went to multiple people for guidance in those streams. We just got one answer from everybody and that was 'Commerce'. I made up my mind for the same as everyone said, 'she is the student of science, if not science, then commerce will be the best option for her. She will get good jobs in companies after her M.B.A or M.C.A.'

But one of my teachers Kartiksir advised me to opt for Arts field. He said, 'Aditi, I have seen your passion for English Language and Grammar. You are made for that. I have read your essays and seen your participation in language based competitions, English language learning is your passion, make it your profession. I am sure, you will rock. Go for Arts with specialization in English.' He advised me to complete my bachelor and masters with English subject. I kept on thinking with my clinging hands. And he continued advising, 'it might cause difficulties in our society for women to work till late night in companies but it would be easier to work in academics.'

He called my parents to his Classes and also explained everything to them by giving various different live examples of girls' career and education. My parents got convinced, too. They were not much aware of academic streams and career options so they always used to get carried away very easily regarding that kind of stuff.

'Thank you very much sir for your valuable advice, we will surely think about it.' said my father shaking his hand with my teacher.

Going home my mother asked me, 'So now what are you up to? I think he is right, there is nothing wrong in being a teacher or professor. In fact, for girls it is one of the safest jobs and easily accepted by the society, too.'

'Hmmm.' murmured I by folding my lips and starring at my mother.

Next day of that discussion, I met my two classmates on the way. We stood for sugarcane juice and were sharing our school memories. We started discussing about streams and I asked them by eating the pieces of pineapple added to the juice, 'What are you going to study further? Arts or Commerce?' I kept on asking the same question to everyone until I selected my field, how insecure I was !

'Obviously Commerce, yar.' they said by throwing the straw on the road and showing high confidence towards Commerce as if they were going to be charted accountants in future.

'Why not Arts?' asked I for my security and with less confidence.

'Arts?' they laughed and looked down upon the field.

'What is wrong with it?' asked I by putting my glass on the table.

'We have got 70 plus percentage, then why to choose Arts. Those who have scored below 60 percent are definitely going to select the same field, who would love to sit with those dumbos, so called students of Arts.' they laughed loudly. Many a times, I met with the same negative answers about Arts which drove me crazy and also drove my confidence down. Sometimes I also thought, how can I select Arts direct from Science?

After few years, I realized that only your inner self-confidence can lead you towards your goals, else people around you would try to lift you up as well as will try to let you down. I perceived, I was seeking guidance from those girls who never wanted to do anything in their lives excepting bombarding and gossiping. But I am very thankful to God who rescued me from being carried away by various people who possessed only fake confidence, nothing else.

Am I going to the right path? I kept on thinking for a very long time and again went to Kartiksir for discussion.

'Sir, I don't know what should I do? I am so confused, everyone is denying me to select Arts field.' I asked it with one breath as I was out of my breath due to fast climbing of the Classes staircase.

'First of all let me tell you one thing Aditi, you are very conscious and sincere about your career. I have not found any sincere student like you up to now in my class. So don't worry about the field. You are going to rock in any field. I know you very well. Now tell me what is the area of your interest?' asked he by putting his spectacles on the table.

'I don't know, I just love English language and I love to be on stage all the time. I love to work among the crowd and to give good speeches. And above all I want to start my career at an early age as I want to help my father financially.' said I quickly.

'Then nothing can be better than Arts field.' replied he by putting his newspaper aside.

'It will give you opportunity to earn at an early age in a noble way. Nowadays, many colleges and schools are in search of English Teachers but they are not finding smart, talented, hard-working, qualified and sincere teachers. If you complete your studies, you will have all these qualities. People will love to appoint you. Not only in colleges, you would also be able to work as a trainer in some multinational companies if you achieve adequate skills by the time.' explained he.

'But sir, everyone looks down upon this field, and my all classmates who got above 70 plus percentage, opted for Science and Commerce stream. Nobody is with me. I am all alone.' complained I.

'Lion is always alone and selects its own path. Don't follow others, follow your passion and choose your own path. It is better, you are alone, you will get job earlier without less competition in the market as very few people would have the same qualification that you would have. When you would be on some good position, nobody would ask about your field or qualification, only your post would matter.' explained he.

'Alright sir. I think you are absolutely right. Thanks a lot. Now I will not change my mind whatever happens. I will go for Arts only.' said I with confidence.

Finally, I went with my father for the admission in the same school where I completed my high school studies. When I left the school with farewell party, everyone in the group was promising to meet with one another in Rajkot for science study as they made up their mind for it before result. I was also one of them so it was little difficult to climb the stairs of the same school for Arts field.

At school, one of my teachers, 'Hey Aditi, you here? I thought you would be in Rajkot for Science, you were a clever, efficient and disciplined student.'

'No ma'am, I don't want to leave my school, I have again come here to take admission.' I told her by hiding my despair.

'Oh! So you have come for Commerce! Good, nothing wrong in that, too' said my teacher.

'No ma'am, for Arts.' said I.

'Arts? Why? You are student of Science and for Arts?' my teacher got surprised.

'I want to be a professor ma'am.' said I.

'But that you can also do in Science, you deserve to be in science school.' she said with determination.

'Yes ma'am but my father is not financially strong, so I will fulfil my dream by giving best in this field.' said I with a mild smile.

'Alright dear, all the best. God bless you.' said she with a little sympathy.

She didn't say anything at that moment but she gathered other teachers and talked about it. They decided to give me scholarship for my science study and also asked the principal to convince me for the same. Their decision suddenly changed my mind and I started having sympathy for Arts field. I thought why the field is so vacant and no good students take admission in this field as teachers and some advisors also look down upon the field which prevents some bright or average students to opt for the field. I made up my mind, whatever I want to do, will do in this field only. I fell in love with the field and started finding good career opportunities in it from the day one.

'Dear, are you sure you want to take admission in this stream? Just have a look at your mark-sheet and and think twice.' conformed the principal before giving me the form.

'Yes, ma'am, I am damn sure, I will take admission only in this stream.' said I with confidence.

'Alright dear. As you wish. Welcome to school again. We always want disciplined students like you.' she told it by giving me the form.

'Thank you so much ma'am.' I filled the form.

'You are very popular for your hard-work and discipline, right.' said my father with proud.

'Yes papa.' I smiled at my father.

It feels really nice when people from outside appreciate you for your good things in front of your family members. It provokes to continue the same thing ahead. I realized that.

Finally after a week, the school started. I didn't require to get my uniforms stitched as I already had that. When I entered the school, we were made stand in the queue for some official formalities. One queue was for Commerce class and one for Arts. I stood in the queue of Arts class. Some of my friends who had 70 plus percentage, who were with me in 10th class called me and tried to correct me by informing that I was in wrong queue. They said, 'Hey, Aditi. Come here. You are standing in a wrong queue. Here is our class – Commerce Class.' I denied and replied with sign that I was in the right queue. Then I shouted from my place that I had opted for Arts field.

'What?' shocked my all most the classmates and went in their classrooms.

When I entered my class, all classmates were literally staring at me and some of them shouted, 'Hey Aditi you here? We thought you would be in the class of commerce or in Rajkot for science studies.'

The bell rang and first lecture started, the teacher took first introduction from the whole class and asked, 'You achieved 80 plus percentage and in Arts? Why?'

All teachers asked me the same question when they conducted their first introductory lecture. I just bowed down and stopped replying to everyone; I just started giving a gentle positive smile in reply. The same question continued being thrown on me for minimum a month as some of them were thinking that I was just joking being in their class but then everybody accepted that I seriously opted for Arts field. But that kind of behaviour from everybody kept me confused and kept on downing my confidence about my selection of that field. Then I also adjusted and accepted the matter strongly. Although it became much difficult to cope up with the students who achieved less percentage and had less seriousness about their studies but somehow I adjusted with them after few months.

I was about to complete my 11th std. I used to come first in the class in all the exams but I never got satisfied as I was an average student but far better than other students of the class so my first rank was natural. Well, I found all subjects of Arts field very interesting but very difficult to clear the exams as all subjects consisted theatrical element so there was not any other option excepting mugging up. But I was very good at it so I managed it. My main goal was to make career in English so my core focus always used to remain on that. I used to read many English books out of the syllabus to improve my English. I continued writing in English to enhance my grammar and vocabulary skills. Kartiksir always supported me for that. Now it was the end of 11th std, my exams got over and result was as usual – first in the class but I didn't take my 11th std much seriously as my entire focus was on English speaking skills. I covered a lot in 11th std as I knew in 12th std, I would have to score well in all subjects to take admission in good college.

Tuition classes of 12th std started in the vacation of 11th std, I also joined and started working very hard for all the subjects. But mischiefs of my younger brother put hamper on my concentration. I loved him a lot but as far as my study was concerned, I used to get disturbed a lot.

'Mom, since two hours I have been trying to concentrate on this paragraph, I am not able to complete it. Baby is disturbing a lot, please take him out, he is coming to play with me all the time, then I also can't control myself.' complained I.

'Alright, wait for a while. Let me finish some household work, at least cooking, it is time for lunch. Let me finish this, till that please play with him.' requested my mother by making the chapatis very quickly.

'Mom, but I have psychology test paper in the evening and I need to finish two chapters, I don't have much time, it is already 1:00 pm.' said I with much tension.

Mom took my little brother out and finished cooking somehow, he was harassing me a lot so he was also slapped by my mom to finish her work as she was all alone for the whole work, and on the top of it, she was supposed to manage everybody's time-table single handedly. I felt very guilty and sorry for my mother and my sweet innocent little brother. But at that time I just focused on preparation for my test paper and finished it successfully.

Again after two days I shouted from the room while preparing for my test paper, 'Please decrease the volume of T.V. I am not able to concentrate.'

'Alright.' replied my father in a loud voice by decreasing the volume.

'Is there any growth in your business or just the same routine, just earning bread and butter, not more than this?' asked my mother to my father in anger.

'Now a days the market is very down, everybody is just able to earn bread and butter not more than this.' replied my father in anger. My father always used the word 'everybody' to defend himself in any discussion.

'I have been listening the same thing since ten years, now our daughters have grown up and we need to do so many things for them, yet you have not settled down your shop, it is in the corner so you are not able to do the proper marketing of your material. There is no marketing – no business, how will you manage daughters' education, their marriage?' my mother started fighting.

'I have been trying, have not given up.' my father uttered half sentence in loud and half one in nervous tone.

'How long will you just try, why can't you enhance your skills? I suggested you not to separate from your brothers; you won't be able to manage financially.' complained my mother.

'If we had been with them, we both would have been living a life of slaves. You would have felt to be in a black jail.' my father yelled by pointing his finger towards my mother.

'This is also not less than a jail. To manage everything alone in less money is not easy, responsibilities of three children, education of them, household work, kitchen work, baby's vaccination, my health issues, I am tired now; I am not able to do it alone. I can't see you suffering for money. I don't want to see you always to pay rent of shop and home loan. Our children also perceive all that, they also spent their childhood in all this matter and have become mature before time. I always find worries in their eyes for their father.' my mother started crying.

'Don't worry, I will do something.' said my father by wiping her tears.

'I served and worked as a servant in the family for seventeen years but what I got, not a single roof for staying. Moreover, I gave my whole gold, else ornaments would have helped us for buying a shop.' said my mother going back to her kitchen work.

'You would have repeated the same thing for other seventeen years, at least you have your self-respect here.' said my father in a relaxed tone. It is said, a husband should always talk in a low tone when the wife's tone is high, it becomes easy for him to win the battle.

'Oh! Yes you have given me a palace for rest and enjoyment. Because of you I am in this situation. You never took any stand in your life, never fought for your rights and mine. Look at your younger brothers, after marriage, they became so smart and fought for their rights and provided everything to their children. My capable daughter couldn't select Science stream because of you.' my mother continued.

Silence for a while.

Again shouted my mother, 'I don't understand, how can your parents and brothers be so pitiless, despite knowing your less skills and smartness, they didn't give you a penny, shop, or house for living. We can never do this with our children. In fact, those who are less smart and less intelligent should be provided more support. I will never forgive them.' said my mom.

'You can never do this, I bet on this. You are the one who respect all of them like anything despite all this. You can't do it so don't blame me. They were not good with you, then also you invite them for lunch, dinner and respect them.' said my father.

'Yes, because I have considered them as my family, if they are like that, God will punish them, if I am wrong I will be punished but I can't disrespect those who come to my place.' said my mom.

'So now where is your fighting spirit.' said my father.

Fight between them kept on continuing, just topics got changed. They brought the topic of family issues from the financial crisis in their discussion. I was listening everything and cursed myself for shouting to turn down the TV volume. It became difficult for me to concentrate on my studies as from one side low music of TV serial reached to ear, from another side words of their fighting, and from one corner, crying of my little brother continued breaking my concentration. I closed my ears to make them isolated by putting hands on them to stop the echo from all directions and tried to concentrate on my studies but I could not make it possible so I went to the bathroom and closed the door, and started reading there. But mosquitoes harassed me a lot and allowed me to survive there for not more than an hour. The same thing used to happen all most the time due to our small house.

Holidays started for fifteen days due to school tour but we were given test papers and lengthy syllabus to complete by the teacher of tuition classes during those days as after that vacation, we were supposed to give our test papers.

'Mom, I am going on the terrace.' said I climbing the staircases.

'Dear, it is too much heat, the sun is on the head, how will you read? You will fall sick, come and sit in the room, we will not make noise.' suggested my mother.

'No, mom I want pin-drop silence. Here, guests and people from neighbourhood coming and going to home, they talk very loudly.I get disturbed, don't worry, I will find a shadow behind the sintex (a water container) on the terrace.' said I.

I started preparing for my exams on the terrace but after two hours, sun-rays started striking on the surface of sintex and then directly on my head. It was March and it was 3:00 pm at noon. So it was obvious to face the dreadful sun. I felt heat to take off my flesh and sit in my bones. The sun was in extreme desire to absorb the energy from my body with the help of the straw put on the surface of my head. I went down and got the bed-sheet to cover my head, sometimes, I also used to bring big towel to cover my head and to protect myself from heat. When I went down at noon, I found pin-drop silence in my whole street. Animals were taking rest in the shadow of the tree, my father came home for rest as no customer was going to come to the shop at noon. When I used to see everybody resting or sleeping at 3:00 p.m in summer and at 3:00 a.m in winter, I literally felt to keep my books aside and to sleep but again I burnt my all boats for my goals, stopped thinking and started studying. I ignored the heat and continued working for the whole days which were not split even by a single nap. Sometimes I used to take books in a marriage functions, I used to dance and enjoyed a lot there but I never involved my time in ladies' unnecessary talks and any kind of gossips. My that kind of sincerity about studies harassed sometimes my parents, especially when I used to make myself foolish in front of everybody in functions. I might not read the carried books but I used to keep them in my bag - full of make-up kit.

'One good news.' suddenly one day my father came and said.

'What is it?' asked my mother.

'I am planning to buy a house which is bigger than this.' said my father with happiness on his face.

'What?' I, my sister and mom got up and got together with happy face.

'But where is it papa?' asked I with excitement.

'It is in the next street to our house. It is Mohan's house, he has given an advertisement for selling it as he is going to buy a new one.' said my father.

'Oh, that house, but the whole house is broken and scattered. How can we buy this? That is the reason they are selling it. Nobody is ready to buy it and you want to be the victim of it ! How easy to convince you, papa.' I gave a daunting smile.

'Oh really ! Thank you my child. Now listen, the house is scattered, that's why he is selling it in low price. We will buy it and then renovate it properly. Think as if we are buying a land only, and at this cost nobody will sell the land in this area.' explained my father.

'That is true, but who will buy this current house? As we will have to sell it first, then only it would be possible for us to buy that one.' supported my mom.

'Ravi uncle, I have talked to him, he is interested in investment and to support us.' said my father.

'Oh! really? How sweet of him.' said my mom by folding her hands towards the small temple kept in a small corner of our sitting-room.

'See, good relations and honesty have played a vital role here. You might not get help from your family members, but God always sends somebody to help you at right time if you are honest in your life.' said my father.

'True. So when are we supposed to shift?' asked my mother showing less interest in any philosophical matter said by my father.

'Just in 40-45 days, it is going to be renovated, then we will shift.' said my father.

'Just in 40 days? But who will take care of the workers and who will buy the raw-material as you are alone at the shop?' asked my mom.

'I will buy raw-material and you are there to explain the workers the way you want it to be renovated.' said my father.

'But how can I be there, who will take care of household work and children? I have small baby and Aditi's final exams are going to start within two months and Harsha is also not well. How will I manage all this?' my mother started.

'It is just the matter of few days, then your struggle will get over. We will have two rooms, one sitting-hall and a big kitchen with a big store room. Please support me for this.' said my father.

'Alright, let's do it. If there is hard-work in my luck, I can't escape from this. After marriage, I have just done shifting of houses and shops, nothing else. It is tough to be on breadlines for the middle class people who are ambitious and expect much from their lives. I get hurt when I see my daughters tightening their belt for each required thing to fulfil their ambitions.' murmured my mother. My father didn't want her to start again so he pretended to listen her with full of attention as if he was listening some terms and conditions of some law.

Finally, he said, 'I agree and sorry' he followed the rule of a husband.

Finally, the renovation started, and mom's hard-work got doubled as workers used to call my mom for each and every minor thing of renovation, for tea and coffee, so she ran on her toe from the current house to that house till the renovation. Finally, the house got renovated in 43 days, it was looking small and beautiful. Although it was not full of many facilities, but at least better and little bigger than the previous one. All members from the neighbourhood came to see it and appreciated by saying that it took the form of a small palace from a broken house. Now, it was time for shifting.

'We will shift this Sunday, I will call my friends and brothers for help.' said my father.

'No, papa, I have my exams after this month, I will get disturbed. Please let us shift after my exams get over.' requested I.

'It is not possible as we have to vacant this house on the due date as we are not the owner of it now, and the owner wants to give it on rent from this month. We will have to vacant it as soon as possible. This Sunday is appropriate.' explained my father.

'For one day, you go to Bhanuaunty's house (neighbour) with your books, you won't be disturbed.' said my mom.

'Alright mom, that is a good idea.' I got convinced.

I was the kind of person who always used to feel afraid of wasting a single minute in my regular time-table. Finally house-shifting was done on Sunday. It was the 6th house that we shifted. My mother kept on arranging the whole house for fifteen days single handedly but she didn't disturb me in my studies as there were just twenty days remained for my final exams. Even all women said to my mother that she used to do a lot of work despite having daughters. Some said, 'her daughters are so mean, they don't help their mother.' But mom always supported us by giving them the reason of exams and education. All these things provoked us to do something for our parents.

Finally the date arrived for final exams of 12th std. It was the second board exam, so I was not that much frightened as was in 10th std. I was little confident, this time my enrollment number also got a lucky card. I got my seat number in a nearby school of my place. My parents were also relaxed about it. On the first day, my father came to drop me, I went inside and said bye-bye to him, he also bid bye-bye to me by wishing good-luck. Little by little, I completed all the papers successfully.

Again it was the time for vacation and waiting for result. But this time I was not much excited about the result, I was sure that I was going to achieve at least 70 plus percentage, which was enough for admission in any Arts College. I started enjoying my vacation. On the first day of my vacation, I asked my mother to leave the whole house-hold work on me and my sister. I worked hard in the vacation so I could give relaxation to my mother as she was suffering from some health issues. I learnt cooking new dishes for lunch and dinner, every day I used to make something different to make my parents happy and relaxed, I decorated a bit of my house, started regular exercise, drawing, course of beauty-parlour, watched good movies, played with my brother, went to my grand-parents to spend time with them, my aunts (my father's sisters) came to my place, we enjoyed a lot together. Although we were living separately, but my grand-parents and my paternal aunts were very attached to us, as my mom spent seventeen years with them, that kind of good relations cannot be separated despite having geographical distance. It was looked like exam of the whole family got over. My grand-parents had various relatives in the town. They all were pretty much attached with my parents. They used to come to visit us once in a week, although we were living separately. My grandparents also started visiting our place often. Everybody realized the value of my parents after few years of separation. I and my sister also started taking training of home caring, respecting elders, welcoming the guest, greeting them, serving them, etc. Everyone started appreciating us; it was like we were put in the market as upcoming candidates for marriage. I was the elder one so everyone asked my parents about finding a groom for me as I completed my 12th std, according to everyone, I was very good looking, smart and had good persona, so I would find a handsome guy. In a nutshell, all relatives found a new job of finding a groom for me. Now that was the worried subject of my life's exam. On that day, I realized, vacation never lasts longer. In life, exams continue – one after another.

'Mom, why everybody is talking about my marriage, I told that I am not going to leave you and I am not going to get married. I want to study further, want to work in some good school and college. I urge to make my career, please.' requested I with little irritation.

'Alright, don't get, just relax and start packing for Ahmadabad. We are going to go to mama's place.' said my mom with a happy face.

'Yuppie, are all masis (my mother's sisters) and cousins also coming?' asked I.

'Yes everyone is coming, we are little late due to your exam.' said my mom.

'Oh! But I will have to stop my Spoken English Classes. No problem, I will collect material from sir, and will complete the remaining work there and after coming back, I will get my work checked.'

'Aditi, sometimes, leave your work aside dear. Nothing will go wrong in life if you stop working for few days, at least in vacation. At least enjoy your vacation without work.' said my mom and laughed.

'Foolish people work continuously even in vacation, Kings don't work at least in vacation, sometimes learn something from me.' added my sister and laughed.

'Ya, ya. I am the most foolish person who gets enjoyment from work rather than other things.' accepted I and said it with laughing and continued packing.

'Please also do my packing as you do always.' said my sister.

'Alright, my queen. Anything else can I do for you?' said I with a smile.

We loved a lot our maternal parents. We waited for the vacation so we could go there and have fun with them. We were waiting for two days to go to reach there. Finally, after two days, we got the bus and reached there. We enjoyed up to any extent and celebrated my birthday and my mama's anniversary there. They did a lot to celebrate my birthday - cake, good food and nice decoration. They ended it with nice gifts. I always loved to be there.

Again we were there and it was the time for result. I didn't want my result to come when I was there as again same discussion might break our enjoyment, again my elder mama might fall in serious discussion about girls' education and all that.

'Hey, tomorrow is our result.' said my cousin who opted for commerce.

'Yes, I know.' replied I.

'Not much excited?' asked he.

'Yes I am but not the way I was in 10th std.' said I.

'Why?' asked he to provoke me.

'Don't know, let's go and eat ice-cream.' I ignored the talk and went down.

Actually I didn't sleep on the previous night of the result, but I didn't let that consciousness reflect on my face. Actually I was not much worried about the result, but I was worried about Chimanmama's discussion about that. Finally it was the morning of the result, at the time of my S.S.C board's result, I waited for the landline call from my father but this time we had our mobile phone so I kept it fully charged and carried it in my hand since morning. I kept on waiting for my father's number to come on screen. Finally after waiting for long, I called my father and asked about the result. He said he was in the school only. He asked me to wait for a while and asked me to call him after five minutes. I called him three times in those five minutes and got to know that I secured 82 % again. I was happy to cross above 80% but again it was not up to my hard-work.

'I don't know why I don't get the same reward what I give. I give too much in everything but I always get less.' I was thinking all that and my mom entered and asked,

'What is the result?'

'82%' said I with pessimistic face.

'Alright.' said my mother also with little grieved face.

'This time you are also not satisfied, right mom?' asked I.

'No, it is not a bad result but of course, not up to your hard work.' replied she.

'I think, I am not intelligent. If I had worked less hard, I would not have secured even that much. I can just go with my hard work, I might not be much smart.' said I with dissatisfaction.

'May be we disturbed you a lot, house shifting and other matters of family.' regretted my mother.

'No mom, it is alright. It is nobody's fault. Sometimes, luck also matters a lot. I am hard-working and sincere about all most things, but I might not be enough lucky person.' said I.

'Oh, please don't talk bullshit, the result is very nice, now think for further studies and come out for lunch still you are supposed to face many cards stacked against you.' supported my mom.

'Hey, I have got 74 %, yuppie.' my cousin came from the school with result in his hand. He was jumping.

'Oh! great.' I congratulated.

'And yours?' asked he.

'82 percentage.'

'Hmm. no increment, same in 10th and in 12th.' congratulated he by criticizing.

'At least better than you, both the time.' replied I.

'Yes, it is very easy to score in Arts, but in commerce ...' commented he.

'One day I will show you the books of theory, just mug up all that, and then tell me.' answered I with little irritating tone.

Everybody was standing around, my mother stopped me to fall in arguments. She did it by giving me signs from the corner. I shut my mouth and stopped talking to him. At night, my mama came and continued,

'So are you planning to study further?'

'Yes.' replied I with a mild tone as usual.

'Where?' asked he.

'Rajkot – a nearby city of my town.' replied I.

'Why not in your own town?' asked he.

'As there is no Arts College which provides specialization in English literature and language.' explained I.

'Then don't opt for English, go for some other subject which are offered by your town college.' suggested he.

'No way, only for English, I selected this stream. I was not interested in 11th and 12th std, I was just waiting for this day so that I can enter the world of English literature and language.' said I with little confidence.

'But how will you manage that, will you live there alone?' asked he in front of everybody to show how a girl became courageous just after 12th std. Somehow he wanted to prove, a girl can go at highest extent of confidence if she achieves good education and confident and independent girls are not liked at the initial stage by our society.

'No, I have received some information from friends, there is a very reputed college of Arts and Commerce in Rajkot. The timing of it is from 8:00 a.m to 12:00 a.m., so I will commute from Morbi to Rajkot.' said I.

'Commuting? A girl of our caste? It is not appropriate.' he looked down upon me.

'I am planning for further education, not for anything else, just relax, I will find my group of girls.' said I.

'Sarita, will you leave her alone for further education?' asked he to my mom.

'We will think about it if she finds good company. Actually, it is a girls' college. It would be very safe for her if she gets admission in it.' explained my mother.

'She is a girl, what she will do after studying that much, she will have to make chapattis only one day. Better enjoy today's life and be at home.' said he with loud laughter.

'I have a son, then also I am not planning to send him anywhere and will ask him to be the boss of his own shop as I have a very big shop so he will take care of it, why to study for so called 9:00 to 5:00 jobs. You are a girl, help your mom at home.' added he.

'Your decision is pretty right; you have a big shop so he will support you in that. But we don't have any big shop so I will help my father as well as my mother.' said I.

Chimanmama's narrow minded arguments with me and my mother continued for few days. We ignored it and caught the bus for Morbi after two days. When we came back to my place where air of freedom used to blow, I felt so calm and composed with my parents. Although everybody was so loving and caring there, but when it was time for a girl's progress, everyone showed their opposition. The same thing used to happen here also in my neighbourhood, but we saw miracle when we came back from vacation. We came to know that the families who always criticized us for our thoughts, they all started motivating their daughters to start some good work outside for their progress. The girls who were educated started working in some firms and in small companies, those who didn't have qualification started working in beauty-parlours and in some restaurants for earning and being independent. Some started working at home only, some started tuition classes and home-business. It gave us immense pleasure to know that and also gave us more confidence to go ahead. We felt that we were on right track. Everyone in the neighbourhood changed their lifestyle; they kept themselves busy in their own work and creativity. After few days, we came to know that Chimanmama was also planning to send his son to Bombay in a very good college for his B.B.A. study. We got shocked and happy to listen that. Slowly and gradually, I started understanding the real world, especially the nature of people around me.

It is said in Bhagavad Geeta in chapter-3, shloka-35

श्रेयान् स्वधर्मो विगुण: परधर्मात्स्वनुष्ठितात्।
स्वधर्मे निधनं श्रेय: परधर्मो भयावह:।।३५।।

It is far better to live your own destiny, duties and nature imperfectly than to live an imitation of someone else's with perfection. Even death in your own nature is better; imitation of others is fraught with danger.

I tried to chase my friends and cousins for my dreams but somehow I was saved from following an imitation. I was shown the path for living my own dream in the form of selection of the career of an English teacher. My own form earned me respect, I might not have been able to perform my self on the stage if I had followed imitations.

CHAPTER 6

After few days, my uncles came home and we discussed about colleges for my further education. When they came to know that there was no college in the town offering English as a special subject, they suggested to study in the town only by opting for any other subject. After a long discussion, I convinced them for my admission in Rajkot's college and also requested him to come along with me for taking admission in college. He agreed and we went next day.

We reached the bus-stop early in the morning and caught the bus for Rajkot. Rajkot is considered to be one of the best cities in Saurashtra. I was dying to see that city.

'Uncle will I get admission?' asked I with little nervousness.

'Hope so.' said he.

'Will you be able to manage commuting every day? It sounds interesting in the beginning but everyday commuting is very difficult. You will have to wake up very early in the morning, along with you; your parents will also have to wake up. Will you people be able to manage all this for long time? Physically, mentally and financially?' bothered he.

'It is a government college uncle. If I get admission in it, we will not have to pay much fees.' clarified I.

'I will do it uncle.' said I with confidence after thinking for a while.

Finally we reached to Kansagara Mahila College. To find that, it was a girls' college, my uncle took a long breathe.

'How frightened everybody gets when it is the matter of college! They carry various doubts for college and girls' education.' I thought for a while and neglected my thoughts.

It was a small government college but the best one for Arts in Rajkot. After reaching there, I directly went to the washroom to get myself perfectly ready as my hair got wavy due to the air blowing from half-opened window of the bus. In an hour, my look got awful, so first I combed my hair, applied some talcum powder on face and lip-glows on my lips. I was about to go out and remembered that I forgot to apply Kajal which was the most important thing for me. Finally I came out and saw some of the professors. My eyes found female professors; some were in blazer, some in sari and some in Patialasuits. They were in different hairstyles and make-up on their faces. I got impressed to see them, and was dying to be like them. They were full of beauty with brains. I always used to get impressed by the female who dressed up nicely and carried themselves effectively. I also appreciated them and followed some of their style.

'Where is the admission booth?' asked I to a student over there for the admission process.

'It is here, in the right corner.' she replied by using her hand gesture towards right side.

I turned my face and saw a big banner consisting big yellow fonts 'Admissions Open'. People had already taken their place in a big queue looking like a big snake. I also took my place in the queue and started waiting for my turn. We all were sweating badly due to much hot weather. Everyone was giving a gentle and formal smile despite tolerating bad smell of oneanother's sweat. I was popping up again and again from behind due to my impatient nature. From that much distance, I could see one lady in specs collecting some documents from people one by one. Finally after one and half hour, I reached the window and gave my all documents including mark sheets of 10th and 12th. The lady at the inquiry office looked at me and asked me to provide my birth certificate which I didn't carry.

'I am sorry ma'am, I don't have this, I was not aware of its requirement.' said I with fast heart beats and perseverance on my face.

'Well you must ask somebody about the required documents before coming for admission. Anyways it is just 9:00 a.m., admission booth is open till 12:00 a.m, you go and bring the copy of your birth certificate fast.' suggested she.

'It is not possible ma'am as I am not from proper city. I am from Morbi.' said I with worried face.

Tears were about to roll down from my eyes as I got frightened and insecure about my admission due to that document.

'Ma'am, what about my admission? Will I get it or not?' asked I with restlessness.

'Of course you have got the admission, we need scholar students, your percentage is very good. So don't worry, you just pay fees now and provide the remaining documents, tomorrow.' said she.

I got so calm and relaxed as if I quenched my thirst without a single sip of water.

'Will I have to come again tomorrow?' asked I.

She gave me some weird expressions as if I had made some mistake. Indirectly her expressions gave me the message - I would have to come to college everyday in regular days and I was getting worried just to come back for providing a document. Before she said anything, I said with a smiling face, without showing any kind of worry, 'Why not, I will definitely come. I will report here early in the morning sharp at 7:00 a.m. I will get the bus early in the morning.'

'No, not at 7:00 am, the college will start at 8:00 and admissions process will be commenced after 9:00 a.m.' said she.

'Alright, thank you so much ma'am.' said I and went to my uncle.

'Tomorrow, again I will have to come for providing one document.' said I.

'Oh, god!' reacted my uncle.

'It is ok uncle, that is going to be my routine from now onwards.' said I.

'Your journey of education is going to be struggling as none of our family members is experienced in any academic field who can guide you for proper things. You are the first one who will have to search everything by your own. You will make many mistakes but you will learn a lot and will gain a huge amount of confidence. In future, you will be able to guide your younger siblings but you will have to struggle for everything. It is not as easy as said. Hope you sustain for long. God bless you. All the best.' said my uncle.

'Thanks, uncle. I will give my best for everything.' said I.

'Shall we get the auto rickshaw to reach the bus-station? Hope we get the bus soon.' said he.

'Sure uncle, let us go. And tomorrow I will come alone, nothing to worry as such I will have to do it after fifteen days when my college starts.'

'Are you sure?'

'Yes, of, course.'

Next day I went alone to the college to provide my remaining document and got the admission certificate. I returned home happily. That work of five minutes took four hours to get completed. It took my two hours for going and two hours for coming back home. Now it was time for shopping as college was going to start after fifteen days. So I wanted to buy some clothes and foot-wears for new college life. Attire was my first priority for any new event or occasion of my life. I was extremely fond of getting ready and wearing variety of clothes and foot-wears. Observing my interest in fashion world, many people suggested me to go for fashion designing course as I almost the time used to design different types of cloths for me and they were liked by everyone. But I wanted to choose profession in academics only. When I saw my college professors, they became my role models as far as their appearance was consulted. I was very excited to learn from them, listen to them, attend their lectures and enter in the world of English literature and language.

Finally just a day was remaining to start my college. I finished my shopping but didn't buy any book; as the books were not available at the book-store of my town. The unavailability of the syllabus books made me feel proud about my syllabus, I thought, 'Oh great! How different the syllabus would be! That is why the books are not available in the town. It is English literature boss, not any normal or ordinary books which would be available everywhere! I got so obsessed with my books and my stream. I realized it after few years.

'Dear, tomorrow is your first day of college, how will you go?' asked my mother with worry.

'Of course by bus, mom' said I.

'But your college starts at 8:00 o'clock so you are supposed to reach there by 7:45 a.m. Morbi bus station is at the distance of one and half hour from Rajkot bus station but you will have to catch an auto-rickshaw from bus-station to reach your college. So at what time will you catch bus from here?' my mother started asking lots of questions.

'I will get up at 4:30 a.m in the morning, and papa will come to drop me to the bus-stop tomorrow. I will get the bus around 5:30 a.m or 6:00 a.m., then only I will be able to reach on time.' said I.

'Oh, so you will have to get up before three hours of your college time to reach there on time!' asked my mom.

'Oh! Common mom, it is not a big deal, all students who commute will have to follow the same routine.' said I by looking myself in the mirror and pressing a small pimple popping up on my nostril.

'Have you found any group of girls? How will you sit alone in the auto? If something goes wrong, who will help you?' asked my mother.

'Don't worry mom, nothing will happen, I will keep my mobile phone with me all the time. You can call me any time. I will take your phone with me and you keep papa's phone with you as we have just two mobile phones, so we will have to manage like that only.' elucidated I.

'Yes, that is alright.'

I packed my bag at night by caring a water-bottle, some snacks in a box, a book and a pen in it. I packed it at night not to get late in the morning. I kept my pair of clothes ready; I straightened my hair and applied a night cream on face to make my skin glowing. I completed my each work, but I couldn't sleep for the whole night due to excitement and little worry of commuting. My mother could also not sleep on that night.

Finally the alarm bell rang at 4:00 o'clock in the morning; well I woke up fifteen minutes before the alarm bell. I started getting ready. I wore black jeans and red top with a pony tail on head wrapping a red rubber belt on it. I applied some light make-up on my face, wore a leather wrist-watch and denim shoes, and carried a new bag, spreading perfume on the bag as well as on myself. My parents woke up with noise of perfume spray. My mom got up and got little worried and said,

'Why are you looking so beautiful? It is just your first day of college, dear?' said my mom.

'It is my first day, that is why I want to look beautiful.' said I with a loud laugh.

My father didn't say anything, just smiled and took his scooter out for dropping me to the bus-stop. And mom made tea and thepla for my breakfast.

'Papa, will you come to drop me in this attire? In this lungi and banyan?' asked I with little irritation and showing much hurry to reach at bus-stop.

'Will I also have to change?' asked my father while brushing his teeth.

'Yes of course, please put on good cloths fast as we are already little late.' I forced my father.

'We are just little late, not much. And it is not my first day of college, why should I change?' asked my father.

'Please papa, change.'

'Alright, give me two minutes.'

We left for the bus-stop. My mother stood outside the gate with worried face till my father came back from the bus-station. I kept on bidding goodbye to mom until the scooter crossed the street and until her visibility. I kept on catching her voice in a shouting form - 'Keep calling me.'even in the next street. We reached to the bus-station with the thought of my being isolated at the bus-stop. But the moment we reached there, we didn't found any area vacant of the bus-stop. It was over crowded and we found lots of buses standing there.

'Oh! God! Numerous students, even buses are not visible, they have covered the buses. Just look at the place, I am surprised.' said my father by parking his scooter.

'Yes papa, me too but it gives me huge amount of confidence. I am not the only girl, there are lots of girls. World is growing very fast. Nowadays most of people motivate their daughters for further studies, development and success. We thought our thoughts are at progress, but the whole world is together. See the tough competition everywhere!' exclaimed I.

'But in our caste, there would be very few girls, I suppose.' said my father.

'Nope, this assumption would be our second mistake. We might not have come across those people but there would be many girls from our caste too, they might not be from our town but somewhere, somebody would be having thoughts like us for sure.' said I.

'True and amazing.' my father got surprised as he never went into other world like that, not even thought about it, he was just bound for home to shop and shop to home.

'Inform mom about it and ask her not to get worry.'

We were talking, and suddenly we saw the crowd of students rushing towards one side of the bus-stop. They ran to catch the bus and especially to get the vacant seat in the bus. Those who could run fast could get a vacant seat. I also tried to get on the bus in that kind of rush, but couldn't succeed. I came back to my father. I saw students were throwing their bags from the window to secure their seats in the bus.

'Papa, if every day that happens, it would be very difficult to get on the bus and reach college on time.' said I with little worry and in a loud voice as it was very difficult to listen each other's voice due to huge amount of noise.

The another bus came and the crowd rushed towards that side. I also ran but again couldn't get on it. I was coming back to my father and one student passed by me while running towards the bus and shouted by looking at me,

'Hello miss, every day it is going to be the same scenario. Learn fast running to catch the buses and push yourself towards the rush to find a seat in the bus. If you are not able to find a seat, reach college by standing on bus or prefer to stand here but I am sure you won't get any bus till 9 o'clock. It is my second year so I am used to it.' he ran fast and got on the bus in front of me and I kept on standing there with open mouth.

'It is like Mumbai local train.' said my father

Meanwhile the third bus came for Rajkot; I ran towards it and tried to push myself in the rush but couldn't get on again. It was very difficult as I never did it before. I was feeling very bashful and nervous as there were a lot of boys in that rush; I felt the touch of everybody while pushing myself in that rush. I felt of being a sandwich. Nobody was doing it deliberately excepting few boys but situation made each student get on the bus in that manner as everyone needed to reach college on time. But I was feeling very shy as I never came across with any boy like that and my father was standing there, I was just scrutinizing my father by keeping my head down. Same thing was going on in the mind of my father, too. We both felt little hesitation but we both accepted the situation and finally I got on the forth bus by pushing myself anyhow but I didn't get any vacant seat. I bid bye to my father from the window and wished he would not share this kind of situation of bus-station with my mother as it would increase her worries.

I reached the Rajkot station and got off the bus fast without looking at any boy's face. I was very shy and even little afraid. I asked one of the girls,

'Hi! I want to go to Kalawad road, will you please guide me?'

In between I was getting calls after calls from my mother, 'Hello, you reached safely?'

'Yes, I am at bus-stop and searching for an auto.' replied I.

'Is there anybody with you? Are you alright?' asked she.

'I am alright mom, please call you later.' said I by putting the phone in my bag.

I concentrated on the girl's answer, and said

'Sorry, my mom's call.' said I.

'It's alright. I can understand. I have also received three calls since morning from my mother. Well, I am sorry. I won't be able to help you as I am also new here, please ask somebody else.' her phone rang and she went away by receiving it.

'Excuse me, I want to get an auto-rickshaw for Mahila college, would you please help me to get it?' I asked a boy passing by me with ear-phones in his ears.

'You can get any shutter rickshaw and if you are in a group, you can go by paying only 5 rs per person but if you are alone, you will have to pay 10 or 15 rs.' said he and ran towards an auto.

I tried a lot to find some group of girls going towards my root, but everybody was already busy with their own group. I couldn't find anybody and caught an auto for my root as it was already 7:50 a.m. I sat in an auto alone first time. I sat at the corner of the seat so if the driver tried to take me to the wrong place, I could directly jump. My mind kept on being derived by various unnecessary and worthless thoughts until I reached my destination. My heart was beating faster than its normal beat. I was sweating very badly; sweat started pouring from my eyebrows and entered my cleavage. My hands were shivering due to fear, but I didn't show it on my face. My mom was calling me again and again but I didn't receive as I wanted to focus on the root and the driver. I also had the fear that he might snatch away my phone from me so I didn't want to take my phone out of my bag. How insecure I was for everything!

Going ahead, one lady got on the same auto for going to the same root. I felt so relaxed and calm. Finally I could read the obscure words of my college name from distance. Coming little near, I asked the driver to stop the auto. I took money out of my bag at the same moment I got on auto, as I didn't want anybody to throw his or her sight on my wallet as I was alone and was pretty afraid and didn't want to get late for my lecture. Finally I crossed the road alone which was difficult for me and entered the college after the struggle of three hours.

First and foremost, I called my mom:

'I have reached college very safely, so don't worry and till 12:00 a.m. my phone would be switched off as it is not allowed in the class.' I said rapidly and went to the washroom to see my face in the mirror..

'All ok dear, and how are you feeling? You must be tired.' she started.

'Mom, please bye for now, will talk to you later. I am already little late.' I disconnected the phone and switched it off as I didn't know the option of silence or vibrate mode although it was Nokia 1112.

I combed my hair, applied talcum powder, lipstick and Kajal. I found my class and entered. It was a pin drop silence and one professor's speech was going on in the class. I was late by ten minutes; I took permission for getting inside, found a bench and sat there.

I got very impressed by the speech of that madam and her appearance. She was giving introduction about the stream, career and personality development and also suggested us to speak in English for better practice of language. I rolled my eyes from one corner to another corner of the class and tried to find good company with whom I could develop and flourish myself. I completed my first day of college and I got to know that my all subjects would not be of English literature and language. Those who opted for specialization in English, they were supposed to give total eleven papers for their bachelor qualification. Two papers in first year, four in second year and five in third year. I got to know that there were only two papers of my choice which were in English language, the rest of the subjects were different and they were in Gujarati language. When I got to know that, I requested my professors to allow me to write those papers in English as I wanted to improve my language and enhance my vocabulary.

'Sir, can I write my psychology and sociology papers in English instead of Gujarati?' I requested to the professors of psychology and sociology.

'How many students are you there for the same stuff?' they asked by looking at each other.

'I asked others, but I couldn't find any so I am the only one.' said I in a mild requesting tone.

'If you are the only one, it will be difficult as in the university nobody will be ready to check these papers in English language. Why do you want to increase your stress? Enjoy your two years, after that you will have to work hard for your third year.' they suggested and looked at each other as if they wanted to get rid of my more questions.

I kept on trying for the same but somehow I didn't find positive response from anybody so I gave up. But I used to attend only English lectures; I started bunking the lectures of sociology and psychology as I was confident enough for scoring in those subjects without attending the classes. I thought to invest my time somewhere else rather than attending those lectures. So I used to spend those hours in library and used to read English books, newspapers and magazines for language improvement.

Such as I completed one month of my college. My mother also improvised herself, she reduced calling me frequently as she got confidence that I became independent and eligible for catching the bus and auto rickshaw safely and reaching home safely. After a month, at bus-stop, almost students started knowing each other.

One morning, a boy student sat beside me on the bus and asked, 'Which college are you studying in?'

I looked at him with little ignorance and replied, 'Mahila College.' I opened my book and started reading to avoid him.

'What are you studying?' asked he

'Arts with specialization in English.' replied I.

'Oh, Arts?' he looked little down upon my field.

'Why? What is wrong in it?' asked I with little annoyance and showing obsession for my stream.

'No no, nothing wrong, but I have not found any of my friend in this field. We notice you every day, we thought you might be doing M.B.A or some other course.' proclaimed he.

'We notice you means? Who notices me?' asked I with surprise.

'All boys, many of the boys are interested in your friendship. They talk about your good looks and your dressing sense and your persona. They also talk about your rudeness for boys. According to them, you are a very decent girl and don't pay heed to any boy. You will never consider any boy as your friend. I think they are not right, won't you make me your friend? Can we go for a cup of coffee.' he proposed me for a date indirectly.

'No, thanks. And your friends are absolutely right. And one more thing, make an announcement among your friends that Arts field also has good personalities and it is also well demanded as other fields, so don't look down upon it. I added further, 'I bet you, after five years, everybody would be selling the qualification of M.B.A in the market but very few will be in the field of teaching and holding qualification of Arts so the demand of it would be raised automatically.' I said all in one breath and changed my seat.

Well, that was my first direct proposal. I got many proposals in my 10th and 12th std in tuition classes. I was in girls' school but there was co-education in the tuition classes. Nobody showed courage to propose me directly but indirectly all most boys proposed me. They could never show their guts as I never even looked up and saw any boy in the class or after the class. I always used to keep my eyes down as I promised myself; I would never do such things which would make my parents feel guilty. But on that day, I felt very happy when the guy appreciated my persona and looks, although I didn't reveal it to him but I liked it. I realized on that day, however ambitious a girl is, appreciation is always appreciated and accepted by her. Some reveal it, some might not but it is acceptable by everyone.

I was about to complete my second month of college.

'Hey, Aditi, I am Riya pursuing my B.B.A.' said she by shaking her hands with me.

'Hello. I am sorry. I don't know you, how do you know me?' asked I.

'Oh, common who doesn't know you?' said she with a foxy smile.

'Means? I didn't get you.' I asked with astonishment.

'You just look up sometimes; you will find all boys' eyes on you, dear. All most boys want to be your friends, sometimes give opportunity to somebody. This is your college life; you have good looks and attractive personality, why don't you enjoy it. Even I have a boy-friend. At least make some friends dear, it will make your life full of fun.' she became my advisor without my permission.

'See, I am very happy in my life, my life is already full of fun and I am not interested in all these things. Thanks for your advice.'

'My brother is interested in you; he has also talked to my parents regarding this. My parents also want to meet you.' said she with a request.

'Oh ! god ! please don't pull me in all this, I am here only for my studies. I will never betray my parents. I want to be something in my life for myself, for my parents. First of all I am not interested in marriage and all and I will never get married to a guy who is not of my caste.' said I with irritation.

'Oh, so you are a casteist even in this century?' asked she with disgrace.

'No, not at all. I don't believe in casteism but in my case, yes I am a casteist.' said I with determination.

'In your case? But why? You are getting so many good proposals, then why do you always reject everyone?'

'First of all, I am not interested to be hooked up with any guy. I am not ready for affairs, friendships and relationships. This is not my proper age for thinking about marriage.'

'Oh you are thinking farthest, I am just asking you to have a boy-friend or relationship for fun, and definitely no need to think about marriage at this age.'

'Well I have never ever thought about affairs or any relationships. If I fall in love by coincidence, first and foremost, I will demand for commitment of tying a knot with me. I don't like to move out with boys and waste my time. In our families, girls don't go out for studies and jobs but my parents have permitted me for my further studies by trusting me blindly. I don't want people to look down upon my parents by saying that the daughter took wrong advantage of her parents' freedom and made the parents shy.' said I bluntly.

'Oh my goodness! You think a lot at this tender age.' criticized she.

'Yes, I do and I don't regret for that.'

'So you will never accept anybody's proposal just because the boy is not of your caste, although he is smart, handsome, educated and rich.' asked she.

'No, I will not, money cannot attract me at all in this matter.' said I.

'You are spoiling your age and your precious time. I have seen you all the time reading and writing something even on bus. This is not a school life, it is your college life, babe, just enjoy it' explained she.

'This is my enjoyment, infect I enjoy more than you people.'

'But with whom, I have never seen you with anyone, neither boys nor girls. Who is your company?

'I enjoy my company.' said I with confidence.

'Oh, so you are a big boredom.' said she.

'Nope, I am more interesting even than you but you need to have that eye to see that. I find myself so interesting that I don't need to find anybody for my happiness or to live an interesting life.' said I with firmness looking into her eyes.

'So I should not waste much of my time to convince you, right?'

'Yes, absolutely dear. Thanks for understanding.' said I with mild tone.

'You never became rude to anybody regarding any matter. I have seen many girls fighting with boys on the road due to proposals they get from them. You might have been proposed many a times but I have always seen you solving all the matters and problems with a mild tone. I think that is the reason of getting the tag of 'a decent and calm girl' among the crowd of bus-stop. I am sure you would have left the same impression among your professors and college friends.' she said with a convincing and friendly smile.

Slowly and gradually, I started becoming popular in college as well as among my commuting crowd. Well I always remained busy in myself doing some or other things but I got to know about my popularity directly or indirectly which almost the time used to give me positive motivation to go ahead in my life. Well I remained alone all most the time. I was like a person who was found in the crowd apparently but could never be the part of it, always remained alone even in the crowd. I came to know about my nature at the mature age.

'Mom, I am bored now.' said I.

'Bored? You have just passed two months of your college and you are bored? I think you are tired as you wake up so early in the morning and commute.' said my mother.

'No, not at all. In fact, I am finding some more work.' said I.

'What? Apart from that much hectic schedule, you want to work more? Are you crazy?' asked my mom.

'Yes. I come back home from college by 1:30 pm or maximum by 2:00 pm.' said I.

'But you get up very early in the morning, every day travelling, studies and then you help me for preparing dinner. What else you want to do, do you have time for anything else?' asked my mother.

'You never get time in life for the work of satisfaction, you always need to steal time for it.' said I.

'Oh, nice dialogue. Effect of literature lectures!' laughed my mother.

'Oh mom, I am serious.' I replied by cutting tomatoes for diner.

'But what will you do?' asked my mother.

'Mom, I want to do a job.'

'Job?' asked my mother surprisingly.

'Yes, I want to do part time job.'

'But where and which kind of job? You are just 12th passed out, who will give you a job?' asked my mother while cooking rice.

'That I don't know how, where, what? I want to start something. I get free by 2'00 pm., so I can join something in the evening which will also provide me experience and I will also be able to earn some amount, at least for my pocket money. Then, papa will not have to pay for my bus-pass and college fees, books fees and my pocket money.'

'It is good that you want to be independent but first complete your studies, then start working.' said my mother by moving spatula.

'When I complete my studies, you people will get me married, then what will I do?'

'Then you can start your job at your husband's place.'

'Please mom, again I don't want to fall in any argument. I just want to work, please tell grand-mother, uncles and neighbors that I am not interested in getting married now as I heard you talking to them regarding the groom for me. Please let me focus on my career.' I begged.

'I know, you are ambitious and I also don't want you to get married now but if somebody suggests some guy for your better future, we should not respond them negatively, else they will stop suggesting anybody for you in future.'

'Wow! Is it possible? Actually I want that only. I don't get why people are much worried about my marriage, don't they have anything else to do?' said I with anger.

'Dear, when a girl or boy crosses 17 or 18, they are fallen in the market of marriage. People start suggesting good proposals for them and there is nothing wrong in that, they are your well wishers, don't misunderstand them.' explained my mom by cooling me down.

'Well-wishers? They are afraid of a girl's ambition. They think if I go ahead in my career, I would have my own thoughts, then I will not get married to a guy suggested by them which will cause humiliation to them. To make a girl get married, to make her cage inside the house and to take proud of helping a girl for her marriage, is their main business. It is a great way to show their kindness.' said I with anger.

'Aditi, now go inside, you are talking much. You go and read your books; this is not the way to say anything about your elders. Don't worry first we will take your permission, then only we will get you married. You are young blood, I can understand your anger but trust your parents.' scolded she.

'I trust you a lot, I hope you will allow me to complete my masters and help me to do the job first, Thanks.' I went inside the room by slamming the door.

I kept on thinking for some days about my part time job but couldn't think anything.

I was watching a movie in which I saw a girl starting tuition classes at home at young age, it clicked to my mind and I started thinking about it. But I was just a 12th passed out girl, who would have come to me for tuition? Some schools kids might come but I was passionate about English language as it was my main field to work in future. I thought of starting English Classes at home. I was thinking but again I thought 'Why will the school kids come to me for one subject only?' I should join some

Classes or School. I thought about Mehta Classes to start my job. Then I thought where a big daddy was present, who would like to attend my lectures? I started comparing myself with Mehtasir professionally who taught me English. I thought he was already there, why he would give me a job and why he would need me?

I got to know from one of my friends that Sanjivani Classes was in search of an English teacher. I wanted to grab the opportunity so I went there. It was the same Classes I studied in my 11th and 12th std. for other subjects excepting English.

'May I come in sir?' asked I with respect.

'Yes, Aditi. Come in. How are you?' asked the owner of the Classes.

'I am fine, sir.' I felt very nice when he addressed me with my name. I felt happy to know that he recalled my name.

'So you got good result in 12th. Congratulations.' said he.

'Thank you sir.' replied I with modesty.

'Today I have come for some different reason, sir.' added I.

'Sure, tell me. You want some career guidance?' asked he.

'Nope, sir. I want to start my career from here.' I came to the point directly without beating about the bush.

'How? I didn't get you.' asked he with surprise.

'Sir, I want to teach English here, as I got to know that you are in search of an English teacher. Can you give me an opportunity?' asked I with a polite and calm voice.

'It is very good. You are our ex-student, so we know you very well. You are smart, sincere and very hard working. It will be great to give you opportunity but the problem is, you are just 12th passed out. We appoint qualified and experienced teachers. Students might not accept you as a teacher as they have seen you studying here for the whole year. Almost students might know you as one of the good students of Classes.' clarified he.

'That is true, sir.' I could not say anything else and was about to leave.

'Wait, but we can give a try as you are the student of Mehta Classes; you would have good command over English Grammar. Don't know about your teaching skills, but we will think about it and will give you a call if we want you to join.' he gave me a hope at least.

'But one thing, your volume is very low; you speak very politely and in mild tone. As a teacher, you will require very loud voice to make it reach to each corner of the class.' clarified he.

'Sure sir, I will give my best efforts for everything if I get a chance.' clarified I with confidence.

I left the Classes and kept on waiting for his call constantly. Finally after three days, they called me for an interview. I went there and gave my interview. I was feeling extremely nervous as it was my first job interview at a very young age. Well somehow I completed it very successfully.

'We have decided to give you two lectures everyday. You will teach English subject to the students of std 8th and 9th.' declared the owner.

'Alright sir, thank you very much.' said I.

'I have various works to handle so I will not be present at the class for the whole day. You will have to deal with Priyanksir, my assistance and senior faculty of this Institute. For any matter, you are supposed to consult him. Of course, you have studied under him but now he is your colleague so you are connected professionally with him from now onwards. He is not your faculty, but senior colleague.' said he.

He finished his words and went out by wishing me all the best; he also encouraged me by saying that I was making great efforts at my age. He went out and I kept on smiling at him to get his smile back but he didn't even look at me. I experienced the first behaviour of professionalism.

'Welcome ma'am as a faculty member of the institute.' said Priyanksir.

'Thanks a lot sir.' I replied with a smile.

I thought he would respond me with a smile but he was saying everything by flipping the papers in his hands and arranging the files piled up on the table. He didn't even allow me to feel for a while that he was the same teacher who taught us just before three months. He was behaving as a very professional and strange person. I didn't mind of his behaviour but I didn't know how to react professionally, as they accepted me as a professional teacher of the Classes but I still was a student of it by heart. I didn't accept myself as a teacher. I was feeling very shy even for asking about my salary, before I ask something about it, he told me very straightforwardly,

'We provide 50 rs. per lecture but you are a fresher so we will provide you 35 rs. per lecture.' he spoke in a professional tone.

'Alright, sir. Thanks.' said I with blank mind and face.

'You will be handed over two lectures from Monday to Friday. Your timing of the lectures will start from 2:30pm to 4:30 pm. We are very strict about the timings; you will have to start your class sharp at 2:30 pm.' he kept on clarifying everything by flipping the papers.

'It is ok, sir. I also like to be on time for everything, and I…'

Before I say something about myself, he interrupted me as if he was not at all interested to know anything about myself; 'From Monday to Friday, you will come for giving tutions, and on Sunday you are supposed to come for supervision duty as we arrange test for students every Sunday from 7:00 am to 10:00 am in the morning. So on Sunday you are supposed to be here by 6:45am. All teachers are required to come and arrange everything before the students' arrival.' he clarified that and left the office wishing me best luck for the starting of my career.

I could not ask about the payment of supervision duty as his behaviour didn't allow me to ask anything about it so I made up my mind that supervision was supposed to be done at free of cost. But I didn't mind. I felt so happy that I got my job after 12th std. Now I would be working somewhere professionally. Now I was not only a college student. I went home with a box of sweets and shared the news with my parents.

'Papa, now your daughter is also the earning member of the family.' said I by putting sweets in my father's mouth.

'Oh ! great dear, Congratulations.' said he with happy face.

'Of course, I would be earning less than you but I would be able to take care of myself by my money. I will not demand my fees from you now.' said I with proud and a loud laughter.

'Oh, you really got a job? Will you be able to do it, will you be able to teach the students? Do you know that much English?' teased my sister with loud laughter.

'I don't know what people will say, they might say we are doing it for money. They might assume that we are forcing our daughter to work for money.' said my mom with a little worry as usual.

'Oh mom, my friend's father is a well settled doctor, then also she works in a laboratory, even her mother works in a hospital. Do they work only for money?' replied I.

'They work for their satisfaction and what is wrong if a daughter earns money and helps her father? Please don't think all this bullshit.' said I with little irritation.

'Yes, true.' said my mom taking sweets.

'Mom, today don't cook anything, we will go out for dinner. Every Sunday papa takes us out for dinner, today I will take you out. It is party from my side.' said I.

'Still money is not on hand, and Aditi madam has started spending it.' giggled my sister.

'Today, I will borrow from papa.' said I.

'Papa, please lend me some money. I will return it when I get my first salary.' said I by lifting up my younger brother and kissing him on forehead.

We went out, had some South Indian Food, some chat, Ice-cream and spent a very good time with one another. We did it on Saturday night as from Sunday I was going to be busy with preparation of lectures. I spent my entire day in preparation for my lectures, although it was just an introductory sessions but I was very excited as well as little nervous, too. So I prepared well and slept early on Sunday to start my fresh Monday. On Monday, I got up early in the morning and ended with my college, came back home by 2:10 pm. My mother was waiting outside the door in that extreme heat. I just reached home, got fresh and up, changed my dress. From jeans and top, I came in a simple punjabi salwar suit, hung purse on my shoulder, carried my attendance sheet and Grammar books provided by the Classes itself. I gave a professional look to myself as I needed to perform the role of a teacher there.

'Dear, lunch?' asked my mother.

'Mom, it is already 2:20 pm. and it is my first day. I can't afford to be late. I will have it afterwards.' said I arranging my dupatta.

'But have at least something. you have been working since early morning, you just had one chapatti and tea in breakfast.' said my mother.

'No, mom. I had a veg-puff at college canteen in the recess time, don't worry.'

'But it is noon, dear. How will you be able to teach with empty stomach in this intense heat?'

'Mom please it is fine. I am getting late. Please papa ask her to stop worrying like that. Her worries increase my worries.' said I taking my keys of scooty.

'At least have a chilled glass of butter-milk.' my mom gave it to me forcefully.

'Oh, mom my lipstick will be removed, I will have to apply it again.' said I by drinking butter-milk.

I applied lipstick again and rushed for the class.

'Hai! Look at Aditi. She is looking very pretty in this professional dress with a purse and heeled sandals, with a leather watch and a small ring on other hand.' said my mom to my father.

'Especially the contact specs make her look like a decent teacher.' said my father.

'Absolutely.' said my mom with a smile.

'After all she is my daughter.' said my father with a pride.

'Mine too.' said my mother with tears of happiness in her eyes.

'What are you thinking, what happened suddenly? Why sounding upset?' asked my father.

'I am thinking about her future.'

'Future? She is really working very hard, definitely she will have a bright future.'

'Not worried about that aspect, I am sure she will do best in her career. I am worried about her future after marriage?'

'Marriage?' My father also became silent for a while and started thinking in that direction.

'She is very ambitious, hard-working, sincere and very sensitive as well as emotional. Will anybody understand her skills and her kind nature? In our caste, girls are considered just for house-hold work, they are not even allowed to go out for studies, and Aditi might go very far in her career, the way she is working.' my mom showed her concerns.

'Relax, even in our caste, many boys are turning towards education.' consoled my father.

'But for girls, it might be difficult.'

'Don't think much about it, if her work is sincere and full of honesty, God will send somebody who can understand her nature and her skills very well. Otherwise, we will find somebody from inter-cast.' said my father.

'No, no, what would people say? We allowed out daughter to go out for studies, she might have an affair and parents had to get her married inter-cast forcefully.' my mother got frightened.

'Oh, God. You think too much. You are too much people concision. Let her complete her education first. God will handle everything when time comes.'

'True. But after all I am a mother, so got little worried.'

'Oh ! Common dialogue of all females, as if we-fathers, don't care for our children. Now I need to go to the shop, call me when Aditi comes back and ask her to share her first experience of job with me.' said my father by applying the kick of his bike.

'Alright bye- bye.'

Finally I reached the Classes for my first lecture. I participated in playing the role of a teacher on Teacher's Day many a times but it was very difficult to play a roll of a teacher in reality. When I entered the class, I got my feet cold as there were sixty-two students sitting in the class. Some were shouting, some were having karate with each other, some were throwing planes made by a paper at each other. The whole class was making noise. The girls were busy in gossiping. When they saw me, all of them started shouting.

'Hoooo, Ooooo.'

'Is she our new teacher? Wow, so beautiful and young!' I heard those kinds of words from the students sitting in the corner.

Girls started staring at me and scanning me from head to toe. Some were scanning my purse, watch, my hair-style. I got the feeling of being a public figure. Well I always wanted to be on the stage, but I realized on that day, it was not easy to face the public when you were committed to any professional field.

Before I speak anything, Priyanksir entered the class to introduce me as a new English teacher. The moment he entered and looked at the students, pin drop silence in the class took place. I got surprised. It felt like peace after a thunder storm.

'She is your new English teacher, she will conduct your English lectures from Monday to Friday.' said he by introducing me.

'CCTV Camera is on, if anybody is caught to disturb her, will be called out and punished. She will also give me the complaint letters about your mischiefs.' scolded he in a very strict tone.

'Alright sir.' students spoke in mass.

Well, I didn't like his favour as I wanted to control the class by my own way but it was my first day so I couldn't say anything. Somehow Priyanksir wanted to clarify before the students that I was working according to his guidance and he was the head of the institution. Somehow he clarified to me indirectly on the first day that he could say anything even to the teachers in front of students. I didn't pay much attention on it and focused on my lecture that I prepared.

I was about to start my class, he called me out for a while.

'Ma'am, they are very naughty, have a harsh control on them and make your voice little loud.' said he in a harsh tone.

'Alright sir thanks for guidance.' said I with a polite tone.

He went out to his office.

Finally I started my class.

'Hello everyone, I am Aditi. I am pursuing my college in Rajkot. Specialization in English is my study area and I am the ex- student of this institution.'

I started the lecture with my introduction.

'Ma'am, in which year of college are you in?' asked one of the students.

'First.' I replied just in short.

I didn't want to reveal it as they might not take me seriously if they came to know that their teacher was just 12th passed out. But they didn't allow me to hide it.

Somehow I overcame the question very soon and started delivering the lecture on the importance of English Language.

'She is just in the first year of college and has become a teacher?' I heard some of students murmuring in the corner.

'No qualification? Just 12th passed out?' I heard some of the students' voice from another corner.

'She is just 12th passed out, what will she teach us? Sir might not have found anybody qualified, or he spared himself to provide much salary to a qualified teacher. They might have brought her in less salary.' murmured some girls.

I was listening everything but I ignored each and every sound and word and concentrated on delivering my prepared lecture. Finally I ended with both the lectures in both classes successfully and reached to the office, signed on the attendance sheet of the teachers.

'So how was your first day? How were the students?' Priyanksir asked by folding his hands and looking at me.

'It was very good. In the beginning I was feeling very nervous, but slowly and gradually I got grips on my speech and students also started getting involved.' said I by keeping my eyes down and arranging the books in my purse to avoid eye-contact with him as I was feeling very shy.

'Very good. You must know that your subject is in much demand and will remain in demand forever. Normally English Teachers are not found easily. If you really work hard and give your sincere efforts in this field, you are definitely going to have a very bright future.' said he with confidence.

'I know sir; I have burnt my all boats for my career now. I will surely give my best.' said I.

'Make sure, never get over-confidence and don't leave your studies for earning money. Focus first on your education.' suggested he.

'You are right sir. I will never leave my studies.' I thanked him for his sincere advice.

'And have a strict control on students.'

'Sure sir. I will.' I thanked him again.

'May I leave now sir?' I asked politely.

'Yes, sure. If you want to meet other teachers of this institution, you will have to wait for an hour as they are busy with their lectures, else you can meet them tomorrow.' he informed.

'Sure sir, I will meet them tomorrow. Now I would go home as I need to prepare for tomorrow's lectures and have some college work, too.'

'Oh so you go to college regularly?' asked he.

'Yes sir, attendance is compulsory in my college.' said I.

'Oh it is going to be very hectic for you to continue all together, study, job and preparation for next day's lectures as our job is like never getting free type.' In any situation, you will have to prepare for next day's lecture.' said he.

'Yes sir, that is true, but I will manage.' said I with confidence.

'Alright sir, now I need to leave. Thank you.

'Alright, good luck.' said he.

I reached home by 4:45 pm. and my mom was waiting for me at the door as usual. She was very excited and I also reached with a happy face as if I had made some great victory. I started sharing the first experience with my mom while locking and parking the scooty as I didn't have patience to start my talk after entering the home. I shared each and every thing with my mom.

'So finally, you found a job.' said my mom.

'Yes, I found the work, I was in search of since long.' said I.

'Now, I am going to be very busy. To deliver lectures for two hours, I need to prepare for four hours. So my job is not of two hours only, but it eats my six to seven hours.'

'It is alright. That will increase your experience and you will learn more and more by teaching. It is going to be a great experience.' encouraged my mom.

'Yes, by teaching them, I will also learn many things, especially I will enrich my English vocabulary.'

'Yes, your English speech will be better and you will increase your vocabulary, too.' favoured my mom.

'I am feeling that I am investing my time in some good things, I am not wasting my time.' said I.

'It will demand much hard work, as timing is very difficult, every day I will not let you go without eating anything.'

'Oh mom, sometimes, in commuting that happens. Bus was very late today, anyways you don't worry, I will manage.'

Meanwhile I got a call from my father, he asked me about everything. I told him everything on phone without waiting for him to come home. Although I didn't share the matter of students' shouting for me, as I was feeling little shy about it, excepting that I shared everything.

'Oh, so your daughter has started job?' asked a lady to my mom in the neighbourhood.

'Yes, from today.' replied my mom positively.

'Where?' asked she.

'Here in the nearby institution, as an English teacher.' replied mom.

She asked each and every thing, we felt that we were at the police-station for investigation for being accused of some crime.

'It is really good, now she will be able to earn for herself at least.

'Yes, even she will get good experience for her future career.'

'In future after marriage why she would do a job, a female will not get much time from kitchen work and kids. Now it is her time. Let her do.' cemented the lady.

'True, after marriage female is supposed to be a good cook only, if her husband earns good, why she needs to do a job?' supported another lady in the neighbourhood.

'It is not like that, many women do it for their own dignity, identity and satisfaction. It should be a female's choice if she wants to waste her time or invest. Of course it should not be compulsory for a female to work but if she is able to manage both- work and family, there is nothing wrong if she works. In fact she would remain active and fresh. If we think about financial point of view, life can be easy and better if husband and wife both play the equal role of earning members of the family.

'But we can never escape from this kind of cage of narrow thinking for female. Only a female is required to support a female, then all problems in a female's life can get solved.' I expressed my feelings.

My mom asked me to go inside by giving a sign. After some time, mom also came inside.

'Mom, why in our society people think much about others and always speak negative about others' good work and creativity.' I asked with little anger.

'Different people will say different things, you must learn to ignore it and keep on going ahead.' motivated my mother.

'Mom but why can't they appreciate anybody's good work?'

'This is life. If they don't do anything, you should also favour them in their unnecessary talks, else they won't allow you to be the part of the society or group.'

'To hell with this society and group. But I never interfere in anybody's life or work, in fact I always appreciate good work of everybody. I never feel jealous about anybody's progress.'

'As you are interested in progress, else you might have done what others are doing. But forget that and look at yourself, where you are at this age. You don't have even time for thinking much about other things excepting your work which is truly a good sign of progress.' encouraged my mom. 'Anyways, put all aside, still you will have to listen a lot. When you listen more than enough that means you are on progress. Ignore it and get ready we need to go for a reception. All relatives are going to come.' said mom.

'Thanks, mom. You always motivate me. I can't do anything without you.'

'Alright, now go and get ready. We will go there by scooty, papa will directly come there from shop.' said my mom.

'Alright, what should I wear.' asked I.

'Wear whatever you like, you are a teacher and you select dresses even for me all most the time, how can I tell you about your dress?' said my mom with a smile.

'Alright give me 20 minutes, I will be ready.' said I.

I got ready wearing a black long skirt with pitch top by keeping my hair open. I applied brown lipstick and red earrings and wore black bracelet, black watch and black heeled sandals. We reached for the party.

'Hello beautiful, nice dress, looking very pretty.' appreciated one of my cousins at the party.

'You always grab the opportunity of being the centre of attraction in any function or party. Really you have very nice dressing sense. We love your all dresses, from where do you buy all that?' asked my another cousin.

'From the town only, dear. Well you are also looking very pretty, nice ring.' We fell in deep talk of fashion. 'Fashion is one of the areas of my interest.' I said.

I started my dinner with some of my cousins and friends. My aunties passed by me but they ignored me due to my beautiful attire. I used to face the same problem of female jealousy frequently. But being elders, I acknowledged them and asked to join for dinner. They smiled and then talked for a while for formality. I couldn't understand why they were comparing me with them as I was eighteen years younger than them. I ignored the matter and started enjoying my dinner and dance.

'Hello, I have heard that you have started a job.' asked one of my close relatives, my father's mama.

'Yes, just before a week.' I replied gently.

'Oh, good. Devang will not face the lacking of a son, now. So what do you do there and how much are you paid?' he inquired about each and everything.

'I work as an English teacher there and my salary is 1700 rs. per month. I give my two hours everyday to the institution.'

'Only 1700 rs.? What do you save then?' he laughed.

'But I go just for two hours. Not for the whole day'

'But what about savings, better to sit at home and enjoy watching T.V.' he said in a satiric tone.

'I am just 12th passed out, it is just my beginning. I do it for my experience, not only for money.' said I calmly by controlling my anger.

'Oh dear, don't work hard for that much only.' he dipped his bhajiya in chattni and put in his mouth while mocking me.

I remembered my mom's words about people's unnecessary remarks. I just smiled and went from there to stop the arguments. I got tired of people's negative comments about others' work and intense gossips about each other. But that was the speciality of small towns. People were found taking much interest in others rather than themselves.

My job started going excellent. I started working very hard for that. Even in college, I used to spend hours and hours in the library for my preparation. I used to prepare even on bus while commuting. I used to carry the books of std 8th and 9th along with my college books. When I opened those books for preparation, students around me always used to ask why I was reading the text books of std 8th and 9th. I told them about my job and they used to wish me good luck and used to appreciate my work which used to provide me huge amount of confidence.

In the library, 'Hey Aditi, we are planning for a movie today evening. Would you like to join us?' asked my college friends - the girls' gang.

'When?'

'Today we are going to bunk the class and for another movie we will go tomorrow in the evening.'

'Oh dear I am so sorry I will not be able to join as today I have to prepare for lectures, then only in the evening I will be able to deliver it.'

'Then come tomorrow evening.' they gave me other option.

'In the evening, I would be busy in taking my class dear; I won't be able to join.' I apologized.

'Take a day off atleast for a day; you didn't even join for the party on that day.' said one of my friends.

'How could I join dear? The party was at night. It would have been difficult for me to catch the bus back for home at late night and my parents might not have even allowed me for that.'

'Then can't you arrange for a leave for a day?' asked she.

'No, dear. It is my new job. I can't do it at the initial stage.'

'Oh, don't you think you have started your job too early? You can't even spend time with your friends; you don't even enjoy your college life. You are wasting your beauty and youth, honey.' my friends made fun of me.

'No dear, this is the enjoyment for me. I enjoy my life a lot.' replied I with gentle smile.

'It is just a hectic life. When do you find time for enjoyment? All the time busy with books and preparation.' said they with little loud voice.

'Anyways, all the best for your career and God bless you.' They got up to go out.

'Thank you all of you for asking me to join for the movie.'

'And so sweet of you for not joining with us.' they smiled, patted on my back and went.

I didn't say anything at that time, but sometimes I used to ask myself if they were really right. Was I not enjoying my life? I kept on thinking in that direction with the pen in my mouth. Again I ignored the thoughts and focused on my work. Finally I finished the preparation and got out of college, reached the stop and got the bus for my town. Like that I spent eight months of college and six months of my job. Both were going simultaneously and going on well. I made a splash and became the crowd puller for my teaching skills and my personality. Students started demanding for my lectures. I also started enjoying my teaching. Well the schedule of life became extremely hectic as I was not allowed to sleep even on Sunday till late morning due to the Supervision duty. In fact I had to get up earlier in the morning on Sunday to reach the institution at sharp 6:45 am. But somehow, with the blessings of God, I managed everything.

'Ma'am, one good news for you.' said Priyanksir sir.

'What is it sir?' asked I.

'We took reviews from students regarding your teaching.' informed he.

'We got 100% positive reviews about your teaching.'

'Oh, really. It is really a good news for me, in fact very motivating one.' replied I with delightedly.

'So we have decided one thing, we want you to conduct the lectures in 11th and 12th std. I discussed it with the owner, he asked me to request you for that.' Priyanksir's requesting tone made me surprised.

'What? Are you sure?' asked I.

'Yes, of course. But sir you already have another English teacher for 11th and 12th std.' asked I with surprise.

'Yes, we have. But students are not satisfied with her teaching, especially with the portion of grammar teaching.'

'Does she know about her? As I don't want to hurt her by replacing her.'

'You don't need to be worry about it. We have also talked to her. And we are not laying her off, she will deal with the text-book portion and you are supposed to deal with the grammar portion as students are not satisfied and it is pure professionalism, don't drag your emotions into it. You are good at your teaching, else you would have also been laid off from the institution. Now learn the steps of professionalism by keeping your emotions aside.' said he bluntly.

I couldn't reply to him in that matter and kept my eyes down and directly came to the point, 'But sir, how will we be able to adjust the timings as my morning hours are already occupied with my college.'

'You don't worry about it, we will manage everything, you just say 'yes'.'

'But sir, I am just 12th passed out, how will the students accept me as a teacher who is just two months elder than them?' asked I.

'I said, you don't need to worry about anything, you just get agree, everything will be managed.'instructed he.'You will be provided 50 rs. per lecture for higher standards. Nobody pays that much in the town but we are very impressed by your teaching skills so the owner has asked me to pay that much to you.' he added.

'Sir, I don't work just for money.'

'We know that but it is a marvellous opportunity for your experience too. You will get teaching experience in higher standards at a very early age.' explained he.

'Alright sir. That is true. But how will we set the time?' asked I.

'You give two hours every day, instead of that give three hours and two hours extra on Sunday, it might be extremely hectic for you but it is our request to you. Please do it for our students, they are very disturbed because of their English Grammar.'

I thought for a while and said, 'It is fine sir; I will try my level best for it.'

'Thanks a lot ma'am.' his thanking tone clarified the extreme need of students for English Grammar.

'You will not allow me to have at least a little time for myself, sir. I will have to do a lot of preparations for all standards. It is going to kill me.' said I with a smile.

'I can understand your concerns but it is the students' demand so please go ahead.'

'It is okay, sir. Let me give a try.'

I went home and discussed everything with my parents.

'Will you be able to manage everything?' asked they.

'It will be very challenging.' I said it with mixed feelings- nervousness and excitement.

'Then, better not to stretch your- self too much, it will also affect your studies and health.' suggested my parents.

'But it is the demand from students, so I will have to do it.' said I.

'I think it would be very difficult then it is your wish. You are mature enough to take decisions by your own.' said my parents.

I thought for few days and finally I took the charge of 11th and 12th std. It became so difficult in the beginning to enter the higher standard classes as there were 96 students in the class. They were looking elder than me and they were very mature students. I felt extremely nervous for few lectures, but I didn't show it on my face. Finally I got grips with the situation and was requested to take the entire charge of 11th and 12th std for English subject. I was asked even to deal with the text book portion.

'Ma'am, students are very impressed by your teaching, so now you deal with higher standards and 8th and 9th std will be handed over to another teacher.' Priyanksir proclaimed.

'It is fine sir. I don't mind. Infect I would be able to learn more from their syllabus.' said I.

I was very happy as my teaching was accepted and I was given higher standards. It raised my confidence too much. But when the students of 8th and 9th std. came to know that I was not going to conduct their classes, they literally rushed into Priyanksir's office and demanded for my lectures. Priyanksir pushed them out by raising his voice and scolding them.

'Mam, please come to our class. We want you to take our English class.' shouted they from the open window of the office. I was standing in the office itself but couldn't speak a single word, nor could I give any expression as I was not aware of the authority's decision. I just kept my head down to avoid their shouts. 'She will come, don't worry.' replied Priyanksir on my behalf.

'On the basis of students' demand, you are required to conduct lectures in all the standards. Why don't you start working here for full time?' asked he directly.

'But sir my college and study.' I replied with little hesitation.

'We will manage everything ma'am. We will set the timings according to your convenience.'

That craziness of students for my teaching enhanced my confidence and made me work harder. I couldn't forget those shouts for two days. I found all balls in my court. Well I tried my level best not to convert my confidence into over-confidence. But it was very difficult to understand that at that tender age.

He set my complete timetable for all the standards and made my schedule even more hectic but I was happy doing it.

After a month, 'Ma'am, one good news for you again. The owner has requested you to conduct English lecture in S.Y.B.Com.' informed Priyanksir.

'S.Y. B.com?' I asked with surprise.

'How can it be possible, how can I teach the students who are elder than me? How will I be able to even control them?

'The way you did it before. Just give a try. I am sure you will succeed.' he convinced me somehow.

Now I started teaching English to the all students of that institution. It was a wonderful and unbelievable experience. Sometimes even the teachers used to come to attend my lectures. The students' demand and various opportunities didn't allow me to digest my success and my confidence was converted in to over confidence, well I didn't realize it at that time due to my pretty young age.

I started earning around 5,000 per month after my 12th std. Well money also mattered a lot at that time as it was my first job but I realized that I was gaining lots of experience as far as my teaching, personality and professional behaviour was concerned. I realized that professional life was quite different from personal life. There was no place for emotions there. It was compulsory to be practical enough in each and every step. Well I used to fail in it many a times, as I was not at all practical by nature, but I started learning it gradually. I could not change my heart but somehow I started pretending that I was also practical enough for my profession.

One day could never be forgotten when Priyanksir invited all the teachers to clean the whole institution on Sunday.

'Cleaning of the classes?' asked I with astonishment.

'Yes, any problem?' asked he.

'No, not at all.' said I despite having problem.

I came home and told it to my parents. They also got surprise; they thought why they couldn't call someone for cleaning stuff. My parents thought what teachers had to do with that? There were fifteen classes including one office, small kitchen and two toilets. We were supposed to clean everything. I realized on that day that one was required to drink those kinds of bitter sips of poison in the beginning of career. All teachers got together and started cleaning the class from morning to evening. Such a pathetic condition! Finally, I personally experienced and accepted the professional life

We were forced to do cleaning of the institution, paper checking and supervision duty at free of cost. I didn't have any choice at the initial stage of career. Day by day, exploitation regarding timings, teaching and salary increased and reached at the intense level. I used to work a lot in less money. But career was going on so I accepted it.

Meanwhile, I got a call from a school which was nearby my town. It was at the distance of 20 minutes from my town. They asked me to join as an English teacher.

'From where did you get my number?' asked I with a shock on phone.

'From one of the students of Sanjivani Institute.' replied they.

'We request you to join here for teaching English Grammar especially.' the principal said in a requesting tone.

I felt pretty good to know about my popularity. But I was already running out of time so I replied very politely, 'Thank you so much sir for acknowledging me but I am extremely busy and can't arrange time for coming there.'

'We know about your hectic schedule, but it would be a great help if you could arrange few lectures at least in weekends.' requested she.

'Ammm, let me check my timetable, will let you know about it later.' I replied gently.

I discussed it with my parents and they denied as they explained to me that I didn't need to run so fast in life. They advised me not to bite off more than I could chew. The school was in other town so they were not agree to allow me to go alone. I thought for few days and got to know that they were ready to pay me eighteen thousand rupees just for two days in a week. I just needed to complete the Grammar portion of 10th std. and I was required to conduct a test paper to evaluate their skills. Eighteen thousand was really a handsome amount for me. I didn't want that opportunity to slip from my hands.

'Papa, I want to go and give tuition to the school of that town.' requested I.

'No, dear, we will not allow you to go there alone.' said my father.

'But it is very easy to get a bus from here.' I requested to my father.

'I am just 12th passed out but they trust me and who will give that much salary to just a college student.'

After few arguments and requests, I convinced my parents for that but my mother said she would go with me to that town. She would wait at the campus until I finish my class. I didn't have any problem with that. So finally I accepted the proposal and set the timings in weekends from 3:00 to 6:00 pm. Now even on Saturday and Sunday, I used to remain busy till 7:00 or 8:00 pm. On weekends, my mother also used to remain busy with me. She used to take my younger brother with her and used to sit on the small ground.

I spent my whole year of college in that way. It was an extremely busy year. I didn't have time even to look at myself. But I was so happy that I started my job at a very early age. My salary gave me marvelous feelings of being independent. I stopped taking a single penny from my father. I used to pay my college fees, books fees, money for bus-pass, etc. I used to buy some or other thing for my siblings and for my parents. It was a joy of being independent. I used to burn midnight oil and remain much active. Despite working many hours a day, I used to find time for exercise, watching T.V., helping mom in the kitchen, listening songs. I found just four hours for my sound sleep.But it never bothered me as I loved to be hyper active. Well, according to my classmates, I was not enjoying my college life but for me my career and my learning was the enjoyment. I enjoyed it a lot, I never felt that I was not enjoying. In fact, I felt I was enjoying even more than them by being always busy in some creative stuff. Of course, I used to get tired but it was managed. I became sincere and very dedicated towards my job. I got used to with both the roles - role of a student and a teacher. Student's role was very smooth and easy going while the teacher's role was burdensome, strict and responsible.

I finished my proposal of other town's school successfully and was provided my salary for it. The salary made me forget all the problems that I faced for completing that proposal. It worked as a magical medicine which healed my all wounds.

Finally, the year was about to end, I had to prepare for my final exams as I didn't pay much attention on my studies during the entire year.

'Sir, I want some leaves for preparations of my final exams.' said I to Priyanksir.

'How many leaves?' asked he.

'At least for twenty days. Seven days for attempting seven papers and ten days I want for preparation.'

'But you will not be provided salary for these twenty days as per our rules.' clarified he.

'No problem sir, it is completely fine.' answered I.

'And on the next day of your exam, you will have to report to the institute so that you can assist us in the management stuff and paper checking.' he said bluntly as usual. His tone could take anybody's temper high but these kinds of people teach us to control our temper and remain calm in some situation. I am thankful to these kinds of people for making me mature before time.

'Alright, sir.' said I in a calm voice by controlling my anger.

Of course, I felt very bad the way he spoke to me. There was not spark of decency in his speech. He was behaving as if I was his student. I was tensed due to my exams and he overloaded me with the duties of the institution directly after exams and that was also at free of cost. I was appointed there just for the lectures, not for any other work as I was not paid a single penny for that but I faced it for the whole year. Well on that day, I didn't say anything; I just left calmly and kept on thinking about it while driving to home. I didn't discuss anything with anybody at home. I just had my lunch and tried to focus on my exams first.

After some rest, I went on the terrace with my books and started preparing for my exams rigorously.

Exams were about to start but it was very difficult to commute during the exam time, I didn't have any relatives in Rajkot where I could find my accommodation till my exams. I called some of my friends regarding that and one of my friends let me know that hostel of our college provided the facility of temporary accommodation to the commuting students during the exams. I took permission from my parents to stay in the hostel for eight days until exams get over. I was permitted and my father came to drop me there to see the environment. I shifted there before a day of exam. I felt like a caged bird there, felt so drown and was missing my parents. I started crying like anything. I called them with tears in my eyes, mobile was not allowed so I called them with telephone booth kept at the reception area of the hostel. First time I was away from my parents so it was very difficult for me.

Somehow I focused on my preparation; I used to call my parents two times a day. Finally I completed the exams of my first year successfully. I started enjoying with friends at hostel; food was not good but that didn't matter much for me. I went back home after the exams and felt much content although I was missing my hostel friends and hostel life of eight days. I shared each and every experience of hostel life with my mom.

I started washing my cloths by myself. I cleaned my room and the whole house as I did it there even during exam. If I was in hostel so I had to manage everything by own even in the hectic schedule of exams.

'How dependent we become sometimes mentally and physically despite having much strength!' said I to my mom while eating cucumber.

'I think I should send you and your sister to the hostel for few years. Just look at you, I can find the damn change in you.' said my mom with a smiling face while making chapatis.

'No, mom. I am happy here with you.'

'Hoooo, it is a vacation time after a long time. I don't want to do anything; I just want to enjoy my vacation, my free time.' said I by taking the slice of tomato from the salad plate put on the platform.

'Vacation and you? Will you enjoy your free time or will find some work even for eight days of vacation.' asked my mom.

'No, nothing. Just planning to write some poems, not much.' said I.

'See, I knew you can't enjoy free time, you are not made for it.'

Priyanksir called me for joining the institute directly after my exams. I requested him to give me some days for my vacation. I told him that I wanted to enjoy my cousin's wedding; I also required some days for shopping. Somehow he was convinced and asked me to come back as soon as possible. On that day, I realized 'Success is not free of cost. Praise is always painful.'

'Hey, Aditi you have finished your exams now. Will you please give tutions to my children?' asked one lady from neighbourhood.

'Oh, aunty, I am going to my mama's place as my vacation has started so I will not be able to give time to your children otherwise I would have surely helped them.' answered I with politeness.

'You have become a renowned teacher. You teach in Sanjivani institute and my elder son is your student. He always appreciates about your teaching.' said another lady in the neighbourhood.

'It is very nice; your daughter has started working at a very early age. Otherwise in college days, I have seen girls just partying, moving around and watching T.V., nothing else. She is very sincere and hard-working. You are very lucky to have a daughter like her. Now you will have to find an educated groom for her who values her talent and hard work. Don't get her married where girls' household work is appreciated only.' said the third lady of the neighbourhood.

I realized on that day, 'when you do something different, people will always speak against you but if you keep on following your path with confidence, they will start behaving against you and when you get success in that path, they will start appreciating you. So it is better not to focus much what people think and say about you. But I know it is very easy to say but very difficult to digest people's opposition, especially from your near ones.'

When my relatives came to know that I started earning good amount at an early age, they also started admiring my skills. When I started my career from seventeen hundred rupees, they became the best criticizers but handsome amount of money attracted everyone in the whole community. I became the epitome of ambitions and professionalism. Out of the blue, my father started getting recognized by my name which gave me and my family immense pleasure. Some also sympathized him for being the father of an earning daughter and not having an elder son. Some thought my parents were taking my income for bread and butter but actually it was not at all like that. But I ignored the comments and people's thoughts.

I apprehended on that day, 'When you get busy in your progress, you might not have time even for thinking about yourself but you become the elite topic of discussion in the market. My parents motivated me to focus on the positive reviews of people and asked me to ignore the negative ones. I was immensely blessed with my parents' broad-minded thinking.

I reached to my mama's place to attend the function. We had a very nice time in shopping and beautifying ourselves. All cousins enjoyed a lot.

'Finally you started your college out of the town and even started the job.' said Chimanmama with a smile.

I got a little shock of his positive smile. My mouth stayed open and I starred at him for a while, then replied very politely 'Yes.' I tried to avoid the discussion about education and job.

'It is very good beta. Nowadays girls are doing nice jobs. They have gone very ahead in their career, even than boys. I have also allowed my son to go to Bombay for higher education, let us see what he will do in his life.' said he with a positive note.

I got shocked by his that kind of positive words about girls' education.

'Of course he will give his best for his studies and will definitely make you proud.' said I with confidence.

I didn't want to fall in any arguments regarding the same topic. But I realized he also realized his mistake of commenting everyone regarding their future, career and life. 'When time comes, everyone gets complied with your thoughts if you are honest and determined about your work.' murmured I.

We returned home after a very small vacation. When I reached home, I saw calls from Mehtasir where I learnt my English language, whom I considered my guru.

'Hello sir! Sorry I was on bus so couldn't hear the ringtone of my cell. I saw your missed calls so I called you back.' said I by calling him.

'Yes, can you please come to Classes now?' asked he.

'Now?' asked I with tiring voice as I was very tired due to the journey of whole night.

'Yes, now.'

'Sure sir. I am coming.' I replied without any hesitation.

I requested my mother to make a cake for him very fast as it was his birthday. On his every birthday, I used to ask my mom to make a cake for him as he loved homemade cake made by mom.

'Good morning sir.' I wished him by touching his feet for blessings.

'First and foremost, congratulations for the beginning of your career and succeeding in it. said he.

'Thanks a lot sir, it is just because of you. You guided me for everything and I am giving to my students what has been given to me by you. They are very happy with the method I am using for my teaching. When they ask me about my learning source of this teaching method, I always let them know about your name. Many of them want to see you.' said I with extreme pleasure on my face.

'Oh really, so sweet of you. But you have become my rival now, you are in my competition. Well disciples always go ahead and do better than their teachers; I expected the same from you.' said he with a smile.

'Thank you so much. Everything has become possible with your blessings, sir.'

'But today I have called you for some specific purpose.'

'Specific purpose? What is it sir, anything serious?' asked I by showing little worries.

'Well, I will not beat about the bush; will directly come to the point. I want you to teach here, I require you to start working here as an English teacher.' he said in a requesting tone.

'Here? Are you serious?' I got extremely astonished.

'Yes.' he replied by looking up from his specs.

But sir, you already teach here and students are highly impressed by your teaching. How will they accept me as a teacher? They are very happy and satisfied with their Pizza, why would they want to have Dal-rice? And above all, how will I be able to teach in front of you as it is very difficult to teach before the one who has taught you and moreover, I am already working with Sanjivani institute, so…

'Actually, I have become aged and students are increasing day by day. I am not able to handle all this single handedly. I want some young blood to help me. I think, you deserve to take my place. You are hard working, sincere, young-blood, exciting, punctual and appreciated and accepted by students. So I want you to take my institute on top in the town. I will pay you even more than them.'

'Sir, it is very difficult to take your place but I can't even resist your proposal.' I said by being perplexed.

I got myself tripled to the right field corner. I could not resist his proposal. As such I was not at all good at saying 'NO' to anybody for anything. But it was very difficult to reject his proposal due to intimate relations with him. I thought a lot for taking any decision and figured out two benefits. If I work with Mehtasir, I would be able to learn more under his guidance and the second one; I would be able to get rid of the exploitation of Priyansir's fake professional rules. I decided to ask Sanjivani institute to increase my salary. If they did it, I might continue there. If not, I would join Mehta institute and would start working under Mehtasir.

I requested the owner to increase my salary per lecture. We discussed for half an hour regarding that matter, they became ready to increase but not up to my expectations. So I told with politeness that I would have to quit my job and would join some other institute or School.

I left that job and started working with Mehta institute. For me, it was the same class, same whiteboard, same marker and same syllabus, the only difference was found in the students. I got used to with that Class just in a month. Of course I used to miss my students of Sanjivani institution as they were pretty attached to me. They were not connected to me professionally only.Things went on for a month smoothly. Then a problem arrived when the students of Sanjivani came to Mehta institute to meet me.

I got shocked to see them and asked, 'you all here?'

'Ma'am, we want you only as our English teacher.' requested the students of 10th and 12th std.

'But, now I am the part of this institute, I can't work at both the places at a same time. And I can't even allow you to join this institute as I will have problem with Priyanksir professionally. Hope you understand.' I said with a chock stick and duster in my hand.

'Then we will come to your home for personal coaching. You give your convenient time. We will come at any time, please ma'am. Don't spoil out board exams due to one subject.' they requested very badly.

'Oh, God what to do now.' I murmured. It was a very tough situation for me. My Guru-Mehtasir, my students and Priyanksir who was extremely angry on me due to my unprofessional behaviour as I left their institute suddenly for my benefit. Well after some years, nobody remembered anything but at that time, that situation became extremely critical as almost the students from Sanjivani institute shifted to Mehta institute just for one subject. I realized afterwards that it was the main intention of Mehtasir to drag me to his Class.

I got scared of that issue. I faced professional problems first time and they were terribly terrible but after six to seven months things started cooling down. I continued working with determination and kept on focusing on my studies. I used to feel very energetic when I used to stand near the black board in the same class where I used to sit on the bench as a student. It was a pleasant experience but I also realized one thing, it was not easy to work under the person whom we know or related intimately. Intimate relations make us handicapped in our professional field. We are not allowed to take our own decisions, of course nobody talks to us roughly there but we are supposed to work even more and exploited more emotionally by them as we cannot say 'No' to anything due to our relations.

Mehtasir started imposing the hold of his classes on me due to his old age. I had to conduct even his classes due to his weakness and sometimes his irregularity. He didn't appoint anybody else for other classes. In the beginning, I liked it as I felt very confident to see his students sitting in my class and enjoying my lecture. Unintentionally, I compared my teaching with him. Students also got used to with me. They didn't mind if I conducted Mehtasir's lecture. That behaviour of students enhanced my confidence about my teaching. But I had to work there for five-five hours, and was provided salary for two hours only. I kept on being exploited till two months with a smiling face as I could not say anything to sir whom I respected like anything but I got extremely tired physically and mentally.

With the blessings of God, I found a way to get rid of that. One of the teachers came to meet Mehtasir and I was sitting in the office. So he happened to meet me also and asked about my experience and teaching style. He got impressed by my informal interview and asked me to give my two hours to the school where he was working as they were badly in need of an English Teacher.

'Sir, for me it will not be possible as your school is at the remote area of the town, it is on high-way. My parents will not allow me to come there alone.' said I while having a sip of coffee.

'Try for few days. Initially you will find it far, then you won't. You conduct the classes at least for two hours, we will set timings according to your convenience and we don't mind if you continue working here.' he tried to convince

'But I am busy with my college from 5:00 am. to 2:00 pm. Due to commuting, I need to get up at 4:00 o'clock to reach college on time and I come back home by 2:00 pm. Then I start my classes here from 5:00 to 8:00 pm. where is the time left sir?'

'Can't you arrange from 3:00 to 5:00 pm.?' requested he.

'Oh god, then my working schedule will be from 5:00 a.m to 8:00 p.m. continuously and after that I will have to prepare for all the classes and for my own studies. Then when to sleep sir?' said I with a loud laughter.

'Please try at least for a week. If you are not comfortable, we will not force you. But I am sure, you will be able to do it. It is amazing the way you are going at this age. We know your strength.' he continued convincing.

I convinced my parents somehow and joined the second job. Two part time job became the full time job for me.

I started earning more than ten thousand rupees per month. Now earning money became my passion. I stretched myself too much for money and experience. I used to reach everywhere by driving my scooty. There was one of the benefits of that job that I used to get free time on Sunday as I didn't have any supervision duty to do so I used to utilize my Sunday for beautifying myself. I used to go to parlour and used to invest my time in which I used to get peace of mind - like meditation, Yoga and Pranayam. Good movies and newspapers made my day on Sunday and used to talk too much with my parents, go out with my father for buying vegetables and fruits. I also used to go to shop to help my father in his work.

Those years kept me on my toes but it was a wonderful life. No time for negative thoughts, just busy in my progress. Although it was a girls' college but we used to enjoy a lot. I used to participate in each and every functions and competitions held at college. I loved to perform on the stage. Stage had become my second home. I didn't feel nervous to be on stage; I used to win competitions and achieved many certificates. Now I accepted my life as a student as well as a teacher. I managed dealing with both the roles successfully. I bought a smart phone with my first salary. It could never be forgotten, such a wonderful phone, very slim and long one! Although features of it were not so good but the model was awesome. I used it for six months and it got stolen from my bag when I was in the library. I cried a lot but could do nothing. I saved my money and purchased another smart phone.

We were very happy. I loved and respected my parents a lot so did they. We were not very rich but I and my sister were provided richness of thoughts from our parents. We got freedom for our thoughts and actions. We became independent for many things as we used to manage everything by our own as father always used to be busy in handling everything at shop single handedly. We didn't have an elder brother to help us for our outer works, so some situations made us stand on our own feet and provided enough amounts of maturity and seriousness about life before the age.

Years passed like a moment, just in a blink of an eye. Now I crossed my eighteen years, eligible for marriage according to my all relatives.

'Dear, we are to go to a wedding ceremony. Come on, get ready fast.' informed my mother.

'I don't want to go.' I denied immediately.

'Why, they personally came to invite us with the whole family. Relatives from so many cities are going to come to attend this wedding. We must go.'

'That is why I don't want to come. People will stop enjoying the wedding and will get busy in suggesting boys for me.' I spoke while doing skipping exercise.

'You think you are a miss-world? They will focus on you by leaving food and other enjoyments aside? And why are you afraid of it, one day that is going to happen. One day you will definitely get married. And who knows you might find some educated and smart guy in this wedding function.' My mom tried to provoke me to join them for the function.

'But I don't want to get married. I am happy with my job and books.'

'Dear, marriage is a good thing. It is a part and parcel of life.'

'Please mom, stop this lecture again. Let's go for the function, else a lecturer will have to attend a lecture on marriage forcefully.' I said it in funny tone.

I wore a blue dress with white salwar and dupatta. I kept my hair open which had brown colour and hung to my low waist. I wore pencil heels sandals and applied some make-up on face, took a purse with my mobile in it. I applied copper colour nail-polish. At last I wore a leather watch and a small ring in the finger of my left hand. I never used to wear many accessories.

'She looks so pretty in a simple wear and look at her figure, so slim and sexy!' appreciated one of the ladies in the marriage.

'She always carries herself with a simple look but she looks stunning.' replied a lady who knew me very well.

'Who is she? Such a nice girl and good personality!' asked a lady staring at me from the corner.

'She is my grand –daughter.' replied my grandmother with a pleasant smile.

'Oh, wow. She looks very pretty and polite. How old is she?' asked the lady while scanning me from head to toe.

'She is pursuing her college studies and nineteen years old. She is studying and also doing job. Very hard-working.' grooved on my grandmother as if she were ready to get my marriage fixed.

'Oh, really great. She is working at a very young age, very nice. She would be knowing cooking, stitching and other-household work also, right?' asked she by keeping the thought in mind that working girls can't handle home properly.

'Yes, she does whole house-hold work, and cooking is her speciality.' exaggerated my grand-mother.

'Oh that is really nice, what is her father doing? Where are her parents?' she kept on asking various questions.

Many people inquired about me and sent proposals for my marriage through various people.

Next day, my grand-mother rushed to home with these words,

'I have come with good news; our daughter is now in the market of matrimony.'

'Means?' asked my parents with surprise.

'Yesterday many people asked me about her, one of my friends has sent a proposal. There is a guy in Ahmadabad. He is in medical, going to be a doctor in future. The mother has selected our Aditi for her son. They are very rich and sophisticated people with good fame in the society.'

'But did you clarify to them about our financial condition, we are not that rich and won't be able to give much dowry.' said my mom.

'They knew everything and they told that they liked the girl a lot, they just wanted her wrapped in one sari.'

'People say it first but then they change their mind-set and in our society, dowry matters a lot. You know it very well. It is my personal experience' taunted my mom. 'And Aditi will continue her job even after her marriage. She is very ambitious, of course she will handle house, it will be her first priority but she will not leave her career so we are in search of that kind of groom and family who consider her generously for this matter. We want broadminded guy and family, their richness and high socialization don't make much difference.' continued my mother while washing cloths.

'Yes, absolutely. So first we will conform and clarify some matters then we will proceed for further matters.' said my father by chewing pan.

'Yes, that is true. There is nothing wrong in that. There should be fair clarification in the beginning of any relationship.' favoured my grandmother.

Before I speak anything, my mother took my ball in her court and put me on the safe side. I became so relaxed and calm after knowing my parents' thoughts and support about my marriage. Now I left everything on them as I realized whatever they do, will be fine for me. My trust and love increased more for them.

After two days, my father again got a marriage proposal for me. My father's mama came to shop with that proposal.

'Hey, Devang, very good news for you. You have met with your best luck.' said he with pleasing voice.

'Why? What happened? Are you going to gift me a shop?' asked my father by touching his feet and with a smiling face.

'Nope, even better than this. I have come with a marriage proposal for your elder daughter Aditi from an extremely rich family.'

'Who are they?' asked my father.

'They hail from Junagadh; they are the owners of very big firms and various businesses. They are involved in numerous businesses and earn crore of rupees. They do foreign trips every month and have too much prosperity in the society. They called me to inquire about your daughter. They saw Aditi in a marriage function and they liked her very much. They are interested in Aditi for their elder son. I think you must think about it.' suggested he.

'They are very rich; our path cannot be the same. We cannot compare ourselves with them. Why do they want to hold my daughter's hand? They can definitely get richer families than us.' asked my father.

'Nowadays, girls are in demand so don't think much about all this and accept the proposal.'

'What is the guy doing? Is he educated? As we want an educated groom for her who allows my daughter to work even after marriage.' asked my father.

'Yes, the guy has completed B.Com but now he is the owner of three shops and he is very smart. And why do your daughter need to do work if she has a rich husband and family?' asked he.

'But my daughter would love to work for her satisfaction even after marriage; I don't think there is anything wrong if she loves to work for her happiness.' said my father. Thanks a lot for this proposal. We will definitely think about it.' my father uttered very politely by saying 'no' indirectly.

Somehow almost relatives started getting on my parents' nerves for rejecting good proposals. But nobody could understand what we wanted. People thought only about money, property, social status and females thought about gold which would be gifted to the daughter-in-laws by their in-laws. But nobody was thinking about the mentality behind that gold and money. My parents had to face much criticism from elders and that kept on happening for many years.

When I was in the second year of my college, one of our closest relatives, Hiteshuncle came with a very appropriate proposal for me. He came with the proposal of an educated and sophisticated family; the guy was an M.B.A and was working in some well reputed bank as a manager. They were very rich. They wanted me for their elder son, Akhilesh but the they wanted marriage to take place very soon. My parents liked the guy and family. It was the perfect proposal as far as our requirements were concerned. The proposal met with our almost expectations. They also didn't demand anything excepting an educated girl. But I was just in second year of my college and was not at all ready for marriage. I started crying and stopped eating.

'Mom, dad, I want to do something in my life. I want to study and do job in some good college as a professor in my future. Please let me live my life, let me fulfil my goals. I have just started working on it. Please ask them to wait until I complete my masters, I am not ready for marriage now. If I am not happy, how will I be able to keep them happy.' convinced I with tears in my eyes.

'Dear but they are ready to allow you to go ahead in your career, they will also allow you to do the job even after marriage and the guy is also very understanding, think about it. Every day we don't get that kind of perfect proposals.' explained my parents.

'That is true but not now please. I beg from you.' I went inside and cried for the whole night.

In the morning, I felt so sick and was not able to get up also. I had severe fever. Tears were rolling down from my eyes. I was not even able to stand properly. My parents got frightened.

'Don't worry dear; we have decided that you are going to complete your studies first.' said my father.

'We have said no to the family for marriage, and also told them they can go for some other proposals so they don't lag behind us. Now happy?' said my mom.

'Now you focus on your third year, final year of college, you are free now. We will not disturb you until the completion of your studies.' promised my parents.

'Yuppie, thanks a ton.' I felt so happy and took the medicine to get well soon.

'But a day will come, you will have to get married.' said my mother. 'Please, don't talk about it. I want to stay with you forever and with my little brother. I want to take care of you forever.' I said.

'It is not possible for a girl, dear. You are supposed to take care of your husband and your in-laws after marriage, that's the reality of a girl's life and we will also feel great to see you doing that.'

'I will do that wholeheartedly if I get married but I can also take care of my parents even after marriage according to the landmark judgement upheld by the Bombay high court.' I said with little seriousness.

'Oh my lawyer! We know you love us so much so do we and we just see want to see you happy and progressive, don't worry about us, we will be happy to see our kids happy.'

'No problem if you don't need me, but I will never leave Tushar, my sweet little bro. I will take him to my in-laws' place.' I cuddled him up and kissed on his forehead.

'Oooooooo.' My mother started laughing and said, 'things are very easy to say but very difficult to do. I used to say the same things to my mother, but couldn't do any of it. Better you accept the reality from beginning.'

'Ok, I will never leave my brother, just wait and watch.' I and Tushar laughed and I added, 'Hey my bro, give me hi-fi, you will go with your di, right?' we made fun of mom while having some snacks.

I got my result of second year. I secured first class even in that year. I wanted to secure first class even in my third year. My third year started. I started working hard for it.

'Mom, now I won't be able to manage job and study together. I just want to focus on my study as it is very difficult to score first class in T.Y. English Literature. I will have to work very hard. I want to enjoy my studies and want to have some break from job and hectic schedule of life.' said I.

'Of course, you must take break and focus on your studies only, very wise decision.' appreciated my parents.

I left the job for my studies and started working very hard for my third year. I wanted to secure first class in that. Now I was just a student so my whole attention was on studies only. I came closer to my friends; I also went for watching movies twice a year with my friends as I didn't need to worry for my classes and job. I was just enjoying my studies, I never bunked a single lecture of my favourite professor, Franymam. One of the best professors of literature. She became the role model of all most the girls. She was intelligent, smart, fashionable and had a wonderful speech. She used to teach not only English literature, but also the moral lessions of life. I could never forget her lectures on marriage, in which she told the importance of marriage life. Her lectures changed my mind about marriage. Now I was ready to get married at right time if I found an appropriate life partner.

In third year, she organized 'English Awareness Day' at college campus. Many girls participated in various events, I also participated in many. I won the first prize in elocution, extempore and essay writing. I also participated in one drama which gave me the opportunity to play the role of a protagonist who was a naughty-mischievous girl of college.

The character's nature was quite opposite to mine but I dealt with it splendidly. The drama became so popular in many colleges that I started getting opportunities for acting. My professors also suggested me to grab the opportunity for acting career but I wanted to be a professor. Eight months passed very fast of my third year. There were just three months left for my final exams. But at home I used to get very disturbed as my little brother used to make much noise so I decided to shift to Rajkot until my final exams got over. My parents also permitted me for that. I found a P.G room with my college friend, Jayshree. We became very close friends. We used to share everything with each other. We were the well wishers of each other.

'Hey, what will we do after this exam?' asked I to Jayshree by carrying the bulk of books.

'Job, what else.' said she.

'You have completed P.T.C. so you will get into some government school, right?

'Yes, of course.' she replied by arranging her books in a book shelf.

'But I want to make my career in some good college.' I shared my future planning with her about my career.

'But for that you need to complete your master degree, then only you will be eligible to apply in any college for the lecturer's post.'

'I know, but what after T.Y. I can't sit at home. I am planning to apply here in some schools as I am accustomed to do job along with my study. I think I should follow the same. I must continue my masters and job together as I have been doing it since my first year. If I continue it, I will have the best benefit. The benefit of it would be - I will achieve my masters qualification as well as experience certificate.'

'Of course it is very nice, but here each school requires master degree even for the post of a school teacher.'

'I know, but what is wrong in just applying? I got job in my first and second year of college before my mark-sheet of 12th std. The same thing might happen if God wishes.' I told her with a very positive hope.

'Touchwood. You can try but it is very difficult.'

'I have shortlisted two schools. I will definitely apply.' I said by putting pen between my teeth.

I applied in those schools. Miracle happened. After a week, I got a call from a Science School, one of the well-known schools of Rajkot. They called me for an interview for the post of an English teacher who could teach English to the students of English medium.

'Hey, I have got a call for an interview, that is on Thursday – Saibaba's day.' I informed about it to Jayshree. We used to have fast on Thursday and used to visit Saibaba's temple near to our room, fortunately they called me for the interview on Thursday which enhanced my trust and faith in Saibaba.

'Are you serious? Which standard?' asked Jayshree with surprise.

'11th and 12th std. Science students but the problem is they have asked me to teach English subject to the students of English Medium. Up to now I have taught English to the students of Gujarati Medium and they ask me to do the same thing for the students of English Medium. That means my entire speech must be in English only. Will I be able to do that?' asked I in a confused voice.

'You first face the interview and give the demo lecture as per their requirement. I am sure you will rock the stage.' motivated Jayshree.

I left my study for two days and burnt my all boats for the interview and demo lecture. After finishing the preparation, I ironed my white dress and blue jeans. I applied brown colour nail paint before the day of interview. In the morning, I got up very early and got ready for it. I didn't have vehicle at that time in Rajkot so I got an auto-rickshaw and reached the school. I claimed the staircases and reached the office. All students and teacher were staring at me as I might be looking very young compared to other staff-members, I assumed that. The premise of the school was very professional and attractive. I was extremely nervous as my entire interview and demo lecture were going to be conducted thoroughly in English language. I knocked the door and entered the office politely by taking their permission. There were six teachers in the interview panel. They asked various questions regarding my field, asked about my timings and expectations for salary. They attended my demo lecture and selected me. They used to offer two hundred rupees per lecture. They offered me two lectures every day. In that sense, per month they would pay me ten thousand rupees and I just needed to give my two hours to the class. I was not required to do any other duties apart from my lectures. They were highly professionals. I accepted everything. I was so surprised to have a job letter in my hand before my qualification. I called my parents on the spot; they also got surprised and felt proud of me.

'Hey, open the mouth. I got selected.' I shared my experience with Jayshree putting dairy milk in her mouth.

'I told you that you will rock the stage. I have seen passion in your eyes regarding your career. You will keep on rocking it for the whole life. Now just find a guy who understands and values your skills. I am little worried as in your community, people might not value your talent and might not allow you to fulfil your dreams. God bless you.' she said by holding my hand and with tears in her eyes.'Anyways, let's focus on exams first and rock it.' added she.

We completed final exams successfully. After exam, we went to watch '3 idiots - movie', had dinner outside and the next day, we departed. She left for her town and I stayed at the same PG room in Rajkot due to my job. I started my new job. I felt little odd to work there as all the teachers were quite elder than me and they became my colleagues. I used to feel very awkward by sharing office with them. I was very comfortable with the students but always used to get uncomfortable with the staff members due to much age difference. I got used to with it and started earning handsome amount in less time. I started saving my money for good.

Result of T.Y. B.A declared, I scored second class. I was extremely upset as I couldn't secure first class despite terrible hard work but I overcame it with short period of time as I was very busy with my job and lecture preparation. I decided not to leave job and joined M.A.with specialization in English from distance learning.

'Mom, I get bored here. I need to go to school only for two hours, then for the whole day I feel lonely.' I talked to my mom on call.

'Don't you have room-mates over there at room?' she asked.

'I have but they have full day college. And I also don't like tiffin food. I survive on magi and biscuits sometime. They provide cabbage sabzi thrice a week as it is the cheapest vegetable in the market.Yesterday, I found weevils in the cabbage sabzi. So I had to take biscuits in dinner. Sometimes, I feel someone is punishing me for moving out of home. It is very difficult to survive here, I miss you all.' said I with crying tone.

'Leave everything, come back and start working here as you did before.' My mom requested.

'No, this job is very nice and I am paid good salary. I don't want to leave it. Anyways I will manage.' I disconnected the call and slept.

My colleagues became my friends who were ten to fifteen years elder than me. Some of them were characterless, some of them tried to tempt me for disloyal aspects of life, some of them were very good pretenders. They acted as if they were the epitome of high characters but later on, I found them wolfs in sheep's clothing. Many of them tried to woo me but I escaped and rescued myself very smartly from all those scraps. I gave my best not to put my parents on shame due to any of my move and I succeeded in that.

'Sir, I want to find another job as I get bored at the room for the whole day by remaining alone. Any vacancy for a visiting teacher in some institution or Schools where I can join part time?' I asked one of my mature and supportive colleagues.

'Give me some days. I will try to find.' responded he positively.

After three days, 'Hello! Aditi, note down the contact number of the owner of the best Language Lab of Rajkot. They are in need of an English trainer. You call him and give my reference. They might call you for an interview very soon.' Shuklasir gave me a call.

'Thanks a lot sir.'

On the same day, I got a call from that language lab. They called me for the interview on the same day. I gave my interview and got selected over there. I was supposed to conduct the classes of IELTS (International English Language Test System) course. I was also supposed to do some paper work and design some portions of syllabus of language learning and teaching. It was completely a new experience for me. The syllabus that I designed and taught was quite different from text book and grammar teaching. It increased my experience beyond my expectation. They became ready to give me 10, 000 for part time. So now I started earning twenty thousand per month after my graduation.

My all roommates used to go out for parties and on date with boy-friends, I never found time for any such thing as I always used to be busy with preparations of my lectures. Sometimes, they used to make me feel regret for my hectic lifestyle at my young age. But I got the habit of overcoming those comments.

After few days, I got a call from the best institution of Rajkot which used to provide the coaching of English literature. They asked me to join their institute and teach English literature to the students of F.Y and S.Y. I also joined there. Then I got a call from K.V.S (Kendriya Vidyalaya) School for providing coaching of spoken English to the students of higher secondary. My hard work and tired feet made me stand on my own feet.

Vacation was about to start so some of the students requested me to start my own institute for 'Spoken English. They wanted to join the class during their vacation period. I always wanted to do that but I didn't have my own house in the city. It was one of my dreams to start my own institute and being the owner of it. On the basis of few students' demand, I grabbed that opportunity and for my own institute. I found a class on rent on the main road of the city. I purchased my laptop, speakers and some other required electrical equipments to start my small institute. I also gave advertisement in the newspaper in the form of pamphlet. 25 students joined my institute just in one month. My time-table of the entire day fixed. Twelve hours for twelve lectures, six hours for preparation of those lectures, one hour for driving from one place to another as I was dealing with five places in a day for my lectures, one hour for my routine work and last four hours for my sound sleep. My work always kept me fresh despite extremely hectic schedule. I used to spend good time with my roommates while having dinner. Of course, I could not involve myself in their all activities but somehow I could manage to be with them. Especially, on Sunday, I used to be very busy in preparation of my lectures of the whole week and used to do my own study. So I could not enjoy many parties with my roommates on Sunday. But after 9 o'clock every day, we used to have dinner together, used to talk a lot - especially 'G talks (girlish talks including fashion, cloths, make-up, sex, labour-pain, periods, affairs, movies, boys)', mock of each other and used to do dance, sing, etc. Sometimes, used to make maggi and chat after 12 o'clock at night. It was such a wonderful and amazing life.

Rekha (One of my roommates) asked me: 'Hai Aditi di, you are extremely crazy and serious about your career. I just imagine how crazy and serious you would be when you would fall in love!'

'Yes, of course, how lucky the guy would be who will get your crazy love!' said other room-mates while having maggi at late night.

'What a joke! I am never going to fall in love. When the hell I am going to find time for it?' I said by washing my plate and fork.

'If a handsome guy might find time for you, then? ' asked they by mocking me and they laughed.

'Why would any guy want a girl like me who might not be able to give him even a single minute in a day.' I said by ironing my dress for the next day.

'Love teaches everything di' they laughed.

'Oh! Experience !' I exclaimed with funny tone. 'Well, I am made for lectures not for love and all.' I laughed.

'Ooooo! Let us wait and watch.' they laughed loudly.

'Sure, let's wait and watch.'

We all laughed loudly and switched off the lights.

It is said in bhagavad Geeta, chapter-2 shloka – 36

अवाच्यवादांश्च बहून्वदिष्यन्ति तवाहिता:।
निन्दन्तस्तव सामर्थ्यं ततो दु:खतरं नु किम्।।३६।।

**Your enemies will deride your prowess
in derogatory terms and say many things
which should not be said;
indeed, what could be more distressing than this?**

If you are on right path or wrong path, people will have to say something. My well wishers always supported me even when I was wrong, they showed me the right path but my enemies spoke dreadful words even for my good deeds. Bhagavad Geeta taught me the path of following my heart by trusting the Almighty God.

CHAPTER 7

Life was going on very busy and exciting. Now Harsha, my sister, also completed her 12th std but she was confused for selecting her field after 12th. I went to my town to help her to take decision about her further studies. Her confusion brought a turning point in my life. The turning point which I never ever thought about.

'I am confused. I have scored 78 % in 12th std. Which career option should I opt for?' asked my sister to me.

'Do you want to go for teaching career like me?' asked I.

'Not at all, I can't hold books for day and night nor can I keep a soft copy of notes of lectures in a phone even in a marriage function. I want to do a job which keeps me free at least after my office hours. After working hours, I can't keep myself busy with books, books, and only books, preparing all the time for lectures.' she said firmly by cutting apples.

'Then go for B.Com, BCA or BBA. It will give you a job as per your interest and requirement or go for CA if you trust yourself.' I suggested by taking slices of apple in my both hands.

'CA? Will I be able to do? But first we should consult somebody who is pursuing any of these courses so that I can have better ideas.'

'I know some of my friends who are in B.com, BCA and BBA but don't have anybody in contact who is pursuing CA.'

Meanwhile one of our close relatives, Pinakuncle came to our place and we discussed much about education and books as he loved reading books and he was always found keen to know about education and technology. He often used to visit our home and our shop. While discussing about streams, he talked about his nephew, Kabir. He informed that he had recently cracked the final exams of CA and got a very nice job in T.C.S - Mumbai. He asked us to call him for suggestions regarding CA. He assured us that he would respond very nicely and would guide us properly. He also assured to ask him anything at the drop of the hat. We were asked to give his reference. He told my father to consider him as a family boy. 'He is very polite and smart.' Pinakuncle appreciated him.

'Alright, please give me his contact number, we will talk to him and take guidance for further education in commerce field.' said my father by offering him plate of fruits.

'Thanks.' he took some grapes. 'Note down his contact number.' he gave his phone to my father.

'Aditi take it and save the number in my phone.' my father asked me to do that.

'Ok, papa.' I took uncle's phone and saved his number in my father's phone. I saved the number by writing his name - Kabir.

My father asked after two days, 'Dear, did you call that guy for the guidance of stream.'.

'No, papa. I was busy in writing my article. I forgot. Let me try now.' I took my father's phone to dial his number.

'It is ringing but he is not receiving.' informed I by trying his number twice.

'Alright, try after sometime.' said my father while having his lunch.

I tried after half an hour again.

'It is switched off. Leave it.'

'Alright, no problem. Keep on trying, else we will ask somebody else.' stated my father.

'I tried three times, it is switched off.' answered I.

After half an hour, 'You try from your cell.' suggested my father.

'No way, we don't know the guy; he might miss-use my number. I will not call him from my cell.'

'She is absolutely right.' interrupted my mother.

After two days, Pinakuncle came to home and asked again if we called his nephew for guidance. We said his phone was out of coverage.

'Let me try. Oh but I have forgotten my phone at home. You can try now as I came to know that he was in Trivandrum for his training so he might be facing network issues. He might have come back, you can try now.' he insisted.

I could not say anything about the strange guy as he was his nephew. My sister was not getting confidence to talk to him so she asked me to call him for the matter. My father was also not at home so I called him from my cell by wishing his phone to be switched off or he wouldn't receive the call. Suddenly a strong muscular voice stuck to my ear.

'Hello!'

I got surprised by the voice as again I was expecting a female voice from customer care - an auto generated response, 'the number you are trying to call is switched off '.

It had been happening since four days but thing turned out differently. He received the call and I kept on listening from that guy,

'Hello! Hello! Hello!'

Finally I replied, 'Hello I am Aditi from Morbi. I got your number from your uncle, Pinakuncle. Can I talk to you for a while, please? asked I politely.

'Yes, sure. Please tell me.' replied he in a very gentle tone.

'Actually my sister has completed 12th commerce. She is planning to opt for CA, we want to have some guidance regarding this.' I talked to him in English language.

My mother, sister and Pinakuncle were staring at me and listening to me with full of attention as if they were in some conference. They never heard me speaking English fluently before that. In small town, people put those ones on airs and graces who speak fluent English.

'It is a nice field. If she is interested, she must join it but with one condition, whatever happens, she is not allowed to leave it in between as it is not easy to crack it with first trial but she doesn't need to give up. There are some classes in Ahmadabad and even in Rajkot, she can definitely join there.' he kept on suggesting accurately.

'Did you pass it with first trial?' asked I.

'No, I could clear it with second one. Now I am in Trivandrum for my training. Will join the office after this month.' said he.

He advised very accurately for each and every thing, his intonation was very polite. Well I never talked to any boy on call before that but there was something in his voice, I thought of him many times a day. Well I didn't reveal it to anybody but something was there in his voice. It was a short vacation period. I was busy with writing my drama at home. Again I got busy in my life and my hectic schedule and my routine activities. I stopped thinking about him.

After one and half month, suddenly I got a message from an unknown number.

'Hi, I am Kabir. Kindly consider my new number.

I hope your sister would have selected her stream and performing well.'

After an hour of the message, I read it. I recalled that guy whom I asked about CA course. I never liked to talk much with boys, chatting with them through messages. I could not understand why I started chatting with him very easily, in fact I felt so glad when he sent me the message. I wanted by heart that he initiates first for calls and messages. He did it without any intention. I was folding my cloths; I left everything aside and replied to his message with much interest.

'Yes, she has opted for CA and joined one of the best institutions in Rajkot.' I read my message twice before sending it to check if I did not make any spelling mistake.

'Alright. That is very nice. Wish her best luck on my behalf.' replied he.

'Yes, thanks. I will wish her on behalf of you.' replied I.

After my reply, he didn't send any message for two hours. In those two hours, I checked my phone for 20 times despite its being on ring-tone mode. My mom also asked me why I was checking my phone again and again. I waited for hours but received no message from him. I wanted him to chat with me. After waiting for few hours, I thought to send him a message to continue the chatting. Then I thought what he would think about me? And what would I send him? I don't know anything about him and don't even know him. I kept on thinking for many hours by doing my work.

'What have you been thinking since morning? You are doing all works physically but mentally you are not here.' asked my mom by wiping the utensils.

'Nothing mom, I was just thinking about my drama, for the further dialogues.' I lied to my mother.

Fortunately, all of a sudden I got his message by the evening around 6:30 pm. I was writing my drama by sitting in the room. I had kept my phone in another room as I was getting much distracted. But when I heard the beep of the phone, I left writing my dialogues in between, put everything aside and rushed to pick up the phone. When I saw his message on the screen, first I prayed to God to say Him thanks.

'Ok.' his replied.

'OK? What is it?' I whispered by getting little annoyed. Then I realized, it was the reply of the last message which I sent him about wishing my sister best luck on his behalf. I didn't reply again as somehow I felt little bad of his quite late reply. I left the phone for a while and didn't want to show my interest in his messages. I thought if he was not showing much interest, why should I?

After half an hour, again I got his message,

'Hi! I liked your English accent; you hail from a small town but your speech is very pleasing. What is the name of your school? Are you an English medium student?'

I couldn't resist myself and replied on the spot, 'No I have studied in a government school, and a student of vernacular medium.'

'Oh really, it sounds that you have studied in some international English Medium School.'

'No, no. Nothing like that.'

'So what are you doing nowadays? In which field are you in?' he typed.

'I am the student of Arts. I am doing my specialization in English literature. I also work as an English faculty in Science School and in English Language Lab. In a nutshell, I am a teacher, I teach.'

'Wow! Lovely! Nice profession, always dealing with young blood and new generation.'

'Yes true. A busy profession, not free even after working hours due to the preparation of lectures for the next day.'

'But it is a noble profession, you are serving the society. Tomorrow's employees are in your hand. Nice job.' he appreciated very positively.

'Thanks for motivation.' I typed.

We continued chatting till late night. Well the topic of the discussion was the same for a long time - education and job, nothing else. But I started liking his thoughts about female education and their freedom. I found some sparks of decency in his messages. We noticed that it was 1:30 at night, and then we wished good night to each other and slept.

I got up at 5:00 a.m. in the morning to catch a bus and to reach on time for my lectures. I first took my phone, read all messages that we sent to each other at night and encouraged myself to send him message again.

'Good Morning. JSK.' sent I.

Then I got ready. I kept on checking the phone for his reply after each lecture but I didn't receive any up to noon. After 2:00 pm. I got his message,

'Very good morning.'

'Good morning? It is good noon.' I replied promptly as if I was waiting in the wings for his message by keeping my eyes on the mobile screen.

'I am sorry. I sent it earlier, you might have received it now.' sent he.

'Oh really?' I sent.

'Sorry, actually I got up late in the morning, and rushed to the office, then got stuck up in the work.' sent he, he also sent the emoticons of a smile through JPG.

'Hey, why to be sorry? I am not your teacher.'

'That is true. But I should not make anybody wait like this.' sent he.

'Well, nobody was waiting. I was also very busy since morning but I have a habit to check my phone after each lecture so that I can reply on time to anyone.' I sent him to show that it was not only he who was given much importance as far as my messages were consulted. I did not want to reveal to him that I was dying for his messages.

'Oh! It is a very good habit, only teachers can be punctual at this extent, else students like me remain careless for all of his life span.' sent he by accepting his habit and clarifying that I would have to wait for hours for his messages if I wanted to keep in touch with him.

But somehow I liked his attitude and confidence. I didn't find him a silly guy who nagged behind the girls after first talk and that really impressed me a lot.

'By the way, what is JSK?' asked he.

'Jay Shree Krishna.' replied I.

'Oh! That is great. Nice and easy short form.' he typed to appreciate.

Our chatting including just 'Good Morning' and 'Good night' lasted for minimum two months. Both of us didn't go beyond that. But we both neither slept nor woke up without wishing each other. We both got the habit of wishing each other but not more than that. If anybody slept without wishing due to any reason, used to wish at midnight. 'Good morning and good night became prime words for our chatting.' But both of us could not understand what it was – just a habit or more than his.

It was Saturday so I headed towards home to enjoy weekend with my family. I reached home and kept phone aside to spend quality time with my parents. On that day, I skipped to send him a message of 'Good night'. He wished me at night and also on the Sunday morning but didn't complain about it the way I did it for two times when he went home and skipped to wish me. Well I felt bad when he didn't say anything for my not sending him message. But I didn't show it to him. Suddenly a thought stuck in my mind. I thought either the matter should go ahead or it should be stopped. All of a sudden I got a thought, why should I send messages to a guy whom I have not even seen? Why to fall in this kind of a habit with a stranger without any reason? What am I doing? I asked various questions to myself.

'May I listen to your voice again, Can I call you?' I couldn't resist myself and sent him a message.

'Sure, why not?' said he.

It was hot summer; my parents were sleeping on the terrace. It was 12:00 o'clock at night. I called him up by gathering courage. I started having butterflies in my stomach. I got sweat on my head as it was first time that I was calling a boy at late night. I was also frightened that anybody would come down from terrace and might catch me red handed. But somehow, I just called him up and started talking to him,

'Hello!' he picked up the phone.

'Hi! I don't need to tell my name, you know it.' said I.

'Yes, I know it. So how are you?'

'I am fine, and you?'

'Me too. So how is your work going on? asked he.

'It is going on up to the mark and yours?' asked I.

'All good. Getting used to with the new job.' said he.

'Hmmm.' replied I.

We stopped for a moment as we didn't have anything else to talk.

'Well you have a very good accent but please talk to me in Indian accent. I am not used to with British Accent.' he clarified.

'Oh, sure.' I giggled.

'Well, what else?' asked he.

'Nothing, you say something if you have anything.'

'Well, same here. Nothing.' I wanted to talk for a longer time but was not able to find words.

'Ok, so let's sleep as tomorrow we both are supposed to get up early.' said he.

'Sure, Good Night. Today oral wishes.' I uttered.

'Good Night.' he wished and laughed.

We disconnected the call but couldn't stop thinking about each other. Finally I messaged him after an hour 'Good night. JSK.' and I got the same reply on the spot. I couldn't sleep for the entire night due to excitement and nervousness. Finally, I slept at 4:00 am. and got up at 5:15 a.m. and got the bus for Rajkot. That morning was different, I found everything extremely beautiful. The roads from Morbi to Rajkot sounded very fascinating. The trees on the road were found green and fanciful. That morning made me wake up with a desire to enjoy the world to the fullest. Fresh air boosted my mind with positivity. I was feeling the spring season even in the hot summer. I arrived at the bus-stop but I lost myself in dreaming about that stranger. I was listening songs and trying to imagine his face. I was constantly thinking about him whom I didn't even see in my life. The conductor shacked me and asked me to get down the bus. I opened my eyes and gazed the reality of crowded bus-stop. I put my ear-phones in the bag, got down and rushed to catch the auto-rickshaw to reach on time for my lecture.

I conducted my all lectures with very happy mood. After conducting twelve lectures also, I didn't get tired. I reached my P.G room. I hugged my room-mates and was extremely happy.

'Hi ! Aditi, you are so happy and fresh, any thing special?' asked my room-mates.

I felt little shy and replied after thinking for a second 'ammmm, yes, I am fresh. Look at the weather, how beautiful it is! Right?'

My roommates looked at the dreadful hot sky and looked at me and asked with astonishment by wiping their sweat, 'beautiful weather?'

'Yes.' I smiled with little shyness on my face and with joyful eyes. They looked at one another and became speechless.

All of a sudden, after a month, problems started in our P.G room due to heavy rain. All girls were requested to vacant the place so we became busy in search of another room. I wanted to call him even in that busy schedule but I could not find any reason to call him.

After few days, while finding a room, I was wandering from one street to another and called him.

'Hi! How are you?'

'I am fine, so what's up.' he responded very nicely.

'Little worried, finding a new P.G room. We are required to vacant our current room as water is dropping out from ceiling due to heavy rain.' I shared my problem with him.

'Oh! That is terrific. Well I am also supposed to shift my room as the owner of our house wants to sell his house so we will have to find another room.' said he.

'Oh! both are in same condition.' I said to enhance my talk.

Somehow we talked for five minutes on general topics and continued our own work. He got busy with his office work and I with my lectures. After two days, he called me. I just finished my bath and came out of the bathroom by wrapping my towel; cloths were also remaining to wear. I heard the ringtone and saw his name on screen. I gazed at the screen twice to conform that it was really Kabir. I sat on the bed and received the phone with wet hands.

'Hello!'

'Hi! How are you?' asked he.

'I am completely fine, how are you? Today in the morning? No office?' asked I with pleasing voice.

'No, we have days off on Saturday and Sunday. It's weekend.'

'Wow, that is so cool, man.'

'By the way did you find your room?' asked he with concern.

'Yes, I found it and going to shift there tomorrow. I will start my packing tonight.' I replied by wearing my cloths.

'That is great. Congratulations. So what else, say something about you.' asked he.

'Why not? But now I need to rush for the class, can we talk later please? I will call you after my classes get over.' I asked in requesting tone while combing my hair.

'Yes, sure, you carry on.' said he.

First time that happened, he wanted to continue and I was in hurry. Well I liked it as I thought it was the time for him to wait for me. It was a cold monsoon morning, it was raining heavily. Despite much cold, I kept on talking to him for ten minutes just being wrapped in a towel. My wet hair was open and water was dropping from it. I was so happy that I got the reason to call him again as I said that I would call him after my lectures, so I was allowed to call him without any hesitation. I got ready for my class and was dying to finish all lectures swiftly. Finally it was the end of the day, I completed my all lectures. I reached to my place, parked my scooty and dialled his number while climbing the stairs. Neither I got fresh and up nor did I drink a sip of water. I just called him up. But his phone was switched off. I tried many a times but it was out of coverage. I felt so bad. I got fresh and up, had some snacks. I converted myself into a fast machine which can finish the work in minutes. I wanted to complete my all remaining work fast so I could give him enough time on phone. In fifteen minutes, I checked my phone for six times. Again I called him but it was out of coverage. I left the hope. I wanted to pack my luggage for shifting but was not feeling to do that as first I wanted to talk to him. I kept on trying but could not approach him. I started to get back to my work. I just opened my cup-board to pack my things and the phone rang. I rushed to pick up the phone and saw my father's number on the screen. I talked to him for a while and again started my packing. I took out my all clothes and books from the cup-board and kept the heaps of them on the floor. I was just thinking about him and the phone rang again. Again I rushed to receive the phone. It was his call. I left everything and received the call.

'Hello, I have been trying since long, but it was out of coverage.' I spoke that in lesser than half second or may be lesser than that. I informed him that as if I missed something extremely precious.

'Yes, I was out and forgot my phone at home. I just charged it and saw your missed calls so called you.' he said it with extreme relaxation as nothing had bothered him.

It was found like he was not at all waiting for my call and got busy in enjoying his weekends. On the other side of the coin, I was just thinking about him even after that much hard work. I stole time to think about him constantly despite my overloaded time-table. I felt little bad but I didn't expose it to him.

'So how was the day? I am sure it would be very hectic as usual.' asked he.

'Yes, but it was nice. And yours?' asked I.

'It was very relaxing. I went to Juhu beach and chowpaty with friends. It was a wonderful day with friends. He shared his experience with me.

'How is the weather there?' asked I.

'As far as monsoon is concerned, you don't need to ask anything about Mumbai rain, it is always awesome.' replied he.

'Monsoon, a romantic season for lovers.' said I.

'Yes, of course. So you can enjoy this rain with your boy-friend.' he asked about my boy-friend indirectly.

'Well I don't have any, and I don't believe in relationship without commitment. I will fall in love with a guy who is ready to tie a knot with me, else I am very happy single.' I replied by putting my books in the bag.

'So first you will demand for commitment, then will you fall in love? Generally people fall in love, then they commit each other.'

'I am little different in this matter or you can consider me odd, too'

'What if you fall in love with somebody, you have gone out with him, you have created memories and then he might resist to get married, what will you do then?' asked he.

'First and foremost, I will never go out with any guy just for fun. I won't move around with anyone without commitment. If I have fallen in love but he is not feeling the same for me, I will not do any kind of time-pass with him. I will forget him. And above all the guy should be of my caste only, else I will not go ahead for this matter.' said I clearly.

'Oh, you are very strict about your love and marriage. You are an entrepreneur - you have made your own laws about it. I have studied law subject but have never studied these rules for love and marriage.' he mocked me. 'But love doesn't happen by selecting the caste.' he said further.

'You are absolutely right but there is a lot of difference between love and attraction. If you are mature enough, you know somebody of the same caste, you try to understand him/her and if there is enough amount of understanding between both of you, automatically you start loving the person. And if it is the same caste, parents will also not deny for marriage and that kind of love-stories last longer and become successful. Well, I am not a casteist but in my case, I won't let my parents put their nose on shy because of my any mistake. My parents have given me enough amount of freedom so I don't want to take wrong advantage of it.' explained I.

'Oh my goodness! You have thought too much about all these matters, great! I like your thinking about your life, career, future, love and marriage. You are more mature than your age.' appreciated he.

'So what is the name of your girlfriend?' asked I.

'I don't have any. I am happy to be single.' replied he.

'That's right. It is very nice to enjoy the freedom of a free-bird but responsibility for certain things at the right age also brings huge amount of happiness and satisfaction.' I said and I felt pleased to know his single status.

On that day, we talked almost for three hours, till 1:30 at night. We talked a lot about our likes, dislikes, interest, family members, family business and many other things. It was raining like cats and dogs. I was talking to him outside the room by carrying umbrella in my hands as everybody was sleeping inside the room so I didn't want to disturb them. It was such a memorable and splendid feeling talking to him for a long time. I talked to the guy whom I didn't know, didn't even see. It was like an amazing imagination. I felt I was just talking to a voice not a person. I kept on thinking about his appearance. I was trying to judge his appearance on the basis of his voice. I was just thinking about him. I kept on feeling the echo of his voice and dialogues in my ear even after disconnection of call. It was already late night so I couldn't continue my packing. I left my scattered luggage as it was and got up early in the morning to pack it for shifting.

On the next day, at 10:00 o'clock at night, when I was preparing for my lectures for the next day, he called me.

I received. 'Hello?'

'Hi, what's up? Finished your dinner? Hope I didn't disturb you? asked he very politely.

'No, not at all. Yes I finished my dinner at 8:00 pm.'

'Oh, yes. I forgot about your punctuality for everything.' said he with a loud laugh.

'Well, Thanks for appreciating.' replied I with a giggle.

'So now sleeping time?' asked he.

'Nope, making notes for tomorrow's lectures.'

'Ya, I forgot you work even after your job. Then I must have disturbed you. Should I call you back or after sometime?' asked he.

'Can you please give me half an hour? I am about to finish my notes, then I will call you.' At least, our relation reached to that stage that we didn't feel any kind of hesitation to call each other. We could call each other anytime for anything or for nothing.

'Yes, sure. Why not? I will wait for you.' replied he.

'Ok, thanks. I will catch you soon.'

Craziness of his words 'I will wait for you' was preventing me to concentrate on my work. I was preparing the notes with smile and little shyness. My mind was recalling his words again and again.

'Di, why are you blushing?' asked one of my room-mates.

'Actually, the story that I am preparing for tomorrow's lecture has many funny characters so...' somehow I managed to hide my feelings from my room-mates by telling a lie to them.

I just finished my work and called him up by carrying an umbrella and sat on the swing which was placed outside the room.

'Hello, so done with your work?' asked he.

'Yes. Well how is weather there?' I initiated with my common question as usual.

'Do you find me a meteorologist? Your first question is always about weather.' said he by making fun of me.

He was right as I always used to ask the same question. On that day also we talked for a long time. It continued for three months. We used to talk to each other every day for hours. We also kept nick names of each other. One day it was horrible rain in Mumbai, I called him but he was not receiving. Well he informed me that he was going for some seminar so it would be very late. But it was almost 12:00 am., he didn't receive my call. I kept on trying for many times, I sent many messages but got no reply. I got so worried about him. I was about to cry and continued waiting for his call. He called me after 2:00 am.

'Hey, how are you?' asked he.

'Not well, it is too late. I was waiting since long. At least you could have called for a minute and your phone was also switched off.' said I with little anger as if I had got all the rights to say anything to him.

'Yes, I am sorry, actually my phone fell in water and it got hanged. I just reached home, charged the cell and called you first. I knew you would be waiting for my call.'

'Thanks for realization. Are you alright? How was the seminar?' asked I putting my anger aside.

'Yes, I am alright and seminar was boring as usual but it was compulsory to go else I don't enjoy these kinds of seminars.' said he.

'But I love to attend seminars and conferences.' said I.

'You are a sincere teacher and I am just a CA employee.' he exaggerated myself.

'Oh now stop making fun of me. And yes I am quite sincere as far as calling is concerned, I call you on time but you always make me wait for your call.' taunted I.

'Look at you! A teacher has started scolding a poor student.' He laughed.

We enjoyed talking on nothing. It was unbelievable for me to talk to a guy with that kind of frankly manners till late night. It felt like the whole world was sleeping; only the dark cloudy sky was with me and the stars were dying to listen our late night talk. I felt the sky was spreading the black sheet on me to hide me from the sight of the world. The full moon was as bright as my feelings; the night was full of intoxication. The moon was awakening with me to give me company. The rain was also feeling colors into our talks while pouring down. The romantic weather motivated us to continue our talks for the whole night. Wonderful days were going on. I was extremely busy in my work, then also I had enough time for his calls and messages.

'Tomorrow my cousin is coming so I will not be able to talk to you on phone.' informed he prior.

'It is alright, no problem.' said I.

I didn't even touch the phone as I was sure that I was not going to get his call on that day. I talked to my parents, kept phone aside and started preparing my notes. I was about to sleep, I got a message from him.

'Hi!'

I thought it would have been sent by mistake as he was busy with his cousin.

But I replied, 'Hi'

'What doing?' asked he.

'Just finished with my notes.' replied I.

'Alright, want to join for movie? Going with my cousin.' asked he.

'Oh, wow. I wish I could. Enjoy and have fun.'

'Well let me know about the weather before you ask, it is raining very heavily. It will be very difficult to get a bus.' informed he by making fun of me.

'Thanks for letting me know about the weather. By the way, don't pull your hands out of the window of the bus keep the hands inside the window and put on rain-coat, don't get yourself wet in the rain, else it will make you sick.' I expressed my care for him.

'I can understand about raincoat and umbrella but what do you mean by keeping my hands inside the window? I didn't get it.' asked he

'If your hand is out and other vehicles are passing by your bus, it might cause an accident and your hand might get injured.' of course, my statement represented me as a moron.

'Oh, God. You are really funny.' said he.

'Yes I am. But please do take care of yourself.'

'Hey my Aditi, don't worry dear. I will be fine. You take care of yourself. Ok bye. Catch you soon.' sent he. I read that line for 20 times as he wrote 'My Aditi' I could not take my off those two words.

I realized that I started caring for him. My care and smile were assuring that I had started taking a shine to him. I was not able to understand what it was. I fell in love or it was just a habit. We both couldn't sleep before talking to each other. We were spending wonderful time with each other. We got on like a house on fire from the start. Then I realized that I was talking to some air as I was talking to a person for hours but did not even see him. I found it odd; so made up my mind and told myself, 'Now some decision must be taken by both of us.' I was just thinking about all that till late night and got his message.

'Hi slept?'

First time, I didn't feel to reply him back. Suddenly I started feeling guilty to talk to a stranger like that. I thought I was betraying my parents. In one minute, lots of thoughts stroke my mind.

'Good night. Sweet dreams.' he sent again after five minutes.

I didn't reply and slept. In the morning I didn't even wish him 'Good Morning'. I continued my routine work with travelling of various thoughts in my mind.

On that night, he called me as usual. I received but my voice was not the same as I always used to have while talking to him.

'Is everything alright?' he understood my voice without energy and asked.

'Yes, all ok. Just feeling little tired.' replied I.

'Then why can't you discontinue some of your lectures? You are pushing yourself too much, aren't you?' asked he.

'I am earning good and I want to help my father financially so I am fine with this.' said I politely.

'As you wish. Who am I to say anything.' taunted he.

'Yes, of course who you are to say all this to me.' said I bluntly.

'All ok?' asked he again.

I didn't beat about the bush and came to the point directly, 'I think we should meet once, else we should stop talking like this.'

'What happened all of a sudden?' asked he.

'I don't know but I think I am right. There is nothing wrong to meet a person whom you are talking to till late night since four months.' said I rigorously.

'Of course, there is nothing wrong in it. So where should we meet? Will you come to Bombay or should I come to Rajkot?' asked he.

'Of course you will come. I am a girl. I can't come that long, definitely you will have to come.' said I.

'You always talk about the equality of girls and boys, what happened this time?' asked he.

He didn't show much interest to come to Rajkot to meet me. I felt very bad the way he said. I thought he would agree on just one demand but it didn't turn out like that. Well I found his attitude right as a neutral person as he was not a guy who nagged behind girls.

'But I am very scared; I have never met any boy in any ice-cream parlour or at any coffee house. I am afraid of my students, colleagues and relatives. What if somebody would spot me with you?' I asked while biting my nails.

'So what to do?' asked he.

'Well, I am going to go to home in this weekend after five months, I will stay with my family for two days. While coming back from home, we will plan something.' suggested he.

'You will go to Patan so your train would pass through Rajkot station. Can we meet at Railway station? I find it little safe. If I come across somebody, they will understand that I would have come to drop or pick up some of my relative or friend. So you enjoy with family. While coming back, inform me about your train timing. I will reach at the platform. We will see each other for a while and will depart. At least we will see the face with whom we are talking since long.' said I.

'Absolutely perfect. My return ticket for Mumbai is on Sunday. Train will reach at Rajkot station around 4:00 pm. I will wait for you.' said he.

'Sure, fine. But how will we recognize each other?' asked I.

'Let's see who recognizes first. Let us wait for that moment.' said he.

We discussed that on Friday, I was very excited to meet him. I went for shopping, purchased a new top and jeans to look pretty. I was not able to concentrate on anything for two days, was thinking about the meeting only. I was extremely scared and nervous. I was also feeling guilty about myself as I was thinking that I was betraying my parents. I wanted to share everything with my mom. I was thinking about his appearance, his personality, his voice, his height and weight. I couldn't sleep properly for two nights. Somehow I just passed those two days; we were not able to talk even as he was at home. Finally it was Sunday; I was desperately waiting for his call, as he promised me he would call me when he would catch the train from Patan to Bombay. On Sunday, I got up at 5 o'clock in the morning and was feeling excessively desperate first time in life. I was getting extremely restless. Finally he gave me a call around 12:15 p.m. and said he would reach at the station around 4:00 p.m. I could say speak only, 'Alright, I will be there.' It was just the gap of four hours for our meeting or for unveiling of our faces. It was just 2:00 pm. and I started getting ready. I wanted my first appearance to remain in his good books for long. I wore black jeans and purple round neck top. I wore a leather watch in my left hand, and a small gold ring in the finger of right hand. I applied some make-up on my face and tied a pony-tail with my hair. I wore very small ear-rings. I applied perfume in much quantity as if he was going to hug me. Finally I got ready and took a small black purse with a phone in it. I took some money. I reached the station around 3:15 pm. and covered my face with a drape as it is very common for girls to cover their faces with it to protect themselves from heat and sun-rays. I did it but for a different reason.

I reached and called him to inform, 'Hi! I have reached to the station.'

'Oh, you reached so early. The train is running an hour late, it might reach around 5:00 p.m.' said he.

'Oh, is it? Train is playing the same role of your calls, It will also make me wait for long.' I laughed loudly.

I had been waiting since one and half hour but still train was not at the station. Those hours were felt like years. I was worried about my make-up, it was too hot and my face was covered. I did not want my Kajal to be smudged. My eye-sight was steadily moving from my watch to the railway stripes. I got up at the arrival of each and every train. Finally after huge amount of waiting, he called me,

'Hello, I am just five minutes away from the station.'

'Alright.' I replied in a nervous tone.

My heart started beating fast; I got up and uncovered my face. I kept on extending my eyes farthest to gaze the train. The whistle of the train blew up. I saw a train coming from distance. The closer it came, my heartbeats kept on increasing its speed of beating. I was feeling cold-feet. Finally, the train arrived. All the passengers started getting down. I was going from one compartment to another to look for him. He got down and started looking for me. Finally someone addressed my name, 'Aditi. Right?'

'Yes, and you Kabir?' asked I with supreme excitement on my face.

'Yup, so finally we are here.' said he with a gentle smile.

We kept on looking into each other's eyes with amiable smile. We both couldn't speak a single word. We were just staring at each other. He was in a travel suit - blue trousers and black round neck t-shirt. He carried two phones in his hands. One from which he used to call me, and another one when he used to use while coming to Gujarat. He was in simple slippers, it was quite apparent that he did not at all pull his finger out to impress me. He was looking extremely simple. He had a nice face and pink lips. His height might be 5:09 and has masculine body which was giving him a perfect and handsome look. The way he was looking into my eyes, I was feeling shy. I kept my eyes down but he didn't take his eyes off my face. It lasted just for one and half minute and the whistle blew up.

'I need to rush now. It was really nice to meet you.' said he by looking at the train.

'Yes, same here.' replied I by staring at train's whistle.

'Would you like to come to Mumbai with me?' asked he.

'But my luggage? My clothes?' I asked silly and stupid questions as if I was really going with him.

'Don't worry. Get in. We will manage everything.' he invited me wholeheartedly. We could talk that much in half-a-minute.

I smiled graciously and he rushed to get into his compartment. He was bidding me 'buy' by standing at the door of his compartment. I couldn't move from my place and was bidding him farewell with a smile. The train caught its speed; we kept on looking in each other's eyes until the train took its turn and got disappeared. I still wanted to be there but I realized he had gone. I left the station and drove my scooty to my room. During the whole way, I couldn't stop my heartbeats running fast. I kept on thinking about that meet of one and half minute.

I reached home and after few minutes I got a call from him,

'Hi! Reached to your place?'

'Yes, just reached.' I said by drinking water.

'Finally, we know each other by face also. Now we won't feel that we are talking to air. We can visualize each other's face while talking.' I said by breathing swiftly.

'True. If I say it was not me but was my friend, then?' asked he.

'What?' reacted I furiously.

'Please calm down. I am just kidding. It was me only.' he made fun of me.

We chuckled and continued talking until the batteries of his both mobile phones got discharged. We didn't give up despite severe network issues. The phone got disconnected again and again but we didn't stop calling each other and the call lasted for three hours without any matter of discussion.

He called me in the morning after reaching Mumbai home and wished me 'Good Morning.' He informed me that he reached safely as it became our habit to inform each other before going or coming anywhere. Then I also got back to my work.

Five months passed. We were in touch of each other and used to hang on phone till late nights. Once I realized it was not right. We were just talking to each other as friends; we also used to care for each other. Whatever we were doing was not appropriate just as friends. I thought, 'No friends would be talking till late night every day. Either there should be future of this relationship or it should be stopped. There is not any name of it and attachment is getting increased day by day. Being a boy, he is not initiating for anything, then how can I? 'But I always wanted a guy who doesn't nag behind me, as almost the time I have found the guys nagging behind me. He is not like them. Kabir is decent, mature enough, possess good qualification and above all, he is of my community.' murmured I.

'It is me who is thinking all this, he might not be feeling anything for me. I might be just a friend and fun for him.' And why would he go ahead with me? He is a smart guy with good qualification, he might find better and richer girl than me. I am not a daughter of a rich father. This relation might cause problems afterwards. Better I must stop everything here. I must not force him for falling in love with me. I know I can't live without him but I will have to. That will be good for both of us. I must stop calling him. Whatever I am doing with him, only my husband deserves it from me. Nobody else deserves my time and my talks.' I asked so many questions to myself and came to a conclusion of ending all that with him.

It was 10:00 pm. My call was ringing, it was he. I didn't receive for two times.

'Good Night. Sweet dreams.' he sent message.

I saw but I avoided and didn't reply. I waited for sometime but couldn't resist myself and called him.

'Hello. I called you two times but I thought you might have slept.' said he.

'No, was reading. Well, can I tell you something.' said I.

'Tell me. No need to take permission.' permitted he very easily.

'It is a serious matter. Reply honestly.'

'Oh, madam is going to take my exam today?' asked he with laughter.

'Yes, it is exam of life.' replied I.

'Do you love me?' asked I directly.

'What?' asked he with astonishment.

'I know you like me, everybody likes me but do you love me?' asked I with little hesitation.

He became silent for a while and replied, 'I don't know.'

'Then why do you call me every day? Why do you sleep after wishing me Good night and wake up after my wishes? Is it love or just a habit? I need to know it.' I asked with sensitive voice.

'Can we sleep now? It is late; we need to wake up early in the morning.' He tried to avoid the matter.

'Yes it is very late, we must have discussed it earlier.' I said with little annoyance.

'I am coming on this Saturday; I would like to meet you. Will you please come to Imperial Hotel? We will meet for coffee if you don't mind.' he asked with request.

'First give answer of my question.' I became stubborn.

'Let's meet face to face and will discuss, please.'

After thinking for a while, 'Alright, fine.' his request encouraged me to say yes for the meeting.

I was very happy; I thought he would come to meet me to take some decision about our relationship. He came to Rajkot and reached to the restaurant of Imperial hotel. I went to meet him secretly by hiding myself from the world's eyes. We ordered coffee. We talked a lot on general topics like education, jobs, business, friends, family, etc. It was face to face talking after a long time. But he didn't start anything about our relation, nor did I. We departed without having any discussion regarding our relationship and again we started talking on phone as usual. I tried to stop all that but somehow I failed. After a month, again he came to meet me and we met secretly at the same place, same restaurant, same table and had lunch together but just as friends. He used to come to meet me from Mumbai to Rajkot but we used to meet as friends. Despite few meetings and constant phone calling, we were still were friends. Either I wanted to go ahead in the relationship or I wanted to put a lid on it which had no future. I realized that

I was breaking rules of my life. I felt that I was betraying my parents and was not keeping the promise that I gave to myself regarding love and marriage. I realized all of a sudden that I was going astray.

'Now it is enough. Please stop calling me, it is too much now.' requested I driven up by the wall.

'Oh, so you want to break our friendship?' asked he.

'Do you talk to your each friend till late night, till 3:00 am.? Or I am the only victim?' asked I.

'Please don't blame, you also call me and like to talk to me.' he saved himself very smartly.

'Of course, I like you and love you and it hurts me now. It has started creating problems for me. I can't think any moment of my life without you. But if it is one sided, I want to stop it soon. I will not force you to give me commitment. But it is a request, please take some decision. Either 'Yes' or 'No' as I can't talk to a friend like this till late night; I don't want to meet any guy by hiding myself. All these things are for my husband only. If you are ready to give me commitment for marriage, then only we will go ahead, else let us stop everything. I feel very guilty; I feel I am betraying my parents and my future husband. You are a nice guy but this is not right. Please try to understand.' said I with crying loudly on phone.

'Please stop crying, please. I have not thought anything about it.' replied he.

'We are about to complete six months of our intense friendship and still you are thinking and taking it lightly. Anyways you think about it. Let somebody else bring marriage proposal to my father for me.' I started bombarding with loud cry. 'Better you leave it and let's leave all this. Let's forget everything as if it was just a dream. You will get busy in your life, I will be in mine.' I switched off my phone by crying like a small baby.

I cried for the whole night and couldn't sleep. I was so attached to him that was not able to think anything excepting him. I didn't want to go to my job as I was not feeling well. I had severe headache due to much crying but I didn't ignored my responsibilities and got ready for my lectures. I was not prepared for my lectures on that day but I managed the day anyhow and completed my work as usual. I switched on my phone and saw 11 missed calls from him. I controlled myself and didn't call back. It was the third day; we didn't talk to each other. By heart I was waiting for his call with some decision but he didn't take any decision. I understood his silence and tried to get extremely busy in my life, again I started making much fun with my room-mates. I made up my mind that it was just a beautiful dream. I started forgetting him rigorously although it was extremely difficult for me. It was seventh day we didn't talk or send message to each other. I got surety about his reply and got busy in my life again. Again I became the same strong girl, in fact came out as a little practical person, too.

All of a sudden I got a call from him after ten days. I didn't want to receive but I couldn't resist myself and received his third call.

'Yes.' I replied in a strong and normal voice, the way I used to reply to my other professional calls.

'Hi, how are you?' asked he in the same friendly tone.

'All good, and busy in my hectic schedule as usual.' replied I.

'Yes, teachers are always busy and....' said he and wanted to continue our amusing talks that we used to do always.

'So, anything urgent? I have to rush for my class.' interrupted I by showing not interest in his talks.

'Oh, so now I can call you only if I have some work.' taunted he.

'Yes of course, I don't talk to strangers without any reasons.' said I in a strong tone.

'Oh, madam is angry today.' somehow he was trying to making me laugh.

I disconnected the call and went to the class. I wanted to hang on phone but I controlled myself. I was so happy by doing that. He called me again after an hour but I didn't receive. After reaching home, I called him,

'Please I don't want to fight; it is a request to stop calling me. I have controlled myself after lot of difficulties. Please don't make me emotional again. Let us focus on work. I am begging.'

'I called you to inform you that I am coming to meet you on this Saturday.' said he.

'No, I am sorry. I don't want to meet you. It is not right Kabir. Please I am not that kind of girl who feels alone and needs a guy in her life for enjoyment and fun. I am already happy in my life. I love to be busy and I have a very good family, I won't to be able to behave in the same manner as I did before. Please I am not for you.' I said kindly while arranging my books.

'I am also not that kind of guy who meets girls and talks to them on phone calls till late nights, don't take me other way round.' replied he in harsh voice.

'I know you don't have such intentions, better we depart with positive reputation for each other. I am not coming as I am going to Morbi in this weekend.' I said politely.

'Alright then I will come to meet you there. Come on, stop this now. Can't you cancel to go home on this weekend? I am coming and will wait for you at Imperial restaurant at 4:00 p.m. I hope to see you there.' he disconnected the phone after informing that.

'So much attitude! His request is sounds as arrogance.' I whispered.

It was Saturday, I was in the dilemma, should I meet him or not?

Up to 2:30 pm. I was not ready to meet but felt his physical presence around me, just at the distance of two hours. I tried to control myself not to go but again I could not resist myself to see his face. I wanted to bite the bullet. I thought of meeting him for the last time and then thought of deleting his contact number forever. By thinking all that, I got ready. I washed my hair fast, I made them dried. I wore a black top and blue jeans. I wore black sandals with high heels. I kept my hair open. I kept my appearance extremely simple. I reached there around 3:35 pm., always before time.

'I am here.' I called him.

'Thanks a lot, I am on the train still, it is running late by half an hour.' informed he.

'Tell me something new, your train always runs late like you.'

'I am slow and steady person dear, but I always win.' said he with firmness.

I laughed but didn't make him hear. I ordered orange juice and was constantly staring at my wrist watch and the restaurant's clock to compare the time. I started counting the minutes for his arrival according to the restaurant's clock as it was showing the time little early than my wrist watch. Finally he reached; I got emotional to see him.

'So how are you?' asked he by sitting on a chair.

'I am fine, so what is new at your end?' asked I with little sad face.

We talked for some time on current job, education and good places in Mumbai. We ordered Pizza and enjoyed that. The waiter came with the bill, he took his wallet out for paying, I stopped him and requested to allow me to pay. I wanted to show that I was just an ordinary friend of him, so didn't want to be treated as somebody special. I went Dutch. I thought to leave. Pizza got over. He wanted to stay there with me but he didn't talk anything about our relationship. 'He will never initiate.' I murmured.

'Shall we order a cup of tea if you don't mind?' asked he so that we could stay here little longer.

'I will have lemon-juice.' said I by gazing at the menu.

'Sure'

'Why have you come here, Kabir?' initiated I as usual by making strict eye-contact.

'To see you.' said he normally as usual.

'Do you go to see your each friend often at the distance of sixteen hours?' asked I by being emotional. 'Why do you want to keep in touch with me if you don't love me.' asked I with tears in my eyes and hitting the fork on the table with little anger.

'Who said I don't love you, I love you that is why I have come that long, can't you understand that?' said he.

'Are you sure? But you never said it.' asked I with surprising face.

'Certain things should be understood, and I was about to tell but failed against your impatience.' said he with a cute smile.

'Do you really love me?' asked I.

'Of course, dear. I have come to meet you all along the way so that I can propose you face to face. I took enough time to understand if you are my love or my habit. I couldn't stop myself thinking about you. I love you so much, even beyond your imagination. But I took some time so that I can give you the final commitment. Now we are committed.' said he holding my hand.

'Finally.' I couldn't speak much; tears started rolling down my cheeks.

We wanted to hug each other but we saw the public around and controlled ourselves. We kept on looking into each other's eyes for long and the waiter interrupted us with the bill. We left the hands of each other and he paid the bill. Now I was his girl-friend so I allowed him to pay. We got out from the restaurant and it was his time to go. He wanted to catch the train at 7:00 p.m. He just came for two hours. While going out, we saw a big mirror at the reception area of the hotel. We stood in front of the mirror to see how we looked together. We both were happy to see each other, he kept his hand on my shoulder and we took a photo by looking in the mirror. I asked him to send it through email. I requested to drop him at the station so I could spend few more minutes with him. He had no problem. I dropped him to the station on my scooty and gave him a card which I had purchased for him. I thought it would be my last meeting so I would give him the card of best wishes from a friend and lots of success for career. I gave him the card and he accepted it whole wholeheartedly and he said he would love to have more wishes from me; those were not the last ones. His words increased my trust for him. The whistle of the train blew up and he got into the train. We departed and as usual we kept on looking at each other until the train disappeared. I reached home with the certificate of commitment. That was the best day of my life, the person whom I loved crazily was with me. We started talking until his phone's battery got discharged.

Finally my love life started with full of excitement. We used to work too much, used to talk a lot till late nights, sometimes full nights.

One day, while talking on phone, he kissed me on phone.

'Was it a kiss, yes?' asked I.

'Thanks for understanding. At least I can do it on phone, I can't do it when we meet.' said he.

'Why?' provoked I.

'I get involved into your eyes and beautiful face. Actually I can't gather courage.' accepted he.

'Don't worry, I will initiate even for this.' I said it by feeling shy.

'Let us see who shows the courage first.' said he with laugh.

'Kabir, I want to say one thing, my father is not very rich. I hope this matter will not disturb our relation in future. Will our parents be agree for our marriage?' asked I.

'Don't think about too far, just enjoy your present. And I am also not a millionaire. We are also struggling. Just focus on your work and career, don't bring stress to yourself. I am always with you.' said he.

'Well my friends are calling for movie.' said he.

'Movie, now? It is too late, it is already 1:30 am.' asked I.

'Some movies are good to watch at night only.' said he.

'Which are these movies?' asked I although I understood everything.

'Blue films, now don't tell, you girls don't watch it with your room-mates.' said he.

'Blue films? Which kinds of films are these? Is everything seen blue in it?' asked I with full of surprise.

'Oh, a big lie and that is also to me! If you watch it, nothing wrong. In fact, that proves that you are normal. Now tell the truth, you must have watched it with friends, right?' asked he with full of confidence.

I couldn't lie to him and said, 'I have not watched it with friends but alone.'

'You! Lying to me! Finally you came to senses my dear. All in blue colour? Nice dialogue! In fact girls watch even more than boys.' said he with laugh.

'Now you sleep. My friends are waiting for me. Bye, see you in dreams. Good night, Sweet dreams, Love you. Kiss you. Miss you so much. Take care; my love.' said he in a very melodious tone.

'Good night, Sweet dream, Love you. Kiss you. Miss you so much. Take care; my love.' said I in the same tone.

Our naughty talks started. We always used to sleep by dreaming about each other. We used to meet in the morning and at night through the phone. I used to call him almost after each lecture. So it was like we were together for the whole day despite a lot of distance.

It was the time for Diwali; I was going to go home for 15 days. I had a small vacation.

'You teachers are very lucky; you get vacations and tours at free of cost.' said he.

'We also get supervision duties and paper checking at free of cost.' replied I.

He laughed and said 'Hey, want to see you soon. Missing you. What are you doing this weekend?'

'Going home for fifteen days.' said I.

'I am also going home for four days. We have holidays for two days and two days I will take the days off and will return on Wednesday. How will you go?' asked he.

'By bus as usual.' replied I.

'Can you catch a train from Rajkot to Morbi? Can you go on the same time when I would reach there, then you get in the same compartment at the same time. We will be able to spend time at least for one an half hour. I would be able to wish Diwali to my girlfriend in advance. I will book your ticket in the same compartment if you don't mind.' insisted he.

'Alright, I will be there. Well it sounds very nice when you say I am your girlfriend.' I told him.

After two days, I packed my luggage. I was more excited to meet him than going home. I purchased Dairy Milk Celebration for him as a gift. I got into the same compartment. He gave me his hand to lift me up. I hold his hand by being frightened as I didn't want anybody to spot us together. We sat in front of each other on the train.

'So finally I am meeting my boyfriend.' I said by feeling little shy and looking into his eyes.

'Yes, my girlfriend.' he said by staring at me without any shyness.

'Happy Diwali.' I wished him by giving him the chocolate.

'Same to you, my love.' he wished me by giving me a gift that he brought for me.

He opened the chocolates on the spot and shared with me. It was amazing time. The window was open and the wind was blowing inside. The wind was spreading the fragrance of romance. Our hair got scattered due to the blow of wind. Gusty breeze was adding fuel to the fire of our naughty intentions. We were talking and looking at each other. We wanted to kiss each other but none of us could gather courage. In the middle of the talk, he flashed at my clothes, shoes and chest. In the blink of an eye, he started looking into my eyes. He thought I didn't realize that but actually I didn't make him realize that realized that. There was nothing wrong to be lusty in true love, I thought for a while.

'Hello, sir. Ticket please.' T.T. of the train came to Kabir.

'Yes sure, sir.' He showed the tickets of both of us.

'Show me your I-cards.' the T.T demanded.

'Here it is.' said he by showing it.

'I don't have my I-card. I forgot to take.' said I with getting frightened.

'Then get down or pay the fine.' ordered T.T.

I looked at Kabir with very nervous face. He asked me to be relaxed by giving some signs.

'I will pay the fine, don't worry.' said he.

He paid 500 rs. for the root of an hour.

'In first meeting, your girl-friend has become costly for you. I am really sorry.' said I.

'It is alright, next time keep your I-card with you. You need it anywhere. And don't worry about this fine; it was my advance donation of Diwali.' said he by making fun. We departed at the Morbi station.

I reached home but I couldn't find myself in me. I was completely lost in him. Half of my mind and heart were with him only. I was not able to forget him for a single moment. He reached home but he didn't call me. The whole day passed, neither he called me nor sent a message. I called him up and wished him Diwali.

I was at home. I was waiting my mother to go out for a while so I could call him. Luckily, someone called my mother for a while and she went out. I was making chapatis but I switched off the gas and called him directly by popping out to see my mother, 'Why have you not been calling me since two days?'

'Family members were around so I couldn't call.' replied he.

'But you could drop a message at least, no Good night and no Good Morning.' said I with little anger.

'I had some work so I was out with mom and in rush hours so I forgot.' said he.

'By next Diwali, you might forget me.' told I by showing little irritation.

'No, don't worry. My memory is not that much weak.' said he with calmness.

'Ok bye, mom is coming.' I said in hurry, disconnected the call and rushed to the kitchen for making the chapatis.

He returned to Mumbai to come back to his work after four days and I stayed at home as I had a small vacation. Although I was at home, I continuously sent him messages even at night. I used to spend time with my family, along with that I used to be with him, too. But he could not keep in touch with me when he was with his family members or with friends. I never did it. We used to fight a lot on that matter.

'I don't think it will work any more.' I combated.

'Oh god ! you have started giving me pyar ka punchnama nowadays.' he said in little anger.

Our fights continued. Sometimes the matter used to reach to the break-up level but our love never got reduced for each other.

Diwali vacation ended, I got busy in my work again. I also started preparing for my final exams. After two months, we decided to meet again. We met at a resort a wonderful place in Rajkot city including various special zones like, Rutya Mandir, Selfie Zone, Indoor Games, Spa world, Adventures sports, vast restaurant, Garden and many more. It was situated at the distance of the city. We decided to meet there. I kept a day off at work. He came at 10:00 am. in the morning, we entered the resort. We shacked our hands with each other. We found a place in the corner of the resort and sat there to have a lot of talks. We talked for hours, we laughed a lot. We were sitting beside each other. In the middle of the talk, I burnt all bridges for romance and kissed him on his left cheek as I was sitting at his left side. After that, we both got shocked on my deed.

'Finally I initiated as usual and showed my courage.' said I by covering my eyes with my hands.

'You are really courageous than me, now I should also learn from you.' said he with excitement on his face.

He held my hand and kissed me on my forehead first, then on nose and then we smooched. It was our first kiss. We both were shocked by our act. We found the whole world was blind. We kept on kissing each other as if nobody was around. We felt heaven on earth with us. We listened to some sound of some workers working around. One of the workers came towards us to take his plough. We sat silently for a while until he went from there.

'Carry on. It is your time. Enjoy.' said he and went away.

We got more courage and started again. Then he slept in my lap and said,

'I have never felt such calmness and relief in my life. I love you so much."

'Same to you, Kabir.' I said by kissing on his forehead and combing his hair with my fingers.

We had lunch together, had a lot of fun and it was time to depart. He was supposed to catch a train by 9:30 pm. We got out from the resort around 8:00 pm. We did not want to depart.

'Still we have one and half hour.' I said while opening the lock of my scooty.

'Let's have a long drive on your scooty.' suggested he.

'Nice idea.'

I started driving and saw a very dark and lonely street. We both were expecting to go inside. We entered that dark street. Parked the scooty and came closer to each other. We started smooching each other vigorously. We saw some light of a vehicle; we stopped for a while; and started again.

'Your face is glowing like the moon.' appreciated he by touching my lips.

'As I am in your love.' I replied by putting my hands on his cheeks..

'Oh, baby. Don't stop kissing.' he held me tightly.

We dropped the veil of decency. Our slow heart beats raised and we let the breaths move in to each other's breaths. We both became lusty. We felt as if we were walking on air. We found all the stars had fallen in our laps. After sometime we realized it was time to leave. I dropped him to the station and we departed. It was a Kiss Day for us; we could never forget our first kiss. We never thought it would be that much lusty and sudden.

'Hey, please don't take me other way round. My love is more than this; lust is just a part of my true love for you. I love you so much. I respect you a lot.' said he on phone.

'I know I trust you blindly. No need to clarify anything, I love you.'

We continued talking till his phone's battery got discharged. Next morning, we both got busy in our work. I called him but he didn't receive, I tried to call him many a times but he didn't receive till the evening. He called me at 11:00 p.m.

'Where have you been for the whole day, we just met yesterday, enjoyed a lot, were you not missing me?' asked I in anger.

'Yes of course I was missing you but I was busy in the office.' said he.

'Was I free? Did I have not any work? But I called you at least and you behaved for the whole day as if you didn't even know me and that is also just after the next day of our exciting meeting. How could you do that? How could you survive for the whole day without calling me? I couldn't resist myself without thinking about you for a second. I kept on calling you? I became furious.

'You have come home now?' asked I.

'No I came back at 5:45pm.' said he.

'What? At least you would have lied. You are at home since evening and you didn't even call me! Why do you do always like that? What will you lose if you call me for a while? At least on next day of our meeting? I was dying to talk to you.' I fought literally.

'Oh, common leave it now. Now if you have called, can't we talk calmly?' asked he.

'But that happens every time. I have also my work, my family, my friends but I reach to you wherever I am and you forget me easily. Am I not special for you? Don't I deserve more time of your life than others? You don't even send me a single message. Why do you behave like this? I know you love me a lot then why you create problems for me with this kind of behaviour. Don't you miss me the way I do?' asked I in crying tone.

'Now will I have to follow your way to love you? I don't have habit of calling and sending messages again and again. I call once a day, isn't it enough? You are multitasking, I am not. I am just a normal person, not hyper-active like you. And it is a natural difference between a male and female, I suppose. Males can't hang over phones all the time like females. I suggest you to read a book 'Men are from Mars and women are from Venus written by John Gray.' You will understand the natural difference between our attributes. It will make our relation better and more understanding.' he said in little harsh voice.

'And why have you stopped your writing and reading after our commitment? I have not read any of your articles since long. Please don't fall in love, rise in love. I am never going to go anywhere without you. I am always with you.' said he firmly.

'But now a days, we don't talk much, we just talk for a while and then sleep.' complained I.

'If we don't have anything new to talk, what to do? Better to spend quality time with each other rather than fighting on unnecessary things. And you have extreme stamina, I don't have that. I have my physical limitations, I get tired after work. But you don't get, you have unlimited stamina. What can I do in that?' he disconnected the call in anger.

'He is right at his end; I should control myself being in fairy-tell romance and continue being immature many a times. My love has touched the top ladder of craziness; I should not think about him continuously and must not miss him righteously. He has become the centre of my life. I should not cry at least just to listen his voice. He has become my first priority but I should not give less importance to my friends, family, parents, siblings and even to myself. I am falling in love despite rising.' I murmured with tears in my eyes.

After two days, he called me and said, 'Wait I have prepared a song for you, listen to it. These are not only words but my feelings for you.' he sang a song to reconcile me and to make my mood fresh.

> *'Na hai yeh pana, na khona hi hai*
> *Tera na hona jane, kyun hona hi hai*
> *Tum se hi din hota hai, surmaiye shaam*
> *aati, tumse hi, tumse hi*
> *Har ghadi saans aati hai, zindagi kehlati*
> *hai, tumse hi, tumse hi*
> *Na hai yeh pana, na khona hi hai*
> *Tera na hona jane, kyun hona hi hai*

I threw myself into fantasy - in the world of imagination. I fabricated myself as Karina Kapoor and him as Shahid kapoor. It was a dreamy moment for me.

We used to fight a lot. He was more mature than me; I realized it after some years. But I was in the time of craziness and fancy. For me his love, his phone-calls became the first priority. If he called, I would leave everything for that. His company became more precious even than my parents' company. He also knew it very well that I loved him crazily.

'Do you think will it work? We have started fighting, it is just two years of our relationship, and see where are we standing? will it work for the entire life?' asked I.

'No problems, we will keep on fighting but will live together. Commitment is commitment. We will try to overcome our fights on small and non-sense things but we will not break-up.' conformed he.

'You are right. And that happens with every couple.' said I.

'Ok, then keep fighting with me on non-sense things, sometimes I think I should sell my phone, then I won't have any worries.' taunted he.

'Oh, now I have become a worry for you.' said I with laughter.

'Not you, this stupid phone. At office – my boss and at home – you. Both are too much.' said he with a laugh.

After few days he came to meet me and we went for a movie. It was dark in the cinema, we booked corner seats. We started kissing each other with the beginning of the movie, we stopped kissing in the interval, and again we started. Two hours passed as two minutes. We always used to find the cinema a safe place for satisfying our lust.

It was around six and half months, we didn't meet. It became little difficult to maintain long distance relationship. We decided to meet at a resort in Rajkot on his birthday. The place was very famous and known for its excellent food, distinguished hospitality, magnificent banquet space and many other aspects. I purchased a t-shirt for him as his birthday gift. Well we didn't go with the flow of giving gifts and chocolates each and every time we met. We used to give gifts on some occasions like birthday and Diwali. We didn't follow the custom of giving cards to each other. I gave him two cards first time. We used to repeat the same cards on our each birthday and used to write good wishes in the same cards. We met at resort in Rajkot. I kept my day off. We were very excited to meet each other as we were meeting after long time.

I waited for him at the spot; he reached half an hour late as usual. We went to the place together with the help of my scooty. We sat on a table in the resort and just kept on looking at each other. We didn't take our eyes off each other for almost fifteen minutes. Then we ordered Masala dhosa, enjoyed it and had a lot of talks.

'Kabir, we are about to complete three years of our relationships. After a lot of fights, we have not stopped loving each other. Will our parents accept our relationship? Will they permit us for marriage? At my place, my parents know very well that we are good friends and we also talk sometimes on phone. What about your family?' asked I with serious face.

'There are 11 members in my family and they are little conservative. My uncle's family is going to shift to Ahmadabad for good; they are planning to set up business in some mega city. Then there will remain only five members at home including me. I hope it will be easier to convince them. Actually they know you as we are in some community but they have heard that you are a little modern, working and independent girl.' said he by looking into the menu.

'Yes, according to our society, independent working girls are not cultural and they are not considered good as daughter-in-laws. You are saying, your family is little conservative. Will they allow me to work after marriage? You know how ambitious I am! I am very serious about my career and my work; I can't sit at home without doing anything. I don't mind working in the kitchen and do the house-hold work, that will be my first priority but I also need some creative stuff to do, else I will get into frustration. I am a modern and independent girl, but that doesn't mean that I don't like to be with family. I would have to leave my family, my parents after marriage so I will definitely consider your parents and family as mine. I also need a family; in fact, I am a family oriented girl. I love people around me. I enjoy sharing my happiness and sadness with them. I do all with my parents and my grand-parents. I can't live alone.' I said by taking few sips of sambhar.

'I know and I trust you. I am sure you will handle everything nicely. Your love and respect for elders will also convince my parents easily, I am proud of you for many things. So just relax and don't worry, just enjoy your present.' he said by offering a flower decorated in the jug kept on the table.

'I am worried as I am not just passing my time with you, my love. I want to be the part of you and your family as well.' said I with tears in my eyes.

'Of course, you are and please stop crying. I think crying is your hobby. said he by giving the tissue paper.

'One last question please, I am very fond of cloths and carrying myself nicely. After marriage, if I am supposed to go for some meetings, conferences or seminars, I would be required to wear blessure with jeans, will I be allowed to wear that?' asked I.

'Of course, why not. You will do anything what you want. You are a girl of 21st century and I myself would love to have an independent and working wife who carries herself very nicely. And which boy would not like to have a wife like that?'he motivated me with great confidence.

'But your parents?' asked I.

'Don't worry. When time comes, everything is accepted. Before your all relatives were against your study and job but now they have started following you. They come to take your guidance for their daughters' education. See the live example. Just relax and enjoy this moment, you really think a lot.' said he.

The waiter came with the bill and I requested to pay it as I didn't want to continue the custom of paying the bills only by the boyfriend. If I used to talk about equality of girls and boys, then everything should be equal, even the payment of the bill. I paid the bill. I offered him a gift that I bought for him. He opened it and laughed.

'What happened?' asked I by narrowing my eyes.

'This t-shirt is very funny. A cap is attached to it.' he said while opening it.

'So?' I asked with smile

'Sorry, it is for college guys, I don't wear this kind of t-shirt.' said he by keeping it on the table.

'Oh is it, at least you could have lied for making me happy that you liked it, then you could have donated it.' said I by tapping on his shoulder.

'Yes, I could have done it. Then you would have forced me to wear it next time when I come to meet you.' laughed he.

'Ok, give it back to me. I will return it and bring something else for you. Your birthday gift will remain pending, better I should have given you cash in an envelop. How mean you are! You returned the gift to a girl.' said I with laugh.

'I don't do it with anybody. I can be that much impudent just with you as I want to look what I am, don't want to pretend in front of you for any matter.' said he.

We kept on walking and talking, along with that we were also finding a proper place for kissing each other. Well we didn't tell it to each other but we both were spreading our eyes from one street to another. Finally we found a lonely street, covered with half walls. We entered that street. It was around 12:30 at noon; we were also getting frightened that somebody might catch us. We were looking at each other. Then we gathered courage, he came close to me. I got myself stuck to the wall, he held my hands and started kissing me from forehead as usual. Then we smooched each other like anything. By kissing, we sat down. I also scattered his hair with my fingers and lust made us to be on the top of the world. We were enjoying that lusty moment and we heard the noise of a bike. They were police-inspectors. They caught us red-handedly during that time. We both got shocked and could not speak a single word. We both set our hair which became extremely wavy.

'Crap!' the same word slipped out from the mouth of both of us.

'We are sorry, sir. It will never happen again.' requested Kabir.

'Shut up. You, young blood, are the curse for your parents. What is your name and where do you work? Where is your residence? We will call your parents and will take you to the police-station. You will be cultured if you are locked in the jail.' shouted the inspector.

'I am sorry, sir. Please forgive us, don't tell about this to our parents. We will spoil our earned reputation because of this mistake. Please sir.' requested I.

'We can spare you if you pay something.' the inspector demanded for the bribe indirectly.

'Please take this sir.' Kabir gave them 500 rs.

He looked at us as if we asked for his kidneys. Kabir again gave him 500 rs. He took it and went by warning us that it should not happen next time.

'Thank God! We are saved; else we would have lost everything, our reputation, trust and love of our parents. I am worried. What would happen if they print our act in tomorrow's news paper.' said I to Kabir.

'Check tomorrow's news-paper and tell me. Don't worry that has happened many a times in Mumbai with my friend. They take some amount of bribe and forget. So just chill.' he said with confidence.

We departed with little worry but somehow we realized it was a venture for both of us. We laughed a lot on that act. He got his train and reached Mumbai, I also got back to my work. Next day, I checked the news papers but I found no news regarding us.

It is said in Bhagavad Geeta in chapter- 9, shloka-26

पत्रं पुष्पं फलं तोयं यो मे भक्त्या प्रयच्छति ।
तदहं भक्त्युपहृतमश्नामि प्रयतात्मनः ॥२६॥

**I accept with love, all of the offering that
my selfless devotees present to Me (devotedly)
in the form of leaves, flowers, fruits and water.**

I considered Kabir as my God and started loving him unconditionally. I wanted him to accept my present which I presented devotedly in the form of my emotions.

CHAPTER 8

I was supposed to clear my final exams of masters, just two months were remaining for it. I always wanted to work in some good college; I got tired of running from one place to another one in extreme heat, heavy rain and severe cold. I wanted more reputed job in some good college but I was required to acquire at least Master qualification or might be more than this. I thought I have always got jobs before qualification. Why not to try once again? 'Well it might be impossible but there is nothing wrong to apply.' I thought for few days and applied for the post of a lecturer in three reputed colleges of Rajkot.Then I got busy with my previous job and preparations for my final exams. Suddenly after few days, I started getting calls from all three colleges for interviews. I got surprised. I gave interviews and demo lectures in those three colleges. One college was in the requirement of a visiting faculty for English Language and Communication Skills. I got tired of being a visiting faculty; I wanted to have a secure job at one place only. I didn't want to run from here to there. I wanted to work as a permanent faculty. I got selected in all three colleges. I eliminated the first college which was offering me eighteen thousand for the post of a visiting faculty. I was supposed to take decision from other two colleges. I appeared for the interview and got selected in one of the two colleges.

'You have been selected, feedback from the student is 98% so we want to appoint you and want you to join here as a lecturer of Communication Skills Department.' informed the dean of the college.

'Thank you so much sir, but I must clarify that the result of my final exam has not been declared yet.' said I.

'We know that but our students are very satisfied by your teaching style, your personality and your speech so you submit your result to HR department when you get it.' informed he.

'Thanks a lot sir.' said I by signing on the joining letter.

'Now the main question, what is your expectation?' he asked by folding his hands.

'As per the norms, sir.' replied I with little hesitation.

'We provide around thirty seven thousand to a PHD holder but you are just a fresher and Masters holder so we can't provide you that much.' he clarified it.

'Sir, I am already earning thirty plus, my demand is at least more than this.' said I with little confidence.

'Alright, thirty one thousand.' he negotiated before I speak anything.

He saw my pleading facial expressions and said 'Alright, last thirty five thousand, I can't go beyond that.'

'It is completely fine sir; I will give my best as a faculty of Communication Skills.' I promised him with my happy face.

I would have joined even in twenty thousand as I wanted to work in some reputed college after my Masters. It was unbelievable for me that I got the ball in my court. God became more faithful and favorable to me by providing me that much amount. I thought, 'honesty, hard-work, punctuality and my sincerity favoured me. Experience of my early age career showed a magic.' I was feeling over the moon, I wanted to jump but I controlled myself.

'We want you to join from Monday, the day after tomorrow.' insisted the dean.

'Sir, I have just completed my exams before a weak, I want to have a break at least for a week, can I join from 1st June, please?' requested I.

'It is ok, No problems. Complete the formalities and submit your required documents at HR department.' he said by taking the bundle of files.

'And congratulations.' added he.

'Thanks a ton sir, I am pleased to get a job here. Thanks for giving me the opportunity to work with this great institution.' I told him by taking my purse and keys from the table.

I got out of the office, finished the formalities and finally got the joining letter in my hand which was displaying the salary of thirty five thousand that was directly after completion of my Masters. I got even that job before my result. I was proud of myself, before my proud and confidence converted into ego or over-confidence, I kept the letter in my bag and visited the entire campus. It was such a wonderful college including specious classes, vast library, gigantic seminar halls, amazing conference halls, expanding canteens, very big play-ground, attractive dance-rooms and authentic language labs. I felt extremely glad by considering myself the part of that amazing campus. For me, it was like an unbelievable dream which came true before time. I thanked a lot to Mehtasir for suggesting me to opt for Arts field before five years.

I left college with my room-mate, Komal Vaja, who accompanied me for my interview. We came back to room by driving our scooty. For the whole way, I was recalling my performance in front of professional and experienced professors. Lots of thoughts were travelling in my mind.

My all room-mates were waiting for me, I reached to my room. I showed them my joining letter, and they all jumped with joy and demanded for the party. All girls motivated me by telling me that I was their role-model for so many things, as far as my hard-work and sincerity about my career was concerned. They said that they also wanted to start something and do something in their lives.

I called my parents and informed about my new job. I informed about my salary and they couldn't believe. I informed them, 'I am coming home after two days.'

At last, I called Kabir for long talk.

'Hi love, I have been selected and got the joining letter.'

'I knew, you will crack it. Congratulations. Now my teacher has become a professor.' said he with proud.

'Not yet, I will become a professor after my PHD and after the experience of many years, now I am just a lecturer or you can say an assistant professor.' I said by washing my cloths.

'At least you have started, but it sounds good to see you at ground-feted. Keep this positive attitude up.' he motivated me.

'Did you inform your parents about it?' asked he.

'Yes.'

'They would have been very happy, right?' asked he.

'Yes, extremely.' said I.

'I am going to home after two days for few days, then I will have to join college from 1st June.'

'Sure, be with your parents and enjoy with them.'

I enjoyed the small vacation at home. My relatives came to know about my job, they got surprised and believed in my hard-work and also came to congratulate my parents and me. They said to my parents it was really nice that they educated their daughters. Some of them confessed, 'Nowadays girls are doing very well in all fields. We have also started motivating our daughters to go ahead in their education. We suddenly found the world laughing with us, instead of at us. All of a sudden, we saw changes in people's thoughts, they were found to follow our path for girls' education and freedom. Well, some people can't help them to be Iago so they ignored my hard-work and spotlighted my luck for my success. Some of my friends came to meet me and regretted on their decision on selecting Science field as it became very difficult to get jobs in that field. They said, 'the field requires a lot of money.' Eight day of vacation passed very fast with family.

It was 1st June, joining date of my new job. It was the first day of my college. I was very young for my post. I found my students elder than me. I wanted to look more professional and mature than my age before my students and colleagues. I wanted to give a professional and serious appearance to myself to create my first professional impression. So I wore a maroon coloured long kurta and white salwar with white dupatta. I wore very simple cream colour sandals and a leather watch. I wore very small ear-rings. I kept my hair open and wore spectacles. I took a simple purse and got the institution bus which was provided by the institute only. The moment I got on the bus, all students started scanning me. I got nervous and thought, 'I might be looking very young or smart.' That assumption kept my confidence high and I took a seat.

It was my first day in college as a lecturer. I was all alone as usual without any group. I inquired about my sitting area in the college. They allocated me a full furnished office which I was supposed to share with my colleagues. I was given my personal laptop.

'Ma'am would you like to have tea or coffee?' the peon entered with two thermoses in his hands.

I didn't have that kinds of services in my previous job so I kept on looking around, then realized he was asking me only. I got surprised to receive that kind of hospitality. I hid my surprising feelings and replied to him with little attitude, 'I will have coffee.'

He poured coffee in my mug and opened the door to go out.

I greeted him with gentle smile, 'Thank you for the coffee.'

He didn't even consider my etiquette and went out just by giving a normal look to me. I found his surprising expressions for my words. It was their routine work to serve each faculty member so none of the peons had that kind of etiquette to reply back. I realized it after few days and stopped saying 'thanks' to any peon who came to serve water or anything else.

I met with my colleagues. Many fresher faculties joined on 1st June. All the faculty members were from entire India. Up to now, I had worked with only Gujarati people but I came in touch with people of North, South, East and West. Everything was so new to me. First and foremost, I came in touch with a lecturer, Neeta Sharma-from Electronics department. We talked a lot. Slowly and gradually, I met all the faculties of all departments. We used to share the office, used to have break-fast and lunch together. It was such a wonderful experience. I tried to start internet. I didn't even know how to work on Google and didn't know anything about face book or twitter. I learnt that from my colleagues. I used to call them by names, but they used to address me as 'Madam' although I was younger than them. Then I got to know that they found me little serious and sincere than them. I realized that they didn't share any of their vulgar talks with me which took place among them. Well I liked their respect and fear for me. We all became very good friends. The college arranged a 'Faculty Development Program' for a week. All new faculty members were supposed to attend it together. Various experienced and qualified professors were invited as expert lecturers to conduct the sessions. They shared their number of experiences about their teaching career and education. They shared various teaching methodologies with us. We were given unlimited activities to enhance our teaching skills. I used to prepare a lot for presentations to perform better. I worked hard to hit the stage. Just in few days, I became very famous for my Presentation skills and my dressing sense. The training program lasted for eight days, we enjoyed it a lot. I completed my first month and earned my first salary. I donated some amount to few Ashrams and went to temple with a coconut and some incense sticks. I called my parents and Kabir to inform about my first salary. I was extremely happy. I wanted to work harder to fulfil my all dreams and to do something better even this. I got huge amount of confidence. I got my hair straightened from my first salary, had some shopping for my family members.

After a month, our sitting arrangement got changed. All new faculties were asked to sit with their own Department. I was allocated an office with the faculty members of Communication Skills Department. There were 11 faculties in the department. Five senior faculties and six junior and fresher ones. I was a fresher. I showed my respect to the senior faculties and told them that I wanted to learn much more from them. They got impressed by my behaviour. They provided me many reference books for preparations of my lectures. They also guided me for my classes.

Now the vacation got over for students and college started from 1st July. It was my first lecture of Communication Skills. I prepared very hard for it on previous day of the class. The college was so big; I could not remember the directions of the classes. I asked one of my colleagues to help me to find my class. Finally I reached there and entered the class. It was a wide class of Mechanical Engineering on 2nd floor. I entered with confidence on face and nervousness in heart, stood on the stage, gave my introduction and started conducting my lecture by keeping the reference book on the podium. Students were staring at me and increasing my nervousness. But with the help of my prior experience, I managed it very accurately. Slowly and gradually, I got used to with almost the classes and lectures. We were also given other subjects to deal with. I got busy in preparations but was very happy that I was learning new things and was quite satisfied that I was dealing with college students. I was given hold of many classes. I dealt with them very successfully and with confidence. Students started enjoying my lectures.

I passed two months in the college; one of the faculty members of Mechanical Engineering came to my office when I was alone. His name was Kamlesh Virvani. Well we were not unknown to each other as we were supposed to team up for the presentations in the training. He was very smart and good looking, his talks were very sensible. He asked about me, my family, my likes, my dislikes. I was feeling little uncomfortable due to his lots of questions about my personal life. After two days, one of his colleagues of the same department, Prof. Priya Bootani, came to me. She was also my friend. She asked me my liking about him. Indirectly she was trying to tell that he was interested in me. I was new so I didn't want her to know about my commitment with someone else that news would have become the breaking news for the entire college and I would have become the prime topic of discussion among faculties and students. So I told her firmly, 'Sorry dear, now I am not interested in any such thing. I want to focus on my career first. I am just twenty-two years old.' Indirectly I told her that I was not at all interested. She forced me by informing me that he was of my caste only. She continued convincing but I left the office by saying politely, 'I got to go dear, I have a lecture.' She must have figured out my unfavourable response from my facial expressions and entire body language.

I focused on my work and got mingled very nicely with my department. It became my team. In the beginning, we had very less work but slowly and gradually, responsibilities started increasing. The work made us run on the toes. We were given various classes and various subjects. Preparation for all new subjects kept us busy even after working hours.

I was trying to get to the grips with the professionalism of college. One of the faculty members, Animesh Luhana, from Environmental Department came to me to give me the papers of students. He was the junior head of the department and was very sincere. I worked under his guidance until the head of our department was declared. I just collected the papers from him and suddenly he said,

'Ma'am, if you don't mind, can I take your two minutes as I want to discuss something very imported and personal.' he requested by staring at me.

'Yes, sir. Please. Anything for students? Please have a seat.' I offered him a chair.

'It is not about the students or college.' said he by pulling the chair towards him and sitting on it.

'Then?' asked I by checking the papers.

'Actually, I got to know that we both are of same caste and we know each other since two months. I have secured good post here, so have you. I like you. Can we go ahead for commitment of marriage? I am sure our parents will also support for this.' he directly proposed me for marriage.

I got shocked by his direct propose, but didn't get nervous as I got used to with the direct and indirect proposals.

'I am sorry sir but I am committed. Please keep it up to you only as I don't want the matter to be spreaded around.' said I cordially.

'Oh, I am sorry. All the best.' he left the office by saying that.

Then onwards, he stopped talking to me even for the professional matters. He used to send his assistant even for major matters regarding students or their work, else before he personally used to come to me just for minor matters. He also started looking through me. Well I was least concerned about it. I didn't focus on that matter, I didn't even share anything with any of my colleagues who were sharing office with me as they were already much interested in gossips of the entire college. If I had shared it with them, they would have created the hype of everything. I was not interested to take gratification of two proposals. I never liked to share my personal matters with anybody; there were just few selected people who might know about my personal stuff. Again I ignored everything and started passing my job days with satisfaction.

I used to call Kabir by standing in the lobby of the college. I didn't prefer to talk to him by sitting in my office as I didn't want to reveal my relationship. My office mates caught me hanging on phone frequently and asked me about my frequent phone calls. I didn't respond them properly so they started taunting me for hiding things from them. I didn't mind if they came to know about my relationship but they would not keep that up to them only. They were so much interested in scoop of college's dean, director, faculties and students. They were much interested in college campus, amenities, hostel problems, canteen issues, etc. I always found them sitting in the circle and enjoying gossips of the whole world after finishing their lectures. They used to spend half of the working hours in scandal only. I started feeling suffocated in that office. I tried a lot to change the office but I couldn't find any other vacant office. They started taunting me for each and everything as I was not walking on their paths and never showed interest in their gossips or in anybody's personal life. I tried to get into their matters but my topics of discussions were rejected by them as they included good books, good movies, and some religious matters. They disqualified me from the list of the girls of 21st century. According to them, I had good looks and good dressing sense but by nature I was like an old fashioned girl as I didn't drink and didn't attend parties till late nights or I never hanged out with friends and had fun. They always found me remain busy with either books or some cultural things. I couldn't change my office but I found one escape from their gossip and that was library. I used to finish my lectures and used to sit in the library for two hours every day.

One of my colleagues suggested, 'Hey Aditi madam, you love to keep yourself busy in creative things, right?'

'Yes, ma'am. I have got nice grips on the lectures. I am satisfied the way I deal with my students and my subjects. It has become my routine work now. I am finding something else to learn more.' said I while heading towards library.

'I know. You will never stop your learning. You are very dissatisfied soul as far as your learning is concerned. You always want more and more in the area of your learning.' appreciated she.

'Yes ma'am, thanks for distinguishing me accurately.'

'Why don't you continue your study? Why don't you go for research? Join P.H.D. It is pretty appropriate for you. P.H.D. demands not only hard work but also sincere work. I am sure you will crack it. If you do it, it will increase your knowledge, will give you high reputation in future and above all, you will be able to guide your students more properly and perfectly as far as your subjects are concerned.' said she with great hope.

'You are right madam. I must do it. But I don't know the process of it. Will you please guide me for its process and even to find a guide?' asked I with respect.

'Sure, why not. Come to my office at your convenient time.' she went to her office by saying that.

I went to her office and discussed much about it. She helped me to find a guide, also helped me with some required sources to get into my research. Finally I started my P.H.D. After that, I kept on remaining even busier. My that busy schedule always kept my mind busy and kept me away from all the political issues happened in college. Well I also became the victim of some normal and major academic issues regarding classes, attendance, supervisions, lectures, etc. I made some mistakes as I was learning my work. I started learning high professionalism and somehow I overcame all the issues soon as I thought I had more important work to do than those issues. Slowly and gradually, I started becoming professional, and put the lid on my emotions as the place was highly professional and full of politics. I realized the reality of all work-places. Exploitation was the common problem for all employees. It was very common everywhere that senior staff members got more rights for everything, they also had rights to exploit their junior colleagues. I faced the universal rule in reality as a fresher, - 'a big fish always eats a little one.' The institute never followed the method of diagonal communication which caused various problems for all junior staff members and fresher faculty members. It was not easy to work there as sometimes the authority used to ask us to remain present in the first shift at 6:00 o'clock in the morning and leave in the third shift at 6:15 p.m. But at the end, high amount of salary motivated us for the hard work for next month.

I came to know that there were lots of students commuting from Morbi town, so the college transportation department got ready to provide the bus facility to Morbi from College campus itself.

'If they are providing bus facility, you must utilize it.' said Kabir.

'But if I start staying at home, we will not be able to talk at night as I share room with my sister.' I said by changing my cloths.

'No problems, we will utilize whats-app. Nowadays whats-app has become a very nice facility. Don't think about me, at least you will have an opportunity to be with your family, you can have home food. You must use the transportation facility. Well commuting will be the trouble but you can utilize that time in listening audio books, reading the news-papers or books as you used to do it before.' explained he.

'Well I will think about it.' replied I with little anger as he showed no possessiveness for my calls or my company.

We used to talk to each other till late nights since two to three years. It was very difficult for me to stop that all of a sudden but I didn't find that much possessiveness or fascination in him for my calls and company. I was so obsessed with his calls; I was struggling in P.G room but was not ready to use the bus facility to home. I didn't even discuss that with my mother as I was sure if she came to know about it, she would force me rigorously to use that.

After few days, my parents saw the institute bus in the town and came to know about it.

'Aditi, don't you know about the bus facility provided by your institute?' asked my mother.

'I knew, and was thinking to use it.' I lied to my mom.

'What you mean that you are thinking? Use it as soon as possible and please come back home, it is a wonderful news.' said she with full of excitement.

'Yes mom, I will take the form from transportation department and will start utilizing it soon.'

I loved my parents a lot, but I also got used to with my struggle of P.G. rooms. That struggle also became the part of my life. I started enjoying all those problems of food, sharing things, scolding and soreness of the owner, managing everything by own and many other things. I got used to with that freedom. I didn't want to go back. I was so possessive about my relationship with Kabir. I started becoming insecure and thought if I started staying at home with my family, we wouldn't be able to talk freely on phone and distance of our distant relationship would increase more. I thought a lot then I thought about my parents.

'Finally I have decided to commute and be with my parents.' I informed to Kabir.

'Well, wise decision.' he encouraged.

'But there is one problem.' said I.

'What?'

'I have two cards given by you. I can't take them home. Where should I hide these cards?' asked I with little worry. 'Can I send them to you? As I don't want them to be misplaced.' asked I.

'Yes, but you know that I have shifted to Bhavnagar now and it is a government company, and the quarters have also been given by the same company. So you will have to use a good courier service for this.' Kabir said.

'Sure, send me your proper address, I will send them to you.' said I with firmness.

He sent me the address. My love was whimsical and I was in fairy tale romance. I wrote 'I love you Kabir' for 100 times on those cards. I wrote it at mid-night by keeping the flashlight of mobile on as I wanted to hide it from my room-mates so couldn't do that in front of everybody. Finally I sent him those cards through courier.

From the next week, I started commuting. Again I had to get up at 5 o'clock in the morning to reach college at 8 o'clock and working hours of college were up to 4:30 pm. but I used to reach home after 6:30 pm. due to severe traffic. Sometimes we were forced to do double shift for supervision duty so the timing of my job remained from 5:00 am to 8:00 pm. In the beginning, I used to get awfully tired and used to complain a lot as I used to fall sick and used to have severe back pain. But slowly and gradually, I overcame my pain by doing regular exercise.

I used to do my exercise after 8:00 p.m. and also started working hard for my P.H.D on bus while commuting. So I got that satisfaction that I was not wasting my time in regular travelling. I must confess, I completed my almost research work on bus during commuting. I used to switch on my laptop at 5:00 am. and switched it off after 8:00 p.m. after reaching home.

I started taking my exceed trouble of commuting and hard work load at college very positively and enjoyed it. I helped my students in all their activities excepting studies. Like, dancing, singing, writing script for their act of stage, wrote speech for them. I helped them for their Youth Festivals. I got the opportunity to do anchoring in Navratri functions and Fashion Shows held at college campus. I enjoyed each and every day of my job. I also hosted many academic activities with students and other faculty members of college. We visited many colleges for the external viva of students. Day by day, I started increasing my professional contacts than friends.

I used to share my success, failures, happiness and sadness with Kabir. I thought I was doing everything for him. I was crazy after him. He also used to love to listen to my stories but sometimes he used to get tired of listening but I never got tired of speaking a lot.

'I have been selected as an anchor for the Navratri Function of college, which is going to be held at an amazing party plot.' shared I with Kabir.

'Oh, great. Your life is full of enthusiasm, everyday there is something new to do.' said he.

'Yes. True. It is just because I take interest in everything.'

'Yes, my restless buddy.'

'Despite that much hectic schedule, I never fail to call you or miss you. But you fail almost the time.' I started complaining.

'Again fighting start.' annoyed he.

I was talking to him by pulling blanket over my head as my sister was sleeping beside me.

'Wherever I am, I always manage to reach to you, not like you.' said I with little anger.

We fought a little and then slept after wishing each other.

Next day it was Sunday, we were having tea in the evening and watching movie.

'Papa, don't you think we should renovate our home, it is so small and we should get two rooms built upstairs.' I said while cracking a biscuit.

'You are right but it will require much money.' said my father.

'I earn good. I will pay for the renovation.' said I.

'But, dear. You save your money, it will be useful to you in future at any time.' said my parents by showing no interest in my salary.

'What if I get married?' asked I.

'You can also use your saved money after marriage, it is your money. you have earned it, dear. How can we take it?' denied my parents.

'Oh! Now it is my money? Who made me earn this? Who supported me? Who is working hard for my abilities? Have I ever helped you much in the kitchen after this job? Who provides me everything on time- my cloths, my food, and all the required things? Can I do that without your support? Now tell me who is earning money? Only me or we all together?' asked I these questions with little anger.

My parents looked at each other. Somehow I convinced them on one condition for renovating the house. One condition was put by my parents which was about purchasing some gold for me. I accepted and went for shopping of gold to a nice jewellery shop. According to them, it will be useful to me during my marriage and even in future.

I forced my father to find the workers soon and get the renovation started as soon as possible. I started the journey with my father to renovate our house from beginning. We found the workers, selected the tiles for floor and the staircase of my choice. I made step to step with my father for that work. I went with my father to select colour and wood for the furniture. My parents trusted my choice, and also knew I would purchase the good raw-material with good price. I used to provide my salary to my father every month. Finally after few months, the whole house got nicely renovated. I was extremely happy for fulfilling my dream of renovating the house for my parents. I was not feeling any regret for my brother being too younger as I did whatever I could do for my parents as a daughter. I paid twelve lacks for renovation and purchased gold of four lacks from my savings. Still I was working and then I started saving money for my marriage as I did not want my father to pay a single penny as usual. I didn't want to bother my parents for anything.

I shared everything with Kabir and he was so proud of me and also asked me to be down to earth and explained me not to allow my success to get over head.

'I am just worried for one thing.' I said to Kabir. 'My mom has got tired a lot as she has not taken rest in her life. She has always worked hard for our education but now she is not able to even do house-hold work. Even in the evening, she gives her time to my little brother for his education, she herself teaches him. She doesn't have time for her own life. She is very active but can't do anything for herself because of our development.'

'I can understand that, then ask your sister to leave the job and help your mom in house hold work.' suggested Kabir.

I suggested but my mother said, 'After marriage you both sisters will be individual personalities, whatever you are doing is going to be useful to yourself only. Every individual has the right to live his/her life the way he/she wants.'

'Well she is absolutely right, very nice thoughts.' appreciated he.

'I don't know how I will be able to live my parents after marriage, I can't leave without them.' said I with tears in my eyes.

'I can understand, don't worry I will come to stay with you, fine? Will your parents accept me as live-in-son-in-law?' asked he to make me laugh.

'Don't get upset. Let's meet, we have not met since five months.' said he.

'I also want to see you but where will we meet? Now I am not staying in Rajkot. I won't have scooty in Rajkot.' said I.

'Why don't you come to Bhavnagar at my room?' asked he.

'Me? But how can I come? What will I tell my parents?' asked I.

'You go for many seminars, it can be one of the reasons.' suggested he.

'But I go with my colleagues; I have never gone alone anywhere.' said I.

'You will have to arrange that, you convince them by telling that you are going with your colleagues.' suggested he.

'Means, a lie?' asked I with little fear.

'Lovers are liars, honey.' said he.

'If I am coming to Bhavnagar, I will have to stay there for a night? asked I

'So? I will not eat you.' told he by being mischievous.

'Remember our lust. When we meet, we glue to each other even on the road. If we are alone in a room, just imagine what can be happened?' said I with a loud laugh and little shyness in my tone.

'We will control, don't worry. Trust me. We both are mature. Now leave if and buts...I am going to book your ticket for this Saturday.'

'Alright but remember the condition, nothing beyond the Kiss.' I promised him.

We both laughed, one of my colleagues entered the office. I disconnected the phone and rushed for my class.

I realized one thing that my office-mates started behaving very nicely with me all of a sudden as I found an escape from their business, that really worked. They all got bored with the unnecessary gossips and started getting busy in new activities apart from lectures. They also started reading good books and undertook some courses. They also realized that I was right. To achieve success, we are required to give enough amount of time to our work and career. Finally all relation turned out very healthy and even better than before.

It is said in Bhagavad Geeta, chapter- 3, shloka 21

यद्यदाचरति श्रेष्ठस्तत्तदेवेतरो जन:।
स यत्प्रमाणं कुरुते लोकस्तदनुवर्तते।।२१।।

**What a noble person does, others also do the same;
the world follows the standards set by him.**

The aeroplane of my career flew in right direction and got the height. Some of my friends and cousins also wanted to be the passengers of the same aeroplane. According to my mom, I set the trend of teaching career at a very young age and increased the value of Arts. I asked my mother to keep her proud for me as it was, requested her not to convert it into ego as I was just a normal human being not the Almighty God who sets the rules for this world.

CHAPTER 9

It was Saturday morning. I got the bus for Bhavnagar. I was little upset as I lied to my parents that I was going for a seminar. But I also thought about Kabir who was my life. I reached Bhavnagar at 4:00 pm. He came to receive me at bus-stop. We hugged each other; I was not worried of any of my relatives as I didn't have any contacts there. He took me to a very nice restaurant; we enjoyed Punjabi food over there as we both were hungry so we hogged the food. After that, we enjoyed chocolate ice-cream. He took me to his quarter that he was provided by the government company. We reached there; it was a very big quarter including three big rooms and one sitting hall. He asked me to take rest for a while. I wanted to change my cloths and wanted to get fresh after the journey of seven hours. I was opening my bag to take out my cloths; from behind he came near to me and hugged me tightly. I turned back and supported him to hug me tightly. We smooched each other for a long time without fear of anybody as first time there was nobody around, it was a closed room. Then I got fresh and we talked for a while, we went out to watch a movie. We visited two shopping malls, did some shopping. He showed me the company and the campus of his working area. It was around 8:00 pm. We went to a restaurant and enjoyed our dinner. It was like a dreaming day for both of us. It was 10:30 pm. We entered the room, we both were alone. We looked at each other and gave mischievous smile to each other. We both got fresh and up and came into comfortable night wears. He wore light green t-shirt and black trousers and I was in black loose top and blue trousers.

'Tomorrow I will go; I will miss you terribly.' I said by sitting on a chair and looking at him.

'Same here, darling.' said he by offering me a glass of milk.

'I don't want to go, just want to be with you all the time.' I said by keeping the glass on the table and by holding his hand.

'These days will come soon, dear.' said he by keeping his hands on mine.

There was just one bed.

'You sleep on the bed; I will sleep on the floor.' said he.

'Don't be mad, it is winter season, it is too much cold you will fall sick. We both will sleep on bed, after all we know our limitations.' I said pulling his hand and taking him near the bed.

It was winter; too much cold. We might have fallen sick so we both slept on the same bed by keeping our limitations in mind. Lights were off. We felt the silent desire hidden in the heart of both of us. We heard the chilled breeze complaining with its silent tongue about the distance between us. It was like, we were so thirsty and water was in front of us but we were not able to drink it. It was very difficult but somehow we controlled our thirst. Then we thought what would go wrong if we drink few drops of water to satisfy our little thirst? We could not be satisfied fully but at least few drops of water would let us sleep peacefully. We looked at each other; it was severe dark in the room, only little reflection of light from the small night lamp was pouring down. We both were not visible to each other clearly. We came close to each other and touched each other. We could feel the touch but could not see each other clearly. He came over me and kissed me on my forehead. I did the same. He kissed on my nose, and then we smooched each other. I hugged him tightly and combed his hair with my fingers. We enjoyed each other for a while and controlled ourselves for going ahead. Finally we got satisfied with few drops of water and slept till the morning. Sun rays fell through the window to spy us whether we were awaken or not. We opened our eyes and kept on looking into each other's eyes. I kissed him on his forehead, so did he. We got up, got fresh and up and then he dropped me to the bus-station as I was supposed to get the bus. It was very difficult for both of us to fall apart. I kept on thinking about all those moments that we spent together during the whole way. I stopped my thinking after reaching home. I saw my parents and felt a little guilty then I thought, 'lovers are liars.'

We met number of times, enjoyed and became the life and breath of each-other. Day by day, it was becoming difficult to live without each other. We had a lot of love and respect for each other. We were sure to get married.

'Payal (Kabir's sister) is in your town.' said Kabir.

'Oh, really? When has she come and where?' asked I.

'To my aunt's place, she will go by the evening.' informed he.

'Can I go to meet her? After all she is my sister too. Well we met in some wedding function before few months, so I know her. I also tried to talk to her. I don't know if she remembers me or not?' asked I.

'She must be knowing you, but she never said anything about you.' said he.

'Should I go to meet her?' asked I.

'Yes, go and meet your sister-in-law.' he permitted.

I went to Sudhaaunty's place with my father. Sudhaaunty was also my relative. So I just went there and pretended that I came there co-incidentally. They introduced me with Kabir's sister and we talked for a while. We also had dinner there. But somehow I didn't find her much responsive towards me. She was not talking to me properly and didn't pay much attention on my talks. I thought it might be her nature and let the things go on, didn't even say anything to Kabir.

Now I was completely put in the market. One of my relatives came to our place with many proposals of educated boys for my marriage.

'We should not get late now, it is the right time for Aditi to get married.' said my mom

'You are right.' replied my father.

'She has become mature enough and has also completed her studies. She will also complete her P.H.D soon. We must respond to our relatives who come with appropriate proposals.' said my mom.

All of a sudden, my mother burst into tears.

'What happened? Why are you crying?' asked my father by going near to him.

'I told you on the first day that people would criticize us for allowing the daughter to do job. I told you that they would point out by saying that we utilize our daughter for expenses of home.' answered my mom while crying.

'What happened? Did anyone say anything to you? Our daughter is a lecturer, she has got a very prestigious job. People are dying to have her job. She is not doing anything wrong and she is doing for her happiness, we have never forced her to work for our needs. Even daughters of our friends and relatives are also inspired by Aditi and they have also started studying hard and have started finding jobs like her.' explained my father.

'Your friends and relatives' financial condition would be better than us. If their daughter work, nobody points out finger but our each act demands explanation and clarification as we belong to middle class family. If our daughters work for their ambition or happiness, it is always considered to be a need.' cried my mother.

'We have always ignored people's comments and see where our daughter is standing today!' my father motivated.

'It broke my heart when I heard from few relatives and neighbours that Aditi is a golden goose who lays golden eggs, then why would her parents want to get her married soon? If she gets married little late, it would be very beneficial for her parents.' said my mother with huge amount of pain in her heart.

'I can understand your pain as a mother. Don't worry; tomorrow I will call Ankitbhai for the meeting. He has always suggested us appropriate proposals.' said my father by consoling my mother.

'Before you call him, I want to tell you something about Aditi's marriage.' said my mother serving food in his plate.

'What is the matter? Please tell me.' asked my father putting one morsel in his mouth.

'Aditi once told me about that guy – Kabir. They are good friends and also talk on phones frequently. They have also met once. If they both are fine with each other, we should think in that direction first. She is mature enough to choose her life partner.' said my mother.

'So better to talk to his parents, we should ask Seemaaunty who is a common relative of both the families, we should take her help in this matter.' said my father.

'I had a word regarding this with her two-three times when Aditi told me about his friendship with him but she said Kabir's parents will find a bride for their elder son first, then they will think about Kabir. Somehow they didn't respond properly. I talked to her before six to eight months still there is no response. I think again we should talk to Seemaaunty or we should think about other guys.'

'Kabir I am so worried. My parents are in hurry for my marriage, they don't mind about our relation. According to them, if your parents are not ready, they don't want other good proposals to let go. I am so frightened, why can't you talk to your parents about our relation?' asked I.

'I have told them, but first they want my brother to get married.' said he.

'You are saying it since one and half year. Are your parents agree for our marriage?' asked I with little insecurity.

'See, I am trying my level best but I am not getting proper response so I am also waiting for my brother's marriage. My sister got married before two years, so they want me and my brother to get married together.' said he.

'They are absolutely right. But at least request them to give some official commitment to my parents so my parents stop finding a groom for me. They have started meeting guys, what would happen if they select someone for me? I can't live without you.' I started crying.

'Please, stop crying. I will have a word with my parents again.'

After a week, he said,

'I have convinced my parents. They are ready to give official commitment, they will ask Seemaaunty to give this message to your parents. Somehow I convinced them for commitment but we would get married after they find a bride for my brother.'

'It is completely fine. I am also not in hurry for marriage but we will be able to shut everybody's mouth for my marriage.' said I with satisfaction.

After three days, Seemaaunty, common relative of both the families – mine and Kabir, came to our place with a proposal from them.

'Hello! Good news for you. These people are ready to fix the matter. They are coming to just fix the matter on this Sunday, rest of the ceremonies will be carried out afterwards.' informed she with a happy face.

'Oh really! It is really a good news!' my parents exclaimed.

'You can go and see their home as nowadays parents of a daughter go and visit the place first, talk about some matters regarding dowry and then finalize the matter. You have that right if you wish.' Seemaaunty informed us about it as our well wisher.

'Well, we know the people since many years and we trust you. We have got all positive reports about the guy so we don't want to ask and see anything. We want you to ask a matter regarding dowry as in our caste that matters a lot.' said my mom.

'Well, they have said not to bring anything on this occasion. Before engagement they won't take anything. They just want to give commitment so the matter gets finalized.' said Seema aunty by putting cashew-nut in her mouth.

'Both are educated and working, so it is quite appropriate proposal for both of them. All formalities regarding engagement and marriage can be discussed afterwards. Get ready for this Sunday. Aditi be ready and confident, we all are with you.' Seema aunty said it with a smile to make me shy.

'Finally, we are meeting on this Sunday without hiding ourselves from anybody. We are meeting officially. I am very nervous.' said I to Kabir.

'Yes, we are meeting finally to be bound forever; still you have time, think about it. We are different and we both are not going to change our nature, will you be happy with me?' asked he with laugh.

'I am alright, are you ok with me? Asking for last time, else afterwards, you will have to be ok although you are not.' asked I with loud laughter.

'I am always alright, you complain all the time about phone calls and messages.' clarified he.

'Oh, leave it. That happens in all long distance relationships, it is common, I suppose. Just think about five years of our relationship will be converted into the official one, won't it be like a dream coming true?' asked I with extreme excitement.

'Yes of course, but now sleep and don't think much about it. Let's not get much nervous and excited.' said he.

'Good Night. Sweet Dreams. Love you.' wished I.

'Good Night. Sweet Dreams. Love you.' wished he.

It is said in Bhagavad Geeta in chapter- 18, shloka-65

मन्मना भव मद्भक्तो मद्याजी मां नमस्कुरु।
मामेवैष्यसि सत्यं ते प्रतिजाने प्रियोऽसि मे॥६५॥

**Repose your mind in Me and be My devotee;
offer your yagya unto Me and bow to Me alone;
thus shall you attain Me, this I promise you,
for you are dear to Me.**

I reposed my mind and heart in Kabir and became his devotee. I wanted to attain him crazily.

CHAPTER 10

It was Sunday – day of our official meeting for engagement. All my uncles and aunties gathered at home. In our community, a girl and a boy are supposed to meet at some temple or some other place for their fix-up but not at a girl's place. We decided to invite them to a nearby temple. We booked two rooms for their refreshment. Nine people were about to come from their side including Kabir. We bought sweets and dry fruits for them. We got it packed in a nice way. We made all the arrangements. I wore a very simple cream colour dress with a watch on my wrist and a small ring in my finger. I kept my hair open and applied some make-up on my face. My father hired a big van and we reached the temple. There were eleven members from our side, including my grand-mother, aunties, uncles, my sister and other relatives.

We reached there before time. They told they would reach around 4:00 p.m. So we reached there around 3:00 p.m for arrangements of their warm welcome.

It was a very special day for me or I could say a turning point of my life which changed my whole life, thoughts and mentality about various aspects of life.

We had been waiting in the room upstairs since three hours; they came around 7:00 pm. instead of 4:00 pm. My all family members went down with flowers and bouquets in hands for their warm welcome, the moment they saw their car. Everybody got down from the car, my family members welcomed them by giving them a lot of respect. They hugged each other. During that moment, everyone was happy excepting one person, and that was Kabir's mother, Chandrika Tanna. She didn't even smile and was found agitated. My mother hugged her but she showed cold shoulder to my mother and walked towards upstairs. My mother felt very bad in the first meeting itself but she couldn't judge anything. There were two rooms, in one room males were sitting and in another one, females were supposed to sit. I was asked to sit in the ladies room by keeping my head down. I was very nervous. The ladies of Kabir's family entered the room. While entering the room, his aunts and sister looked at me and gave a gentle smile but his mother looked through me and didn't even smile at me. I felt very bad. I gave a gentle smile to everyone but didn't receive back from his mother. All ladies were in Punjabi dress and their heads were covered with dupatta excepting his sister. I figured out the daughter-in-laws in Kabir's family were supposed to cover their head with dupatta in almost the functions and festivals. All ladies wore too much of gold from head to toe. I was feeling suffocation by seeing them. Everyone was literally scanning me from head to toe. I was extremely nervous; my heart was beating very fast. My grand-mother started some general talks; they were talking on customs and rules about their families. My mother was busy in serving snacks and tea to the guests. I saw nervousness even on my mother's face, she was also found little sad by the behaviour of Kabir's mother, even my sister felt the same. She informed me by her signs, 'Something is wrong.' On the other hand, males' room was found full of laughter. Everything was normal in that room. Finally Kabir's father asked my father about the private meeting of mine and Kabir. Both of them knew that it was just a formality but our fathers pretended in front of everybody as they knew nothing about our relationship. I was asked to come in males' room with all the ladies. I entered the room and came in the limelight. Everyone's eyes were on me. I looked up for a second and looked down again. Me and Kabir looked at each other for a while in front of everybody and pretended as if we didn't know each other.

'You can ask them questions whatever you want.' said one of the relatives from his side.

'Why to ask questions? We know everything about both of them, then why to get them nervous?' said his mother as if she was not at all interested to know anything about my education, job and my progress.

'Alright, then give them some time to underrated each other.' said his father.

'Alright, let's go to the garden and you talk in privacy and take your decision.' told my uncle and he took us to the garden downstairs to give us some privacy.

At that time, I realized about the greatness of Indian children who take important decision of their life just in ten to fifteen minutes.

'So how are you feeling my official fiancee?' asked he by looking at me.

'Very nice, my fiance. Well we have nothing to talk today.' I said by keeping my head down.

'That is why I used to tell you to remain some content but you were in hurry to finish all the talks on phone.' said he by laughing.

We were making fun and decided to keep on talking until somebody came from upstairs to call us.

'It is time to increase their herat-beats, everybody would be waiting for our decision.' Kabir made fun of all our relatives.

'Are you happy, love?' I asked by looking into his eyes.

'Yes, of course.' said he by looking into my eyes.

'Is everybody happy at your home?' asked I by staring at him.

'Yes.' replied he after a while.

'Is your mother happy with this relation?' asked I.

'Yes, why are you asking that?' asked he.

'She seems to be unhappy with this relation. Her face and behaviour represent her unhappiness. I found gloomy on her face.' said I.

'Common, it is your day, enjoy it to the fullest.' ignored he and we got up to go ahead.

'So how do you feel? Did you ask him whatever you wanted?' asked my uncle.

'Yes uncle.' said I by showing little shyness on my face.

'So 100 % or 110%?' asked my uncle.

'110 %.' replied I by showing modesty.

My uncle went to the room and said 'yes' from my side. His uncle also came with the same reply. So our love marriage finally took the first step for being converted into arranged one. We got many congratulations from everybody; everyone clicked our photographs by making us stand together. We were made eat lots of sweets. I was given gold earrings and I gave him a gold- pendant in gift. According to everyone, we made a perfect pair. They appreciated our pair by saying that we both were good looking, having good persona, equally qualified and working at reputed places. All were happy but his mother was not happy. I felt it each and every moment, even my family members felt the same, especially my mother and sister. We took them for dinner in Parasnath restaurant and then we departed. We also discussed to arrange 'ring-ceremony function' after few months. When we went to fix-up, we were extremely happy but when we returned after good news, something was wrong with us. Each of us felt it but we didn't realize any reason behind it.

Next day I went to my college with sweets. I informed my colleagues about my engagement and distributed sweets.

'Hey, what doing my love?' Kabir called me.

'Just routine work at college' replied I

'Not missing me?' asked he

'I miss those whom I forget.' I replied while feeling attendance of the students.

'Oh, heart touching dialogue my honey although it is worn out.' he made fun of me.

'You..... I will not say anything for you from now onwards.' said I with laughter.

'Yes, don't say anything, just sing a song for me, please.' requested he

'Now?'

'Yes, now only.'

'But I am at college now. Everybody is around, man.'

'I know honey. It is a challenge. You say you can do anything for me, then do it. I am waiting. My ears are dying to listen your song. Remember, You challenged me for kissing you in front of everybody when I was in office, I can expect at least that much from you.'

We used to these kinds of mischiefs all most the time with each other.

'Alright man!'

I came out of my office and rushed towards the gallery and entered the washroom to sing a song for him.

'Tu hi toh jannat meri, Tu hi mera junoon
Tu hi to mannat meri, Tu hi rooh ka sukoon

*Tu hi aakhion ki thandak, tu hi dil ki hai
dastak
Aur kuch na janu mein, bas itna hi jaanu
Tujh mein rab dikhta hai
Yaara mein kya karu
Yaara mein kya karu'* I sang for him.

'Oh my baby, don't make me God. I am just a normal person.'

'For me you are everything, my love.' said I being emotional.

'Thanks for loving me so much, my love. I love you so much, I adore you' said he

'Same here. Anyways now I need to rush for my lecture. I am already late by seven minutes.' I came out of the washroom by spreading my eyes everywhere to conform nobody was listening my talks by standing there.

'Ok my time table, go. Love you. Bye.' said he.

'Same to you. Bye.' I entered the class by saying that.

From beginning, I had a habit to initiate in any relation. I took my mother-in-law's contact-number from Kabir and after reaching home; I didn't even get fresh and up and directly called her.

'Hello Namaste! how are you? How's everybody at home? How is your health?' asked I with a very polite and excited tone to build a new relation.

'Fine.' replied she in a rough voice.

'I just came back from college. I was missing you all so called you.' said I with frightened voice.

'Hmm. well I have some work now, talk to you later.' She disconnected the call by saying that.

I called her on the next day and she behaved in the same way. I asked Kabir about it but he didn't focus much on it and ignored it. But I was very sad and upset.

I didn't call her on third day neither she called me. I could not resist myself and called her on fourth day.

'Hello mom, how are you?' asked I with a pleasant voice.

'Fine as usual.' said she in sneering tone.

'I just came home from college, so called you. So what is new at your side, mom.' I enhanced the talk.

'We don't go out every day by leaving our house, so we can't have new everyday like you girls.' said she in very rough and taunting tone.

My hands started shivering and heart beats increased by listening her choppy answer. I couldn't resist myself and asked,

'Are you not happy with this relation mom?' asked I.

'How dare you to ask me this question? I left my elder son and came to see you for my younger son, isn't it enough for you people?' shouted she on phone.

'Oh, that is the matter. I am sorry mom, you are right. It is very sweet of you.' said I.

'No, this is not the only matter. I never wanted you as my daughter-in-law. I never wanted a working girl as my daughter-in-law. I wanted an educated girl but she should not be allowed to go out for any work. A female is just supposed to stay at home to take care of elders, husband and children. That is the only job of a female. A working girl can never handle home properly. She cannot manage both together- household duty and job. And working girls always carry the ego of their earnings. I wanted my friend's daughter for my son who is educated but is not working outside. I also talked to my friend regarding this.

She is qualified but not like you, full of proud and ego.' shouted she.

'Proud? Who said I am full of proud and ego? Why are you talking to me like this?' asked I with frightened voice.

'As you have trapped my son in your false love, you and your family. My son is educated and smart and works in other city so people like you are always in search of that kind of boy. You trapped him to stay alone, away from in-laws to have all the freedom of life. You are very smart and full of proud. I never wanted you in my house.' she kept on talking rubbish.

'I have not trapped your son, he was also interested in me, it was not only me. And my family didn't even know about it.' said I in a very low voice with tears in my eyes.

'You didn't even bow down to me; you did it to everybody while we were clicking the photos. You have bewitched my son. He has also started following you from now onwards but beware; in our house, girls don't get that much freedom. However educated you are, you will have to live the way we want you to live. You might live away from us but you can't find escape from our customs and rules. Let me check how you perform at our place. We were getting proposals of daughters of millionaires but my son is blind in your love so I can't do anything now, else you don't deserve us.' said she in anger and disconnected the call before I speak anything.

I started crying like anything and closed the room. I directly called Kabir with a loud cry and asked,

'Have I trapped you? You are with me forcefully?' asked I.

'Why are you talking this rubbish? What happened?' asked he with astonishment.

I told him everything and asked to go for break-up if his family was not happy with our relationship.

My parents were listening to everything, they got shocked and my mother said,

'We will find better proposals; you will never be able to happy in that house. Whatever you do, you will be proven wrong. I have never heard these kinds of words for my daughter, in fact everybody appreciates our daughter for her sincerity, kindness, politeness, hard-work and decorum. I will talk to her. If they are not happy, still nothing has gone wrong. We can end the relationship.' said my mother with tears in her eyes.

After sometime, Kabir called my parents and asked for forgiveness on behalf of his mother.

'Why didn't you inform us before if your mother was not ready for this relation? We never forced you for anything. How my daughter will live there if she is behaving like this from beginning?' asked my mother with tears in her eyes and in a very polite way.

'Please give me some time. I will set everything; please don't even think about ending up the relation. I really love your daughter by heart.' said he with calm voice.

My mother called his mother next day, in the morning,

'Hello, Namaste!'

'Namaste!' responded she in rough voice as usual.

'I heard everything yesterday on phone; I want to conform about your willingness for this relationship.' asked my mom courteously.

'Oh, you people also care for my willingness! If they both are happy, then who am I to interrupt?' said she in a loud voice.

'Means, you are not happy? My daughter will not get married only to your son but with the entire family. She wants love and respect from the entire family, not only from Kabir.' my mother said in a requesting tone.

'You people don't want family, you just want my son. You know that due to his job, he will not stay with the family so your daughter will take the advantage of having freedom, no burdens of family. You - mother and daughter are smart enough to trap any guy.' she shouted.

'Well, we did not at all think about it, honestly. First; he is your son, then my daughter will have right on him. There might be any girl, she would have definitely stayed with her husband, nowadays this generation goes out for studies and jobs so it has become the trend. Nobody has said that my daughter is egoist and full of proud up to now, why do you feel so?' said my mother with a loud cry.

'All mothers find their daughters bestowed with all great qualities, so do you. But she was never my choice; I wanted another girl for my son, my friend's daughter. And I was getting better proposals than your daughter for my son.' she continued rubbish arguments.

'We were also getting better proposals, but if our children are happy with each other, we should be happy in it. Now the world is changing. If we have given freedom to our children for going out, having education, they should be given permission for choosing their life partner. They are mature enough to take their own decisions.' my mother responded to her argument politely.

'Changes and freedom are for the daughters of your house but our daughters and daughter-in-laws remain in their limitations not like yours. They are not even allowed to go out alone like you people leave your ladies.' she kept on criticizing my family, our rules and customs and disconnected the call before my mother said anything.

My mother sat there by holding the phone receiver in her hands. She kept on thinking without speaking anything for a an hour. Tears were rolling down her cheeks.

Next day, my parents heard through grapevine that Kabir's mother was little difficult one to handle. We had to be very careful. By listening that my father had severe fever but he didn't show his grief for me and my life.

After all that melodrama, I went to college next day to follow my routine but could not concentrate on anything. I applied for a half-leave and came home early. Kabir also couldn't concentrate on his work and applied for a leave and went home early. We both were feeling sick and were not able to concentrate on anything. He shared all this with his father and brother.

'Whatever your mother has done is very bad, she must not have done it.' said his father to him.

'It is completely wrong, she can't hurt anybody's self respect like this.' said his elder brother.

My father-in-law called me, 'Hello! Dear, How are you?' he talked to me in a very polite manner.

'Yes, I am alright papa.' said I in a very depressing tone.

'I came to know that you have fever, it is the favour of happiness right?' he tried to make me laugh and tried to make the difficult matter lighter.

'Yes, it is.' I laughed with little grief.

'Dear, ignore the things and focus on your goal and education.' consoled he.

I felt little relaxed after having a word with his father. But I didn't feel like talking to Kabir. I thought so much about the future of our relation and stopped calling him. I didn't even receive his calls.

'Why no calls? Do you want break-up?' asked he

'Yes, I think that is the only way out. I can't stay at the place where I don't have my self-respect. I love you so much; I will never get married to anybody else in my life. I will keep on loving you till my last breath but will not be able to stay at your house. I am sorry. If the beginning is that much horrible, you just imagine about the future.' said I firmly.

'Nothing will happen; you can't leave me like this. We will handle everything together. And I will not force you to keep in touch with my mom. Next week I am going to home, till that you don't call any member of my family, excepting me. Let the matter calm down.' said he strictly.

Eight days passed, he reached his home and talked to his parents regarding this.

'I don't like this girl.' said his mother to him

'But, what is wrong with her? Then why did you come for engagement?' asked he.

'For your happiness only.' said she.

'Then go ahead for my happiness only, please.' said he.

'I found her very fashionable and stylish. She is pretty intelligent.' said she

'So what is wrong with that? Nowadays people want that kind of daughter-in-law only who is good at everything.' said he.

'But she cannot rule my family by her smartness. I am the only boss of the family and will remain forever, nobody can replace me however intelligent and decent she is.' said she by showing her superior complex and insecurity.

'Oh! That is the reason. So you feel inferior?' asked he.

'Not at all, I am the smartest one. I might not have qualification like her but I am not less than anyone.' said she by showing the ego.

Somehow after lots of arguments and discussions, he convinced his mother to accept me as her daughter-in-law; else he would not get married to anybody else. He said it to his mother.Then he called me and handed over the phone to his mother to have a word with me. We talked for a while very calmly on some general topics. Somehow we passed a month like that.

Every alternative day, I didn't stop facing the bows of taunts thrown from her for one or another thing. Kabir asked me to ignore the stuff. Just after a month, they found a bride named Ankita for his brother. I saw the photographs of his brother's engagement, my mother-in-law was smiling and was found much happier in that.

'Why is it happening to me Kabir? I loved you too much, am I getting punishment for this?' asked I with tears in my eyes.

'Please, don't worry; love marriages are always like this in our country. Let me clarify one thing, that girl has not a mother, her mother passed away at young age so my mother's inclination towards her might remain more than you but you are supposed to ignore that.' he clarified.

I disconnected the call without saying anything and sat quietly thinking lots of things about future.

It is said in Bhagavad Geeta in chapter - 5, shloka -11

कायेन मनसा बुद्ध्या केवलैरिन्द्रियैरपि
योगिन: कर्म कुर्वन्तिसङ्गं त्यक्त्वात्मशुद्धये ॥११॥

Yogis perform actions only for self purification,
having renounced attachment with
their senses, mind, intellect and body.

    Sometimes, it is better to continue performing your duties by forgetting your sense, mind, intellect and body. I continued loving Kabir without expecting for any fruits.

CHAPTER 11

It was difficult for Kabir's family to arrange ring-ceremony at both the sides on the same day. My father fixed menu for food, booked a party-hall and made all the arrangements for ring-ceremony. But all of a sudden, we got a call from Kabir's family. They said it would be better to go for marriage directly as both brothers would get married on the same day so it would be little difficult to arrange 'ring ceremony'. So the marriage was fixed after five months in february by discussing with Pundits.

We started preparations for marriage. I wanted everything of my choice. My parents supported me for everything - Wedding booth, music, dance, invitation cards, etc. I and my sister fixed the menu for food. I started shopping with my sister. I and my sisters hit all most the best shops in Morbi and in Rajkot for new wedding collection. I resigned for my job before a month of my marriage. The fare-well party given by my colleagues was unbelievable. I was feeling very sad to leave all that. I cried a lot as I was very happy with my tiring and hectic job. I was also thinking about my parents and my siblings, and used to cry on alternative day.

'Now, don't cry for us, from now onwards we are not your parents, they are your parents.' said my mom by showing the photos of Kabir's parents in the mobile. 'You have always been a good and responsible daughter, now it is time to play the role of an honest and sincere daughter-in-law.' added my mother.

I got a call from my mother -in-law at that time, 'Have you decided your outfit for wedding?'

'Yes, I have given it in a boutique.' said I in a very low voice as I was so frightened.

'Tell me the colour, so we will select the same colour for Kabir's wedding suit.'

'It is cream and red.' said I.

'And have you decided any outfit for your reception, actually groom's family is supposed to buy this, but let me ask you, you want to select by yourself or we buy for you?' asked she in harsh voice.

'I will buy mom, you don't take tension.' said I.

'Alright, now I am free from tension. We will send you 10,000 rs. in which you are supposed to manage your outfit, jewellery, purse and sandals.' said she.

'No need to send money mom. We will manage.' I showed courtesy with scary tone.

'You do what is said to you; don't argue.' ordered she harshly.

'It is alright, mom. Thanks.' said I.

When we went to the market, it was so difficult to find a reception wear for bride in that much low price, somehow after wandering at various shops; we finalized an indo-western suit for reception. I called my mother-in-law and said,

'I have purchased one indo-western suit for reception.' said I.

'Indo-western? I told you to go for an evening gown as Ankita (my sis-in-law) is going to buy that only. And you bought that one? Which colour?' asked she in anger.

'But an evening gown was not getting fit in the budget and those which were fitting in the budget were just giving the look of a long dress, what I have purchased is little unique and it is blue color.' said I.

Before I say anything else, she disconnected the phone in anger. I was so upset the way she talked to me. Just for the minor things, she started fighting with me. What is wrong to wear a dress of your own choice in your own reception? I kept on thinking with a sad mood and again let the things go on.

Now just fifteen days were remaining for marriage. I was feeling down in the dumps but was also excited. Countdown started. I was to get married after two days. All the guests had arrived; all the preparations for marriage were at end. We held Ganesh Pooja at home before a day of my marriage. From the next day of pooja, all the functions started one by one. The first ceremony started with Janoi of my brother. Then we had mehndi ceremony, ladies sangeet and DJ Party at night. All my cousins and relatives danced a lot and enjoyed much. As after a long time in the family, a marriage function took place so everybody was excited. My grad-parents also danced with joy. My friends and colleagues also enjoyed a lot. On the next day, procession came and they were welcomed wholeheartedly by my parents and relatives. I was little sad and was also crying as I was supposed to leave my entire family, friends and parents but the moment I saw Kabir, I forgot my grief. He entered the wedding- hall and we both looked at each other. I went to the beauty parlour and got ready by wearing bridal suit. We both were in red and cream costumes. We matched the colour of our wedding suits. We completed all the rituals of marriage. Then the photographer called us in a room for photo-session. I was feeling very shy to come close to him and to give pauses for photos but he kept on looking at me without shyness. He hold my hands for photographs by looking through everyone around us. Finally we were taken to the wedding booth by our cousins with the flower sheet above us. We were asked to proceed followed by dance and songs, my cousins danced before us and we followed them towards the wedding booth. Our entry towards the booth was very interesting and creative. We planned for it before a month. We selected red and white colour for wedding booth. It was decorated with red and white flowers. It was looking simple and elegant. Finally, we got married with an Indian style. Now it was the time of my fare-well from my sweet home. All started crying to follow the custom of bride's farewell and so did I. They made me throw rice behind as per the Indian ritual. I did it with tears in my eyes. My sister tried to make the moment little light; she made me dance in my fare-well. The car came near and I sat in it with tears in my eyes. The car started by crushing the coconut under its wheels as it is considered an auspicious ritual. I kept on looking behind by bidding bye to my all family members standing in a big group and staring at the car until it turned into another street.

It was my new journey of life with new passengers. I was little nervous in the car but Kabir held my hand and gave me courage. We started our journey for Patan. His relatives were very nice and tried to talk to me and tried to make me laugh, they kept on making fun in the car.

Finally I reached my Second Home.

Our car was welcomed by his family members waiting at the door. They fired crackers for our welcome. Few women came with the Arti-thali. We were taken to the idol of our late grand-parents for taking their blessings. The cousins of Kabir made us dance; they said they would like to dance with new bhabhi.We both were extremely tired but somehow we managed to dance with them and kept on giving plastic smile. Then I was asked to go inside a room for some rituals. It lasted for two hours. It was around 1:00 pm at night. I was feeling suffocation due to much weight of bridal-suit and heavy jewelleries. I just wanted to sleep, my head was spinning. Everybody was very happy excepting one person that was my mother-in-law. She didn't even smile at me on my arrival. But she was behaving very nicely with the other bride (my sister-in-law) means Kabir's brother's wife - Ankita. When she entered, she hugged her and kissed her on forehead and when I bowed down to her, she kept hand on my head as everybody was standing around but she didn't even look at me and went away. I felt much agony on the first day. I was observing everything but didn't tell anything to anybody. Finally, we reached the real charm of the marriage - First Night. We were sent to a hotel room for it. It was the same hotel where the reception was going to be held next day.

When we got in the car to go to the hotel, all relatives were standing outside and looking fixedly at us as if they were wishing us happy sex life. Some of the females wished me all the best. We both were feeling very shy. Finally, we reached to the hotel room, it was a very nice room decorated with red flowers. The bed was decorated with red and yellow flowers. The room was smelling very nicely due to the sprinkling of some perfumes. On the desk, we found two glasses and a jug full of milk. We found all most the required things but they forgot to keep condoms over there. I bowed down to Kabir and touched his feet as I considered him my God.

'Oh my 21st century's old fashioned wife!' he blessed me by putting his hand on my head and requested me to get up.

I stood in front of the mirror, wanted to get fresh and up and wanted to remove all the heavy cloths and jewelleries. I started doing that, and Kabir cuddled me up from behind and he started helping me to remove my hair clips and flowers from my head. Finally all hair pins and hair bun were out from my hair, he opened my hair by shagging them with his fingers. He started kissing me. I rushed to the bathroom due to shyness and closed the door by giving him a naughty look. He wanted to come inside but I slammed the door fast. I took bath. I kept my long hair open. I came out of the washroom. He was staring at me. He lifted me and made me lie down on the bed. He came over me and started kissing me. I was feeling shy and was trying to hide my face and closed my eyes.

He said in a very sexy tone by breathing heavily, 'Let us live the precious moments of life. Open your arms for me. I want to get all relief in your arms. I want to destroy myself in you, my soul mate! Your charm is like gentle breeze, let it touch me. Your blushing face is driving me crazy. Please drop the veil of decency and permit me to cross the line with you. Come closer my love, let me touch your lips.'

His romantic and lusty words for me caused me goose bumps.

He hugged me tightly and we smooched for a long time without anybody's fear. It was our official right on that night. After ourselves, we tried to go further, although we couldn't get success with first trial. It was an amazing and unforgettable night.

It is said nothing is permanent, that happiness also passed just in a blink of eyes. In the next day, both the daughter-in-laws were called for taking blessings from the relatives and for Pooja. Next day, people came to see the dowry given by our parents as it was a custom in our culture. The new bride was supposed to be there to show what she got from her parents. I was asked to wear a heavy worked red dress given by Kabir's family. I was asked to wear huge amount of gold from head to toe. I was feeling very uncomfortable. I was asked to cover my head with dupatta and sit on the chair. I bowed down to all relatives and got the blessings of giving birth to many sons. In a nutshell, real marriage life started after first night. I was feeling suffocation due to so many people around me. I got tired of those scanners. Especially it was unbearable to listen the ladies comparing the dowry of mine and my sister-in-laws. I felt very sad to see my mother-in-law's constant rough behaviour for me, my things and for my parents. She kept on looking through me and was giving much importance to my sister-in-law.

'Take the new brides for the remaining rituals.' said one of the ladies.

We were taken to a pooja- hall for that. Everyone was scanning us and we were asked to sing some religious song, I was aware of all those matters so I already prepared three songs before marriage. I sang them very nicely.

'Oh, nicely sung. She is a professor in a college, and then also knows all these religious songs ! Very nice.' appreciated one of the ladies standing around us.

I figured out the mentality of the females standing over there who believed that working girls can not be civilized and cultured properly, they can't have the knowledge of religion, God or any spiritual things. I said to myself with little irritation, 'Working girls apply the spirituality in their action; they don't just sing the religious songs and make show of being religious.'

I was thinking all that, and my mother-in-law interrupted by saying with sarcasm in front of everybody,

'She was a professor, not now. She was working before marriage, now when will she get time for all that? After marriage a girl's life changes totally, she will also get busy in kitchen work and house-hold work.'

'She was teaching Grammar, right?' asked one of the ladies to satisfy her curiosity.

'Yes, but now don't teach Grammar here, here there is no space for your Grammar.' said my mother in law with confidence as if she had set the goal of her life to subdue me and insult me.

Some of the ladies who were also my relatives, and knew me from childhood directly looked at me with sympathy and also saw some tears in my eyes.

I was trying to overcome it, meanwhile my brother called me up. I received his call. While talking to him, I observed everyone started staring at me with little sarcasms. Then I realized after marriage, I was not even allowed to receive the calls and talk freely with my parents. I disconnected the call but he kept on giving me rings again and again. I couldn't resist myself and went to the bathroom and received his phone.

'Hello! Why are you calling me again and again?' I scolded my beloved little brother.

'Di, I am coming to attend your reception, Kabir jiju has invited us.' he said with full of excitement.

'With whom are you coming?' asked I with little worry.

'I and sister, and we are about to reach to you. I am so excited to see you.'

'Me too missing you all a lot but reception will start at night and it is just noon, I will have to go to the parlour. If you come here, nobody will be free to attend you as everyone is busy. Please go to the aunt's place and come directly to the reception at night, please dear. Please my little heart.' said I with tears in my eyes and in a very low volume to keep it suppressed in the washroom only.

I was feeling down in the dumps as everything changed just in a day. Before a day I was with my siblings and they had all the rights on me but now I was preventing them to come to my place without any reason. I was very scared about the rough behaviour of my mother-in-law towards me and my family; I didn't want them to get humiliated. But I couldn't stop their humiliation despite my hard trials. My brother and sister came to attend the reception with my relatives. She didn't even look at them and did not welcome them. She was welcoming everybody with open arms but looked through my siblings and relatives. I was observing everything from the stage and was getting restless and too much hurt. My relatives and my siblings also felt very bad. The reception was about to end, the new couples were invited for the dance on the stage by the anchor of the musical-party. My mother in law stood up fast and invited her elder son and daughter-in-law for the dance but looked through us. It was very embarrassing moment for me and Kabir. Somehow we pretend to be happy in front of the guests. After dinner, my siblings were going home, but I could not be with them as Kabir's cousins were forcing us to take photographs with them. My little brother was going out and looking at me until he got into the car. I was also looking at me while giving the pauses for photographs. I saw him crying for me but I controlled my tears somehow and continued giving fake smile. My each heart beat was beckoning him. It was the second day of marriage, the reception night of our wedding.

'Why is your mother behaving with me like this?' asked I to Kabir after entering the room.

'What happened?' asked he.

'Stop pretending at least in front of me. You know what happened. At least ask her not to behave like that with my family members; they will fall in tension to see all this.' told I in little anger.

'Please ignore, let it go, all will cool down soon. Let us enjoy our moment.' said he.

'What enjoy? I am letting the things go since many months. I thought, after marriage things will settle down but it is increasing even more. Have I come here to face just humiliation?' asked I by removing my heavy jewellery and bridal suit of reception.

'Please, I respect you a lot, I love you too much. Don't think much. Come let's enjoy the moment and tomorrow we are going for our honeymoon, it is our precious time, let's make it memorable.' said he by taking my hands into his and kissing me on forehead.

I calmed down but I also found him upset. We slept calmly by hugging each other as we were extremely tired mentally and physically.

On the next day, in the morning, Kabir woke up very late in the morning but being the daughter-in-law, I couldn't have that right for sure. I woke up very early in the morning; I had my bath and came down wearing a long kurta and salwar. I kept my dupatta on the shoulder. I bowed down and touched the feet of my in-laws, worshipped the temple kept at home and directly went to the kitchen to help my mother-in-law for break-fast. She was straining tea for herself. I was extremely feeling hungry as I had the habit of early break-fast and tea but I couldn't tell anything neither she offered me. I remembered my mother and father as sometimes papa also used to make tea for me when I was studying or resting.

'Mom, should I help you with something?' asked I with the low and frightened voice.

'Help? Now it is your kitchen, you will have to do everything, not only help.' said she with rough tone.

'Yes of course mom, I will do everything.'

'You will have to do. You must do however educated you are, makes no difference but how you perform in the kitchen shows your abilities. My sister's daughters are also educated but they have never been given much freedom like you girls so they are very respective and do all the kitchen work very easily. I hope you give your best performance in the kitchen and at least feed your husband properly. You are not going to live with us so you don't have burden of your in-laws but at least you will have to do for your husband. Do you know how to make chapattis? Can you shape them round?' she kept on taunting me by giving examples of educated daughters of other relatives.

I was frightened, couldn't speak anything, kept on tolerating all the taunts and kept on making chapattis for break-fast. I felt very bad by knowing my values in that house. I was hurt a lot by knowing that there was no value of my talent, smartness, good looks, education, qualification, my job, and the hard work of my parents. I was compared with those girls who just completed their 12th std and graduation by being at home. According to her, I secured my qualification like them. She ignored my hard work that I paid for my career during my youth. I kept on thinking about my behaviour; I woke up early, bowed down to them, went to temple, dressed as an Indian typical daughter-in-law, went to kitchen, then where was I wrong? Why was I being taunted like hell? I was thinking so many things and she came to the kitchen and ordered roughly,

'Cover your head with dupatta. We are respective people, here daughter-in-laws don't move around without covering their heads with dupatta.'

'Yes, mom. I will do it.' I covered my head and started working in the kitchen.

I thought she might be having that kind of nature, I tried to accept it. Meanwhile my sister-in-law (another new bride of home) came down. She also bowed down to in-laws and entered the kitchen.

By seeing her, my mother-in-law hugged her and said, 'Here is the queen of kitchen. She will handle my kitchen properly and will follow my rituals. She is the greatest daughter-in-law in the family. Dear, please you have some break-fast first, and then start working. You may be tired and feeling hungry.' said she by offering her break-fast.

'No, mom. I don't have the habit of early break-fast, I will do it letter.' replied she.

'Ok, but don't feel hesitation, it is your home. You have it at your convenient time.'

I was seeing all that and got offended. I was feeling to go to my mother; I was missing them a lot. Tears rolled down on my cheeks, but I rushed to the bathroom to hide them.

We had break-fast after 10:30 a.m. Kabir also came down. He saw my sad face which was pretending to be happy but he didn't speak a single word and went out for some work. We had to catch a bus for our honey-moon. To show people that she cared much for her daughter-in-law, she bought me many cloths for honeymoon. We got the bus at 10:00 pm. for Himachal Pradesh – India, the dream place for all newly married couples. The package was for eleven days which included various places of Himachal Pradesh. We took five bags, packed with lots of clothes, foot-wears, accessories, etc. I was extremely fond of photos; I didn't want to miss a single dress and accessory in the photos of my honeymoon. I forgot everything and started the journey of my honeymoon.

Everyone wished us 'Happy Journey' as if we were going for some adventure in space. But it was sounded very nice as for us it was really an adventure. Sex adventure. It was the third day of marriage but we didn't get success for intercourse. Finally we god the bus and our journey started. There were eleven newly married couples on the bus. We started enjoying from the day one. We got the first seat on the bus; we didn't take our eyes off each other. We wanted to sit in one seat instead of two to glue to each other. It was a wonderful journey. We didn't skip a single chance of kissing each other even on bus, especially at night in the dark. We got involved in each other by reaching in the lap of nature. We found Himachal Pradesh an awesome place including the abode of snow, lush green forest ranges, rich flora and fauna, snow covered mountain ranges, etc. It was like paradise for all honeymooners who were with us on bus. We visited various places like, Shimla, Kullu and Manali, Dalhousie, etc. The places were full of deep valleys, glaciers, exotic wild life as well as rich vegetation that filled Himachal with their beauty. We shared moments of intimacy in combination with greenery, snow covered mountain ranges and other natural wonders. We also visited lower bazaar, temples, malls, restaurants, etc. Apart from it, we visited luxurious hotels, resorts, lodges and other accommodations which gave us extreme privacy. We kept on gluing to each other. Dalhousie is considered to be India's Switzerland. We found the place adorable. Khajjar was one of the most romantic places. It was shaped like a saucer and surrounded with endless rows of pine trees and lush green meadow having a diminutive glacial lake and sky touching mountains in the backdrop. Apart from that, an ancient temple, forest rest house, golf course and overwhelming beauty of deodar forests added more spices in our honeymoon. We enjoyed nice hotels, restaurants, valleys, sunset, ice-mountains, nature, garden, water. We also tried a lot of adventures games. Above all, we took a lot of photographs, around four thousand and fifteen. We didn't miss a single pause for photo; we covered almost all the pauses of Bollywood, Hollywood and Normal life for photography. We wore matching cloths for all eleven days to have awesome photography. We walked by holding our hands on the roads. They were the dreaming days and dreaming life. We found the heaven on earth which supported us rigorously for our romance. We enjoyed shopping and brought good things for everyone in the family. Eleven days were about to complete, the dreaming life was on the verge of its end. We returned Bhavnagar after eleven days. Well we got half-success in our sex-adventure even after fourteen days of marriage but we were happy.

It is said in Bhagavad Geeta in chapter- 2, shloka-70

आपूर्यमाणमचलप्रतिष्ठं समुद्रमापः
प्रविशन्ति यद्वत्।
तद्वत्कामा यं प्रविशन्ति सर्वे स
शान्तिमाप्नोति न कामकामी।।७०।।

**Just as the ocean remains calm even when
turbulent waters pour into it from all sides,
similarly a person of steady intellect remains peaceful
even as all desires converge within him; those who crave
for the fulfilment of desire do not find peace.**

We both decided not to let our lust overcome our spirituality and responsibilities of life. We made up our mind to enjoy our lust but not at the cost of our duties.

CHAPTER 12

Kabir was given a nice quarter by the company but he didn't like it so he booked a nice flat on rent. He decided to shift there after marriage. He took me to the flat after our honeymoon. Now I came to Bhavnagar as a married female. He asked me to wait outside the home, then he dragged the luggage inside the home, then he lifted me, closed the door and took me in the bedroom and we again started romance early in the morning. He introduced me to his neighbours. Then we took rest and went out for dinner. From the next day he joined his office and I started arranging the house to make it Sweet Home. I arranged and cleaned the whole house, kitchen and each corner of the flat.

Finally the marriage life started very nicely. I used to get up early in the morning to make breakfast for him. He used to hug me, kiss me before going to the office. He also used to come home for lunch around 12:30 pm. for 20-25 minutes. I used to decorate the whole dining table with different varieties of food; it pleased me when he used to appreciate my food.

'You make all these dishes, I didn't know!' he got surprised.

'Yes, I used to cook in vacations at mom's place and I also take help of YouTube.' said I with laugh.

He used to come back from office around 5:00 pm then we used to go out for fun. Splendid days of life were going on.

'Kabir, it is very easy life that I am leading now but I will get bored soon, I complete the house-hold work then I watch T.V. It is very nice, in fact I feel it is a break for me after a long time, after hectic life that I had but I want to do something, should I start a job?' asked I.

'Of course, why not? First settle down, relax, then apply for job where you want. I will support you for everything and you must focus on your PHD Synopsis, yesterday only your guide has sent you a mail, have you checked it?' asked he.

'Yes, you are right. I must complete it first. From today only I will start writing it.' I replied by cleaning the platform.

'If you are busy and not able to get time for cooking, just give me a call. I will bring parcel for dinner or wait for me, we will cook together. You focus on your work, baby.' he supported wholeheartedly.

'So sweet of you. I am blessed to have a husband like you. No need for parcel, I will study and will also manage time for cooking and cleaning, don't worry.' said I.

'It is alright sweetheart, but don't take stress.' he kissed on my forehead and left for the office.

Life was going awesome and fantastic. I used to give a ring to my mother-in-law every day after completing my house-hold work as I never wanted to be apart from the family. I never forgot what she did with me but she gave me a very nice person in the form of my husband. I must be thankful to her and should not give her the same taste of her own medicine. I again initiated to maintain better relations.

'Hello, mom. How are you?' asked I on phone.

'Fine.' replied she very harshly.

'So how is your marriage life going on?' asked she before I spoke anything.

'It is good.' said I.

For a while, she didn't speak anything. I was waiting for her response, I said 'Hello !' three times. 'I am listening.' said she in anger.

'Of course, your marriage life would be definitely fine as you are living alone without any bondage of in-laws and relatives.' she started again.

'Mom, why do you think so? Please you and papa come here, we will stay together, in fact I also feel alone all the time. We will live together. Kabir's job is here so what to do? I am supposed to stay here with him as his wife.' explained I politely.

'How can we come there, your papa's shop is here, my elder son is here. I can't come without your father and he won't like there being idle without doing anything, he has worked during his entire life.' said she.

'Mom, should I convince brother and papa to start a shop over here so we all can stay together?' asked I in amiable tone.

'Who are you to think all that? And who knows Kabir might get job somewhere else, you people might shift to other city for the good. Guys working in the firms or companies don't stay with their parents due to their constant shifting, and who can know it better than you? That is why you chose a right partner to enjoy your freedom, very smart!' she kept on taunting me.

'Mom, why do you think all this. When I came in touch with Kabir, you all were in a very big joined family, I didn't even ask about all that. And I....'

She disconnected the phone before listening my further explanation. Again I called her next day to initiate for good,

'Hello mom, how are you?' asked I.

'First class as usual, enjoying with my daughter-in-law.' she taunted by talking about my sister-in-law. (Wife of Kabir's brother - Ankita)

'So you got free?' added she.

'Yes just finished of cleaning the utensils and other stuff, now will start cooking.' replied I.

'Oh, so will you cook or will order the food?' asked she with sarcasms.

'I do cook every day, mom.'

'You might be managing home but my son would have more ideas for house-hold work as he has stayed in hostel for a longer time, so he would be helping you in all household works, right?' asked she.

'I have also lived as a pain guest for few years and I complete almost the work before he comes back from office.' I gave explanation calmly.

'Yes, you are only two people, what would be the work and you don't have many relatives there so you would be remaining free almost the time.' taunted she like anything.

'No mom. After my household work, I work on my P.H.D synopsis.'

'Oh! Still you want to study, means you are planning to do a job?'

'Yes mom.'

'But we don't want money, then why do you want to do it?' asked she in anger.

'I don't want to work only for money, but I have worked very hard for my career so can't leave it in between.'

'Well, it is your wish. You today's girls want to be like men but time never changes for women, remember my words...' said she in anger.

I used to call her every day and find myself in the firing line without any reason, and then my mind used to waver only negative thoughts regarding marriages and relations for the whole day. I also started fighting with Kabir because of those mental torments.

'I have told you thousands of time not to call her, then why do you do that?' told Kabir in anger.

'I love them and also respect them. I want a family; so ...' I gave explanation for my calls.

'But nobody loves you and respects you there excepting my father, so you can call him but stop calling my mother.' he shouted by putting his bag on the table.

Situation reached to the crunch. I started crying as he scolded me very badly. He then left the house for an hour in anger. I didn't want our relation to be broken so I stopped calling her and definitely wanted to find a job to keep my mind busy and to keep myself away from all that scrap. I applied in two well known colleges of Bhavnagar.

After a month, my mother-in-law came to Bhavnagar for few days to see the house and kitchen arranged by me. It was Saturday morning, she came. I used to wear trousers and top at home but as she was going to come, I wore a long dress with dupatta. Kabir went to pick her up. She came with two bags. I opened the door and bowed down to touch her feet. She gave her blessings by keeping her hand on my head. She entered the home without smile on her face. I was so frightened that the glass of water fell down from my hand.

'Alright mom, I am going for the office, I am already late.' said he in a low voice.

'Alright dear, come soon. She stood at the gate to bid him bye.

I was looking at him from the kitchen-window but that day he didn't even look at me. From the first day of her arrival, our life changed. She came inside. I was still standing at the window, he was standing there and he gave me a flying kiss. I felt very nice that he did it for me but also got little upset to see him frightened by his mother. I realized our romance kept on continuing as we were living apart from her; else she would have definitely killed love between us.

'Hello, he has gone now. Close the window and come out of the dream world, it is your real life.' interrupted my mother-in-law in my imagination and thinking.

I closed the window and started cleaning the home. I switched on T.V for listening the songs while cleaning the house but her sarcastic sight made me switch it off. I started cleaning house by shutting my mouth. After finishing the work, I took my laptop to write my synopsis.

'So still you want to do job?' asked she

'Yes, mom. What will I do by staying at home alone?'

'If you work outside, you won't be able to handle home.'

'If that happens, home will be my first propriety. I will leave the job.' said I with little confidence.

'You might handle home and job together but relatives, our rituals will not be handled by you.'

'We don't have many relatives here. We are in touch of some friends of Kabir's office and their wives are also working.' I said by trying to make eye-contact with her.

'But you have just shifted here, you will increase the relatives. The girls who work outside become independent and egoist, then they won't like if somebody comes to their place. They would find it disturbance, they love to be busy in their own life, you will become like that only. If you start a job, you will not have time for anybody. After earning money, you will start feeling superior and will suppress us.' said she in anger.

'That is why I wanted an educated girl but never a working or ambitious girl who comes with her own thoughts. That is why my friends said to me not to choose an independent girl, as they will just like to be with their husband not with the family.' She kept on blaming the working girls.

'Ankita is also a graduate but doesn't want to work, only wants to stay at home. She is very respectful.' appreciated she.

I was listening all that without saying anything and continued chopping the vegetables. She kept on torturing me for being educated and ambitious.

'My son is educated so you have come to his life, what is a big deal in it? You don't need to take proud on it. If you consider yourself Rasmalai, my son is also Gulabjamun. My elder son is just 10th passed out and he has got a graduated girl. There is no fault in her; she is so honest and respective. She never showed her will to do job and her parents are also very modest and gave many things in dowry and your parents didn't even ask for the ring-ceremony function to save the money.' she kept on bombarding on me although I never showed proud or ego of my qualification or ambition. 'Especially, the girl like you.' she said sarcastically.

'Girl like me, means?' I couldn't resist myself and asked.

'Just look at the pics of your honeymoon, how stylish and romantic pics. It is your love marriage, else who dares to take these kinds of pics in the beginning of the marriage?'

'They were very normal couple pics, and I wore all the clothes that you bought me. I though you would be very happy to see that.' I said very politely.

She didn't even reply and went inside. I could feel the female jealousy for female. And realized that I would never be able to make her happy whatever I do for her. I tried to keep my mouth shut but I couldn't resist myself when I heard abusive words for my parents. I was thinking to run away from there. I felt paralyzed and felt the burden of marriage. I sympathized myself for getting married to Kabir and cursed myself that I happened to meet that female in my life.

'First of all, bhabhi has never worked in her life. She has just completed her studies from distance learning just to have qualification so please stop comparing me with her. And my parents booked the plot for ring-ceremony function and also decided menu for food and made the guests list but I came to know bhabhi's parents were not ready for the function due to their hectic schedule. And my parents have given the equal dowry what bhabhi's parents have given. Why do you blame me and my parents for each and everything?' asked I with tears in my eyes.

The torturing kept on increasing day by day without any reason. She would sit on sofa and start bombarding on me after Kabir's leaving for his office. The torturing kept on extending since my marriage. I couldn't tolerate much and shared everything with Kabir.

'What the hell is happening to me? If I am a working girl, is it bad? What is wrong with it? And it is not only about my job, she doesn't like the way I get up, the way I walk, talk, smile, my dressing sense, she finds me stylish. I just wear normal simple cloths. What can I do if I look good in any wear? Why is she so jealous of me? She says I am full of freedom, what kind of freedom is she talking about? Have you ever seen me moving in bikini or shorts? Don't I do house-hold work? What is wrong

if I don't poke my nose into anybody's matter, and deal
with my studies after completion of the whole house-
hold work? After marriage, do I need to leave my studies
even after completing all responsibilities of home? If I
interfere with the matters of all relatives, if I spend my all
free hours in their matters, then only am I a caring and
respective daughter-in-law? That means, I should not have
my own thoughts and stop working after marriage even
after fulfilling everybody's expectations. Right? I should
not have the right to give time to myself, am I right Mr.
Kabir?' I spoke all that just in one breath.

He kept on listening by keeping his hands on his head.

I stopped for a while and again started, 'A woman
has always been judged among her family, her career and
her personal life. A woman's status and position in the
society has been toing and froing from century to century.
For instance, ancient Egyptian women had a great deal of
freedom. In ancient Greece, people worshipped goddesses
as well as gods. In rich Greek family, the wife was expected
to run the home and to manage the finances. Meanwhile
Celtic women had a great deal of freedom and many rights.
In 16th and 17th century, women were confined to domestic
work only. They used to enter in the profession like tailors,
milliners, dyers, shoemakers and embroiderers, bakers,
washerwoman, confectioners, brewers, etc. In 18th century,
girls went to school but embroidery and music learning
was more important than academic subjects. In 19th
century, women started getting into education and 21st
century's technological and economical changes inspired
women to get in all professional fields and to have all
rights as men had. 21st century has pulled off various
changes in education, technology, mentality, religions,

society, etc. so a woman's status is also the part and parcel of this change. Today a woman has proven herself a big cheese in all most the fields like sports, commerce and industry, education, health, politics, technology, navy, army, agriculture, astrology, astronomy etc. She has broken through the journey from a domestic servant to a spacewoman. Despite embarking her journey of being a professional person in each field, a woman has not been stopped centering around for various questions, like-

"Can a working woman be a good part of the society?"

"Can a working woman handle both- profession and family?"

"Can a working woman take care of her children and family?"

"Should a working woman be respected?" And above all,

"Should a woman work?"

Today almost working women find themselves in the midst of these kinds of chaotic questions despite having possession of abundant freedom and intelligence.'

He replied after a while,

'It is said maturity leads one to change the world but wisdom leads one to change oneself. If a woman walks on the path of wisdom, she can juggle multiple chaotic traits in one walk because there is no doubt on a woman's strength because it is said, 'A woman is like a tea bag. When you put it in hot water, you come to know how strong she is!' A woman can set herself on the top ladder of professional and personal success by developing high EQ (Emotional Quotient) in herself; means you can monitor your emotions to cope up with pressures and demand by controlling your negative thoughts and actions.

I stared at him for a minute and started again with cry, 'I don't mind if she gives much love to bhabhi. There are no issues between me and bhabhi; I never underestimate her for anything;nor I show attitude. We can be good friends if mom allows but at least I must not be insulted like that and what fault she is talking about? Why can't she understand my feelings and honesty for family? If she doesn't have any fault, which faults she finds in me?'

'As you have gone for love marriage so you will have to bear with all this.' said Kabir bluntly.

'Now love is over, real life has started. And I have already endured a lot. I have my limitations. If I have gone for love marriage, will I have to be insulted like hell during my entire life? Am I supposed to deal with all these only? Don't I have anything else to do? I am the girl of the same community; then what is the problem? And now she wants me to go with her to Patan for a month, how will I survive there without you in this kind of atmosphere?' I asked.

'Mom, are you planning to take her to Patan?' he asked while having a cup of coffee.

'Yes dear as many guests are going to come to stay at our place for few days, she will stay with everybody and will also learn the rituals of our family. If she comes in touch with them, they would also prefer to come here. You can initiate your social life like that.' said she.

'We are already busy in our life, we can't afford much socialization. And she is also busy with her PHD research.' he said very politely.

'Do you want her to do job?' asked she by squinting her eyes.

'So what is wrong with it?'

'But we don't want money.' she said bluntly.

'It is not only for money but to keep herself busy in good things. Rather than poking nose in others' matter, she will be busy in her own work and life. And why we don't need money? If she earns, she will increase one more earning member in the family. The things that we can achieve in ten years can be achieved in five years only, and papa is also ready with this, what problem do you have? In fact you would be able to flaunt in front of your friends that your daughter-in-law is a professor in a good college.' said he with laugh to cool down the matter.

She looked at me with sarcasm. I realized the difference between a daughter and a daughter-in-law. If I had been her daughter, she would have supported me whole wholeheartedly.

'But after children, it is very difficult for women to maintain job and home together.' she continued by not giving up.

'We will think about it, first let children come till that she can work.' Kabir said.

'Oh! That is the problem. She is suffering from inferiority complex but why doesn't she understand my situation? In fact I will finish all work on time and if I am learning new things by working out, I will share it with the family and new things will also enter home.' I gave clarification to Kabir.

'Problems would have been so easy if she understands that. But you will have to go to Patan with her for a month at least; I understand your situation but please support me with this.' Kabir requested.

'But what about my PHD synopsis? I am required to send it within few days.' asked I

'Please carry the laptop over there. When you find time, finish it there.' suggested Kabir.

'Alright, I will go.' said I

'Thanks and all the best for your new adventure with my mom.' said he by taking my hand in his hands and kissing me on my forehead.

We laughed loudly and I started crying, he wiped my tears and again we laughed. We discussed that in the room.

'Anything for you my love.' said I.

Finally we got the bus for Patan and reached early in the morning. I was feeling very uncomfortable with her during the entire journey. I was missing Kabir very much. We reached there at 7:30 am.

I covered my head with dupatta and bowed down to my father-in-law, the best person on earth. I got fresh and up and directly went to the kitchen to help my bhabhi. We had our breakfast and took rest for an hour, and then we were watching the album of our wedding and honeymoon. The cassette of our wedding and reception was also played on T.V.

'Your sister is also looking like a bride. She has applied much make-up, don't you think so? Oh, your mother also is also very fashionable; she also applies lipstick at this age! I take care of my age and don't wear stylish cloths and apply much make up.' said my mother-in-law to me.

We blame the society almost the time but it is we who have made the society. We ourselves make the society handicapped and never allow it to enjoy its freedom. Especially, a female plays the role of an enemy for other females. They can't digest each other's progress, good looks, good personality, smartness, etc.

'But your bhabhi is looking very nice. She is young and wears nice cloths. You organized the marriage function very nicely, the decoration was also fine and your suit looked very pretty, too.' said she to my bhabhi to subdue me.

'My elder brother and bhabhi looked better than younger couple.' added my sister-in-law (Kabir's sister).

When I observed the stuff, everything was same in the cassette but somehow to harass me, they were speaking all negative stuff about me, my family, and our arrangements for marriage function. For me the album and wedding movie became like curse rather than enjoyment. We finished the wedding movie of Kabir's family, my bhabhi's family and now it was time to run my DVD. The moment it started, lot of negative comments started without any reason by my mother-in-law and sister-in-law, they left the movie in between and went to the room for other work to insult me and my family. I was about to cry, I controlled and went to the washroom and cried a lot but not in front of them.

The next day, Kabir's relatives came for staying with us for few days and for attending some wedding functions. There were thirteen people and we five members so in one house, eighteen people were supposed to stay together for few days of vacation. All the guests came; we were newly married so I and my bhabhi were asked to wear a long dress with dupatta to cover our head. We bowed down to everyone whom we didn't even know. It was the heat of March and it was compulsory to wear much gold, dupatta must not be slipped from the head. According to my mother-in-law, a daughter-in-laws should not allowed to come out of the kitchen before guests. They are not supposed to enjoy their lunch and dinner with the other family members. She is supposed to have her food in the kitchen only. I kept on working in the kitchen from morning to night constantly as there were many people so the house became a restaurant which was open for twenty four by seven hours. It was compulsory to wake up till late night even after finishing the work. We were not allowed to sleep as we were required to entertain the guests for at least an hour so it was compulsory to wake up almost for the entire night whether we were happy, not happy, interested in the talks after a lot of hard-work or not. It was such a pathetic condition. I didn't mind doing all that as it was also my family but after doing everything, I was humiliated and not respected, and that response drove me up the wall.

It was morning and time to make break-fast for everybody. I entered the kitchen and started the preparation. When I started working, I came to know that my bhabhi didn't know cooking properly. She informed me that she had never cooked before marriage. But I didn't want to reveal that. While cooking, I remembered my God and used to make food in much quantity, it used to be very tasteful, all guests appreciated that. I used to multiply the ingredients for three times, as I used to make food for four-to five people at my mother's place and here I was supposed to cook for fifteen people. Sometimes, I didn't trust myself that I could do that.

The guests got very impressed by me, my nature and my cooking.

Some of the ladies came inside and were scanning me when I was cooking as it is considered to be the females' habit to scan the work of others and give comments, well I got positive comments. One of them asked me, 'Oh, dear you are cooking so nicely, you learnt the house-hold work and cooking along with studies and job?'

Before I say anything, my mother-in-law replied, 'at our side, girls know everything however educated they are. My another daughter-in-law is also very good at cooking, in fact she has handled everything alone at her mother's place. My daughter, Payal, made Pav-bhaji for twenty people at her in-laws' house on the first day of her marriage. So she is not the only one who is doing this, every girl does that and girls must do it. Both are equal - to run a company and to run a kitchen. So the girls who work in companies can't have proud of it as kitchen also go parallel as far as its management consulted. Indirectly she also clarified her views, 'A lady's job should be only in the kitchen. If a girl wants to do something after marriage and children, she is supposed to manage everything by her own.' Indirectly she clarified if I wanted to work outside even after kids; she would never support me. I would have to manage everything by my own. My mother-in-law put the knife in my matters in front of everybody to decrease my influence on the guests.

Some of Kabir's cousins came to me to have some guidance regarding their career but I was called in the kitchen to do unnecessary work so that I couldn't leave any influence on them of my intellectual property. Due to that kind of behaviour of her, the guests also stopped asking about my education and career. They stopped taking guidance from me for anything. In a nutshell, she gave her best efforts to keep my importance just as a normal woman who had no knowledge, no desire for education or job. She didn't give me any importance for my studies, my job and my ambition; in fact she made others do the same. They used to talk to me regarding my life, my work, education in her absence but not in front of her. I never even dreamed that I would be treated like that after my marriage. I used to miss the respect and love given to me by my parents, friends and relatives, and used to cry in the washroom to hide my tears. I used to miss my husband, wanted to go there. Other relatives understood that and also sympathized me but couldn't say anything. I couldn't find any escape and let the things go on. I kept on thinking many things, 'Why does a woman become enemy of another woman?' 'Why are they found green with envy for each other?' 'Why is a woman always ready to screw other woman's dreams and independence?' 'Can't women be friends and go ahead in life for freedom?' I kept on thinking by sitting on kamod.

Next day, we were supposed to attend the wedding function of our nearby relative in Patan itself. I went up to get ready for the party after taking permission from her as I was not allowed to go upstairs even without her permission. I applied make-up and got ready very nicely by wearing a blue and white suit. My mother in-law first went to my bhabhi's room and saw that she didn't get ready as she didn't even know how to apply makeup and lipstick, so she got her ready and made her beautiful, then she entered my room and I was looking very pretty according to everybody but she didn't want me to get ready the way I wanted. According to her, me and my bhabhi both should look alike. She forced me to change my dress and made me wear another dress of her choice which I didn't even like. She used to do that almost the time, I was not allowed to wear the cloths of my choice after marriage. I literary cried as I never wore cloths of anybody's choice. I loved my choice, in fact every one used to love my choice of cloths and accessories. But here I couldn't say anything and let the things execute.

It was the end of the vacation, all the guests left and the functions also got over. Now I also wanted to go to my husband, it was more than a month.

Meanwhile my mother called me and talked to her, she also fought with her without any reason. Again she started bombarding about the same thing about girls' freedom, education, job, company, kitchen, dowry, money, etc. My mother just asked me one question after her call,

'Dear, are you happy there?'

I couldn't reply, just burst into tears and my mother understood everything. I perceived to hide all that but ultimately my mother got to know about everything.

My mother said to my father, 'We thought, we were not independent so we suffered a lot. Now our daughter is educated and independent but she is suffering for her talent and independence. We made a big mistake by getting our daughter married there. She is not disclosing anything but I know she is not happy there. I am scared if the torturing lasts for longer, she might get depressed.'

After a month, Kabir came to pick me up. I packed my luggage but she was very angry when I went with him. Only my father-in-law gave me blessings, else she just wanted me to leave my career and be in the kitchen only forever. I also got grips with the kitchen work and impressed all guests, despite her unlimited trials to let me down, God kept me up in front of everybody. I thought of continuing my honesty with everybody and for everything in life. Finally, we reached Bhavnagar. I took a deep breath, well I was missing my father-in-law and brother-in-law a lot, as they were very pure by heart and always supported me in Kabir's absence. I shared everything with Kabir; he also became very sad and upset but asked me to focus on my work and career.

'You always advise me to let the things go but it is very difficult to tolerate all the time, what would you have done if my parents had humiliated you like that?' asked I in anger.

'I can understand she has crossed her limitations but what can I do? Why are you fighting with me?' Kabir asked with little irritation.

'Many people go for love marriage, many girls work after marriage; I am not the only one. And I am behaving the way she wants whether I like or not, then also she is not happy. I am totally not agree to cover my head in front of my father-in-law but I do it. I wear typical panjabi suits which don't at all suit me, isn't it enough? Why to cover the head in the heat of March? In fact by doing this, the daughter-in-law is forced to differentiate between her parents and in-laws. I am sure no father-in-law demands that, it is mother-in-laws who force for all this rubbish stuff. If they leave this mentality, we would be able to make two more chapattis for them by heart. At least we would feel less heat in the kitchen. And I was informed on the first day by your mom that, 'There is a difference between a daughter and daughter-in-law.' Now I should also start differentiate between parents and in-laws, right?' asked I in anger.

'See, this is the mentality of my family, I can't help it. You will have to bear with it. And now we are married so it is not good to cry over split milk.' said he.

'If I were aware of your mother's nature, especially for me or for working girls, I would have never got married to you. I had a lot of proposals and you too had. At least, you would have got peace from my complaints and especially your mother would have achieved happiness in her life.' I burst into tears.

'Don't worry about complaints, it is the moral duty of any husband to bear with the wife's complaints. I am not any exceptional, so carry on.' said he by using ear-bird for his left ear.

'I can't tolerate much humiliation, I want a divorce. If I am not in touch with you, I will be free from your mother's tortures.' said I in anger.

'If you want a divorce, then find a lawyer and make him prepare the documents of divorce.' said he.

He knew I told that just in anger, none of us wanted to have a divorce seriously. After that fighting, we slept. Again I woke up in the morning, made breakfast for him and he went to office by kissing on my forehead, again life came on normal track.

After two days, I got a call for interviews from two colleges. I prepared hard for it and gave the interviews for the post of an Assistant Professor in both the colleges. I was called three times for the interview in one college, and two times in another one.

At night when my mother-in-law called, I shared about interview stuff with her.

'Oh, so finally you are up to start your career again! But you won't get handsome amount of salary in Bhavnagar as these colleges take highly qualified and talented people, you might not get even selected. If they select you, they might offer you fifteen to twenty thousand. You lose three four thousand in petrol, then for ten thousand why to spend the whole day? Better take rest at home, do house-hold work and better to increase social relations with relatives which will really be fruitful in future, especially for your children.' demotivated she in a rough tone.

'Let us see, what happens, interviews were very nice but...' said I. 'But there would be thousands of people like you. They might not select you just by seeing your face and personality, they would require actual talent.'

interrupted she by taunting me that I was working in the previous college due to my good looks and personality.

She disconnected the call in anger. Again I tried to pick up the pieces for healthy relation but couldn't succeed. Well now I was also not interested to talk to her. I got fatigued of her constant tortures even on phone calls.

I kept on waiting for the reply from both the colleges. But I realized that I was feeling off colour since few days.

I asked Kabir, 'Will I be able to manage both together, household work and job?'

'Yes, definitely. You will. I trust you.' motivated he.

'I am not feeling well since few days; don't even feel to eat anything. I don't know what is happening.' said I with tiredness on my face.

We kept quiet for a while.

'Do you think I am pregnant?' I asked to him by narrowing my eye-brows.

We both looked at each other for a while without speaking anything.

'I think we should go for a report, should I bring prega-test?' asked he by pinching his chin with his hand.

'But I don't know how to use it.' I said by getting little frightened.

'Description will be written on the packet, so you can use it accordingly and give me the urine sample tomorrow morning, I will also get it checked in the laboratory so we can have final clue.'

'Alright, let's go for orange juice, I feel to eat only sour things.' said I.

We went out for that and I said, 'We have just completed three and half months of marriage, and baby? Isn't it too early? I have also given interviews for jobs. We are in nuclear family, and above all nobody is ready to help me from family for my career. How will we manage all that?' asked I while having orange juice.

'Let the reports come first, then think about all.' said he by taking out money from his wallet for juice.

Next morning, I gave him my urine sample and I also used prega-test but I could not judge anything due to my lack of knowledge of using it. I was waiting for the report from laboratory, meanwhile I got a call from both of the colleges. They informed me that I was selected. I was so happy; both were ready to pay me 40,000 as per my expectation. Now I got confused which college should have been selected. I called Kabir about it, he was also very happy. Then I called few of my colleagues, and had more positive reviews about GMIT (Gyanmanjari Institute of Technology) Finally I selected GMIT. I was sent the joining letter through email, and was asked to come to college next day for some formalities. I asked Kabir to take print out of that and bring home.

It was 5:30 pm. The door bell range. I opened the door and Kabir came with three things. In one hand my joining letter of college and in another hand a packet of Amla and in pocket my pregnancy report which was positive. He came inside and handed over everything to me. We both were extremely happy and shocked for that. We saw tears of happiness into each other's eyes as a new life took birth in my womb as the sign of our love. He put one Amla in my mouth and hugged me by wishing me Congratulations.

'So now three things to manage - home, job and baby, will I be able to manage that?' I asked by eating some amlas.

'You take your decision; there is no force on you. Are you ready for baby now? If not, we will find some solution.

You don't take burden, think and take your time. I am with you in your all decisions.' said he by holding my hands.

'I want to keep the baby. I will not get it aborted. It is a god gift but isn't it too early? We will feel shy while disclosing it. In fact our relatives thought we would give this good news at least after five years of our marriage, as we both are working and ambitious.' I said to him.

We both were laughing on it.

'You can do all, my super lady. God knows your capability so He gave three things to manage together, home, job and pregnancy. But you take decision. If you are fine with this, then only join College else no need to stress yourself.' Kabir said.

'I think I must join as it will keep me active and will keep me away from all negative thoughts during pregnancy and baby will also enjoy college life since his/ her childhood.' said I with laughter.

We were discussing all that and making fun; all of a sudden, I started bleeding. The blood was in much quantity. We assumed that it was a miscarriage. We rushed to the gynaecologist and reported as the emergency case as bleeding was not at all stopping. She checked by using her ultrasound equipment, she penetrated and I shouted loudly. She scolded me to keep my mouth shut and kept on checking.

'Oh, she is very fussy patient. How she became pregnant?' said she to my husband with smile.

'She even shouts.' replied he feeling little shy.

'Very fussy girl.' said the doctor.

I was smiling and looking at both of them. I didn't speak a single word.

'Well pregnancy is still on continuity but heart beats of the baby are not found yet. Give a week to it and come after ten days. I am giving some medicines. Three tablets for swallowing and one you need to put inside you to stop the bleeding and have complete bed rest.' said the doctor.

'Thank you ma'am.' we left with heavy heart.

We came by two-wheeler. He drove it very slowly and reached home safely. We informed about it to the families. All got shocked first by the early pregnancy of a very ambitious girl, then they kept on advising me for taking complete rest, eating good and energetic food, fresh fruits and dry-fruits. Ten days passed and we went to the doctor, she used her equipments again and checked the condition of baby and ended with my shout.

'Well now all well, heart beats are found so you are pregnant but you will have to take bed –rest as in your case, it is little risky. There are chances of miscarriage.' She warned.

I was on bed-rest; nobody was at home to take care of me. I myself used to take a lot of care of myself. Sometimes Kabir used to cook, sometimes I used to do. We kept a maid for other house-hold work so somehow we managed the situation with some difficulties.

I wanted to continue my job as well as my pregnancy but the college was on high-way and we were staying in the city. Every day commuting was difficult for me during the critical situation of pregnancy. I got upset as I wanted to continue my work till my delivery.

'Don't get upset. We will shift the flat nearby your college. Then it will be easy for you to commute.' supported Kabir.

'But I will be able to work only for one semester, and then I will have to take leave for delivery. If we shift, you will have to commute for half an hour every day.' I denied for shifting.

'Any one will have to commute, so in this situation you should not do it, better I do.' said he.

We went to find the flats nearby my college, after seeing many flats; we finalized one which was at the distance of 7 minutes of my college. It was such a wonderful two bhk flat having all amenities like Jim, swimming pool, big garden, small library, safe parking facilities. The flat had a nice gallery from where a nice garden view was visible. Such an amazing place with very nice locality!

'I am on bed rest, shifting will be very difficult, how will we do it?' asked I to Kabir.

'I will manage everything, will take help of some friends, you don't worry and take rest.'

He packed everything, the neighbours got together to bid us farewell. I hugged my all female friends and they wished me good luck for future, for delivery and healthy baby.

Finally, Kabir finished the whole house-hold work as on that day my made was on leave. He packed the whole luggage and we shifted to our new flat. The weather was very bad; it was raining like cats and dogs. Somehow he managed everything, took a lot of care of mine and we reached safely.

Now I was supposed to arrange the whole house.

'Arrange it slowly and gradually, you don't need to stress yourself.' Kabir warned me.

I started arranging everything as from the next week I was about to join the college. My in-laws came to help me out for arranging the house and to stay for few days with us. I was very happy as I got a very reputed job in reputed college and also found a flat nearby. I didn't want to enjoy all that alone without family members, I wanted to share my happiness with my in-laws. I was glad that they were coming on right time.

They came in the morning; I bowed down to them with the dupatta on my head and wore a long suit. I made break-fast and tea, we had some general talks, my mother-in-law also asked me to take rest and she also started helping me in house-hold work. But she couldn't stop her torturing for my job, freedom and all that. I didn't want to fall in any arguments so I kept my mouth shut and my mind calm. She brought many dresses for me and asked me to wear those ones only. I didn't like any of them but I accepted without saying anything.

'These are the good dresses and even cheap ones, we cannot afford costly ones.' said she in rough tone.

I started tolerating again even during my pregnancy.

'Why does your mother dominate me especially for cloths, at least I know about appropriate dresses for my designation as a faculty. I don't want this heavy dresses; I just want simple, professional dresses, in which I feel comfortable and confident. I don't want to wear those dresses which are not of my choice, at least I can wear what I want so what if I am married.' I complained to Kabir in tiring tone.

'You will have to wear, I can't help.' he said.

'Don't worry, now you take it from her, we will buy new ones for you.' he suggested.

Finally I started my job from the first month of pregnancy. I used to get up at 5 o'clock in the morning, used to prepare lunch and breakfast for me and my husband and for my in-laws. I used to pack the tiffins for both of us, well my mother-in-law used to help me. Then I used to get my college bus around 8:45 am, after completing my job in college, I used to come back home around 5:45 pm. Then I used to take rest for 15 to 20 minutes and again used to get back to work. In the evening, I used to wash cloths with the help of using washing- machine and finished some house-hold work, and used to prepare dinner. After that I used to prepare my notes at night for the next day lectures and used to sleep by spending some time with husband and in-laws.

'See, your schedule is very hectic; you don't have time for anybody now. You got busy in your own life and again became independent, now you don't need anybody. But it is just first month of pregnancy, I am sure you won't be able to manage this hectic schedule for the whole semester.' said my mother in law to demotivate me.

'I will try my best, mom.' I said in depressing tone by getting extremely tired of her taunts.

'Today's girls think that they can do anything but how long will they manage? Life never changes for women. One day you will have to quit your career.' said she.

'Mom, I complete the whole house-hold work, give time to everybody and then I manage my work. I give second priority to my work; home is always my first priority. Then what is your problem if I do some creative things? Do you want me to sit at home by doing nothing? What will you get if I stop my career, why do you always up to screw my career? My parents have spent their entire life to make me educated and independent.' asked I with tears in my eyes.

'But you were a girl at that time, you were a free bird. Now you are a woman, you have many responsibilities. You should also take responsibilities to enhance your social relations with all our guests. You must invite them to your place every week. And your parents have spent their entire life, so they think you will rule our family?'

she continued blaming me and my paretns without any reason.

I felt suffocation and took deep breath. 'Of course I will also do it on Sunday. If I quit my job, what will I do at home? I get up so early, finish my work then I go out for my job, what is the problem then?' asked I.

'You can do it as you don't have active social life like us, else you could never do it.'

'I don't mind if guests come, I will behave very nicely with all our relatives.'

'If a female is working and goes out for wandering, then who will come to you? The girl who has always remained out cannot stay at home, she loves to go out and hang out all the time.' She started fighting.

'Wandering? Am I going for wandering? It is a noble profession for your kind knowledge.' said I in a little loud voice as I couldn't bear my humiliation about my character.

'Look at my daughter, the way she is living at her in-laws' place. She is in joined family and spends her whole time in the kitchen for cooking and attending the guests. Look at herself and yourself. See my another daughter-in-law; she cooks for us and stays at home only. They never even go out alone without asking me and you go out with a big tummy, even in pregnancy.' said she by taking proud of themselves and subduing me with high humiliation.

'You just wait and watch. I will bring many guests to your place and will increase your social life too much, then I will see, how do you get time for your study, job, career and all this rubbish stuff?' she challenged me.

'Nobody even comes to Patan frequently.' I said.

'As it is not in the middle of the state; but Bhavanagar is in the middle of the state so they can take the advantage.'

She was excessively narrow-minded and against the girls' education. I didn't say anything and left for college. I could never forget her behaviour at the door. She literally smashed the door when I just went out from home and when I came back; she opened the door with an angry face and didn't even look at me. She used to do it every day as if she was kicking me out of the home, and letting me get inside as if I entered without her permission. She didn't even think about my pregnancy period and kept on behaving like that. That behaviour used to make me cry as I used to remember my mother who used to stand at the door to say 'bye' to me until I got into another street. But I accepted, that was the real life. I also understood that 'women are not happy because of women only.' I used to think all that even at college.

I spent tough days without saying anything to anybody but it went beyond limitation, especially when she blamed me for my character. One day, I said each and everything to Kabir by bursting into tears.

'Mom has crossed the limits. I can't tolerate my humiliation like this. She says, I go for wandering. Am I a prostitute? She always compares me with your sister and bhabhi. She says, I am free and don't work the way they do. What can I do if your sister cooks for ten people and she is in joined family? When time was in her hand, she didn't educate her daughter. Now she feels jealous when she finds others' daughters independent, she starts criticizing them as their life is little better. Why did your mother not get educated your sister? Just to have the fake fame of keeping the daughters inside the home? Just to say her daughter is in her control and very respective? Means the girls who are educated and working are considered to be manner-less? What is wrong if they don't poke nose into anybody's matter and find some time for themselves for some creative work? These kinds of girls are sound egoist to your mother; she doesn't understand that I complete the household work of five hours just in two hours as I have other things to do; that doesn't mean I am free. I get some time for other things as I believe in time management. I follow my timing rigorously for each work. I don't waste time in gossips of all relatives. I never get free mently. And she always talks about bhabhi, what she does? I have seen her doing all the work with a snail's speed as she doesn't have anything else to do in her life. She doesn't have any hobbies or goals. She stretches the house hold work of five hours and finishes it in ten hours. Your mother talks about guests and social life, who goes there? Nobody goes to stay there as our all relatives stay far and settled in mega cities. Then why does she always compare me with them? Everybody is good and happy as per their status. You are educated so I am. If husband and wife work and help each other financially, what is wrong with it? We are planning to buy a flat. If I pay half amount for this, what is wrong in it? She doesn't know about market and expenses of children's fees now days, it is very difficult to manage with the earning of a single person. In fact, they should also start some work at home. They take the leisure of taking nap at noon for four hours, do I do that? Do I watch T.V and serials every day for hours? Do I have that kind of time? I sacrifice leisure, relaxation and many things to balance my job and home together. Now tell me who is free? And I know she likes my sincerity and discipline. She likes the way I finish my work on time, and manage everything but she will never appreciate me. She suggested bhabhi to start the tuition classes at home but she refused and told she won't be able to do that kind of hard-work. Now tell me who is free and who is jealous? I am tired of this nonsense taunts now. Above all, she also fights with my mother and other family members, it is too much now.'

'Why are you telling me all that? Go and blast on her, fight for yourself. I don't mind. I have already given you all the freedom. Did I ever say anything to you?' Kabir told me with full of anger.

'You don't say anything. That is the biggest problem of the world. You don't dominate me by words but you dominate by your actions.' replied I with anger. 'I was getting various proposals, I never knew about your mother as I would have never got married to you.' added I.

'You have repeated this dialogue numerous times.' said he.

I stopped speaking and sat on the bed by putting my hands on my tummy as I didn't want my baby to listen our fights.

'I can understand, but can't help. You are better than them, that is why she is doing marketing of bhabhi and my sister. Now I am also tired of your problems. But I am helpless. I can't change her mentality and her envy for you.' explained he.

'But what is my fault? I don't understand why she behaves with me as a sworn enemy since the first day of our meeting? I have always respected her. My education has become my enemy. How sad it is! How hard I have worked for my career and qualification, don't you know that? After helping her in all the matters, why does she want to stop my progress? Can a mother-in-law be jealous of her daughter-in-law? Am I not her child? Are you not her child? Is she your step-mother? Doesn't she want your happiness? Why papa doesn't say anything to her? At least ask her to stop torturing till my delivery.' I requested to Kabir by crying loudly and by crouching before him.

'Better to get divorce and abort the baby. Let's finalize the divorce as it is never ending problem. I don't want you to suffer more.' Kabir said firmly.

I kept my hand on my tummy and kept on crying. 'The baby has not even taken birth and you are talking to kill the baby.'

I cried for the whole night and went to college as usual. For the whole day, I couldn't concentrate on my work. I loved to be with the family. I loved to share my thoughts, happiness and sadness with the people of my family but now I wanted to live separate from my mother-in-law especially for my baby as she would never stop taunting me and I would never stop fighting with Kabir.

'I was family oriented person but your mother has brought me at that extent that I have started hating family, marriage and love. I am raped and screwed mentally for all relations in life.' said I by being depressive.

He hugged me and we sat for a while without speaking anything. She went back to Patan but this time I didn't feel any regret of her going back. In fact I was very happy. I decided I will take care of myself even better if I stay apart from her. At least I would find an escape from all those tortures.

Slowly and gradually, I got to grips with the situations and managed house-hold work, my job and pregnancy. I got my first salary.

'I want to buy something for each member of the family.' I showed my wish to Kabir.

'But your gift will not be considered. You might also get insulted for that.' said he.

'I know but I have feelings for them. Can I buy?' I responded.

'Better you buy them a new fridge, it would remain as a memorable gift from your first salary but do remember, you won't be given any kind of consideration or appreciation, you might be humiliated so do without any expectations, then don't complain.' he clarified.

'Mom, I have seen few fridges. I want to gift it to the family from my first salary. Please accept it as a token of love.' I called my mother-in-law.

'Who are you to give that? Don't we have money? We are not surviving on your money. Stop doing all that. Keep your money with you. We don't want anything from you, just give some money from your first salary so I can donate them.' said she bluntly.

'Sure mom, it will be my pleasure.' said I.

'Kabir, I have given my best efforts to make your mother happy. I have also tried to live the way she wanted but she is not at all ready to accept anything given by me and still she has not accepted me. She just keeps in touch with me as I am your wife but she has not accepted me by heart. Now onwards, I will also consider her just as your mother not my mother-in-law.' said I.

'But you know you can't do what you say in anger.' said he.

'I know. I think now I should accept it that I am not for the family. I will never be able to be the part of it, whatever I do for her. It would be better that I stop thinking about my complete acceptance by them and must focus on my work.' I accepted with sad face.

'You understood it late but at least you understood.' said he.

'You know Kabir, I used to tell my mom by making fun of her that I would take my little brother with me at my in-laws' place. I will never leave him but today I am not even feeling to buy him a gift from my own salary. I don't know what is stopping me, I always feel what my in-laws would think, what Kabir would think if I help my family or buy something for my siblings. It is true, after marriage a girl's life is changed completely. Government laws might change and take favour of girls but the rituals and bondages of this society can never be favourable to her and sometimes a woman herself gets tired of all that and gives up.' I sad with depressing feelings.

'Please stop thinking much and sleep, I am feeling asleep.' he said by covering himself with the blanket.

My mother-in-law used to come to Bhavnagar every month, used to stay for ten to fifteen days and left. But she never stopped taunting and insulting me for all those matters. She didn't even think about my pregnancy.

'It is alright, our baby will also learn the reality of life from beginning.' said I to Kabir.

'I am sure he/she will learn earlier than you, and will also remain happy and strong by realizing the reality. I want my baby not to be like you, always crying and complaining on the matters. Just accept the reality and enjoy what you have achieved up-to your life. Just be happy. It is your time to be happy and calm. Let the things go on and ignore the stuff.'

'I think you are right. I have earned love and respect of many people, nothing should make difference to me if I don't get it from one person.' somehow Kabir made me accept it and I tried to console myself.

I started enjoying my pregnancy. I started hogging food and made a real pig of myself. I remained active for the whole day. We purchased a car from my savings and used to go out every day for fresh air. We also had nice maternity photography shoot by giving various pregnancy pauses. We kept on making our moments memorable and started dreaming for our new guest. I faced lot of complication in my pregnancy till five months. I used to bleed a lot, the doctor suggested me to have complete bed rest but I kept on working and juggling many jobs together to keep myself away from negative thoughts. I had to take thirty two injections and various kinds of tablets to stop bleeding. We decided to discontinue job after seventh month as I became so heavy due to my weight and was not even able to walk. I got swelling on my legs and entire body.

We were thinking about job and career and my mother-in-law called him,

'We are coming for a small vacation, me, your father, your sister and other two cousins.'

'Most welcome mom, but please can you postpone it for 20 days, as after this month Aditi is going to take leave from her job so she would be able to give her enough time to you. As she is about to complete her seventh month, the college would not allow her to work from eight month. After this semester, she will be relieved by the authority.' informed he.

'No, we will come next week only. We might stay for fifteen days only.'

'Oh! You stay forever, that is not the point.' said he politely.

But she decided to come by next week with the guests. So I made up my mind again to be tortured, this time not only by one woman, but by two. My mother-in-law and sister-in-law. I prayed to God to give me strength for all that.

They came and I bowed down to everyone as usual. I wore a long suit; else I wore trousers and t-shirts at home due to my heavy weight of pregnancy. I used to get up early in the morning as usual, cook for everybody, go for my job, come back after eight years of work, then due to back pain, I used to take some rest for twenty minutes; then go back to kitchen and prepared dinner for all. I must consider my mother-in-law's help in the kitchen. Then we used to sit till 12 o'clock at night and used to have fun, used to go out for some time. I used to get tired a lot but couldn't sleep early at night even after finishing my work. If I did that, they would feel bad so I kept on waking up despite my physical limitations. We enjoyed and they left after fifteen days. This time I ignored the taunts and kept on working without any response.

I gave resignation for my job and decided to take rest at home. I felt quite relaxed. I started watching religious TV serials, started reading good books, used to make different dishes of food at home, started pregnancy yoga, used to spend time with neighbours. With that enjoyment, I completed eight months of my pregnancy. Ninth month started and my mother-in-law came to help me for my delivery. It was my last month so she might have thought not to give me any stress; she kept her mouth shut for few days.

Now it was time to encourage me for normal delivery. But after everybody's motivation, I could not gather courage for final check-ups even in the last month. The doctor also lagged behind due to my less confidence for normal delivery. Finally, we decided to have cesarean or we decided to wait until natural labour pain started.

It was my 2nd anniversary. I bowed down to my mother-in-law and asked for blessings. She did it very well. But she couldn't resist herself and said,

'My son has already wasted much of money behind your pregnancy, at least spare him from paying for cesarean. If you can work for seven months outside with a big tummy, can't you deliver a baby? Where is your courage and confidence now?' scolded she in anger.

'I tried a lot and I am still trying but I am very scared.' I cried.

'What is there to be scared? You people didn't match your horoscopes before marriage that is why you faced a lot of problems during your pregnancy, and because of you, my son also scattered and wasted his lots of money for your recovery.' she blamed me as usual for everything.

'Mom, if we had love-marriage so didn't match horoscopes but bhabhi and bhaiya's horoscopes matched up to 94 %, then why did she have miscarriages for two times?' This time I couldn't shut my mouth.

She didn't reply and went to the kitchen.

'You must have normal delivery as you do some exercise, read good books and also watch T.V else we never had that much time to do all that as we were so busy in handling the family members, you also eat fruits and salad on time, our in-laws never allowed us to do that, even my daughter is in joined family, she also couldn't enjoy all that freely during her pregnancy.   But by chance you found a nice guy with small family, you are enjoying all that. You must have normal delivery.' she kept on taunting me even on my anniversary.

'What is the relation of all that freedom with the normal delivery?' asked I with anger.

We started fighting and Kabir came all of a sudden. He came with a flower and wished me. I was in extreme anger so didn't even look at him. He understood that situation of war of nerves and didn't ask me a single question. He found himself in the war zone. We had our dinner without speaking a single word and without looking at each other. We slept in silence. I wanted him to ask me the reason of my anger, but he didn't ask anything as usual.

'Your mom has never let me enjoy any of my function and festival after marriage. In fact, after engagement. And she will keep on doing it.' said I with anger in the morning.

He gave me a tough look and left the room without speaking a single word. Now it was worthless to share anything with him, too.

Finally, we went to the doctor last time. She advised us to wait for two days. She informed us that if the natural pain didn't start, they would go for cesarean as I was not supporting the doctors to cause fake pains with injection for normal delivery. Two days passed but I didn't face any natural pain so finally we opted for cesarean. I was asked to be admitted to the hospital. The doctors informed me not to eat or drink anything before four hours of operation. I got ready and worshipped the God and my husband and mother-in-law took me to the hospital. I was little nervous but was also very excited to see the face of baby whom I carried for nine months in my womb. We reached to the hospital and I was taken to the operation-theatre. Before entering the theatre, I bowed to my husband and my mother-in-law by touching their feet for blessing. In the theatre, I saw the scissors and knives on the table and I literally got frightened as they decorated all the equipments in sequence to cut my tummy as if my tummy was an apple. I saw another female, they were making him naked by uncovering her bottom. I also heard screaming noise of some female from another room, they might be going through labour pain or delivering the babies. Those scenes terrorized me deeply. I left the room and came out for a while. Then I made up my mind to be confident enough as I didn't have any other option. I went back to the operation room, the nurse gave me to wear hospital gown with snap. I wore it by feeling shy and looking from one corner to another corner of the room. She gave me a miserable and sympathetic smile and asked me to sit on the bed. The anaesthetist came with confidence and talked to me, made me laugh and in between the talks, he asked me to bend for spinal injection. I was given the horrible injection and was lied down the bed. Light of operation theatre was switched on which was above my tummy. They started operation. I was able to see all the doctors using scissors for my operation. I was staring at them and the lamp above me but was not feeling the pain due to injection. I felt my body was dead but my mind was working. I was able to listen their voice, they were talking to one-another in Marathi language so I couldn't understand a single word. All of a sudden, the doctor pulled out a baby from my tummy. The baby started crying, then the nurse took the baby for cleaning. I tried to get up to see my baby but my body didn't favour me. Then I focused on gazing the doctors taking stitches to finish with the operation. They were taking stitches as if they were sewing some cloths. I got astonished to see that and realized they were working on my tummy.

After fifteen minutes, the doctor came near to me and kept my baby to me and said, 'Hai congratulation ! you have been blessed with a baby boy.'

I touched my baby and kissed him with tears in my eyes. The doctor said, 'He has been bestowed the qualities of both the parents - just look at him, he is so fair and handsome.'

I smiled at her with tired face and she asked me to take rest.

She congratulated Kabir and my mom-in-law by handing over the baby to them. Kabir was on the ninth cloud to see him. My mom-in-law called everybody to give the good-news. Everyone became so happy and pleased, my in-laws, my parents, my siblings and all relatives. Everyone congratulated, it was an amazing moment.

The effect of anesthesia got over and I started feeling horrible pain of stitches. But that was natural according to doctors. We were released from the hospital after four days and came home with our new little guest. The delivery rest started, it was very tough time as my health was very weak. After few days of delivery, I fell sick and my veins got pressed. The doctor told if we had not reached to the hospital on time, I might have got the attack of paralysis. There was no one to take care of my baby, from the seventh day I kept on taking care of him. I was missing my mother a lot. Well my mother-in-law gave me delivery food on time, and also took care of me, but she was not able to handle the baby as she never did it before. She didn't like if I asked some baby caring tips from my mother, her ego of being superior in everything used to get hurt. It was very critical condition. One month passed and then we were supposed to shift to Patan for the naming ceremony of the baby. I went there with my in-laws, without my husband as he couldn't take leaves for many days. I didn't achieve my complete recovery. Now I had baby's responsibility and Kabir was also not with me. I was supposed to spend at least a month there till the naming ceremony. It was the month of vacation so many guests came there. I also used to work in the kitchen till late night and at midnight baby didn't allow me to sleep, it was a pathetic condition for me. I didn't even know how to raise a baby, but nobody supported me for that. Everybody got busy in the preparations of function. My sister-in-law and mother-in-law continued taunting me for various things. They said I didn't wash baby's cloths properly, I didn't even take him bath properly and many other things. But they didn't understand that it was just the second month of my operation and I didn't get recovery. The guests also sympathized me but couldn't say anything. All of a sudden, I fell very sick and had fever. I was shivering and was taken to the hospital. I was given some medicine by the doctor. I tried hard to get well soon, one side I was shivering on bed and other side my baby was crying in the cradle. I kept on swinging him with the shivering hand. Nobody helped me though they were free. I got so hurt and wanted to run away from there. I wanted to be either with my husband or with my mother. Finally the naming ceremony took place, my parents and various relatives from my side arrived with lots of gifts for me, baby, and for other members of the family. They also brought gold for me and baby. The function was very nice. My son was given name -Nilkanth. I needed a lot of rest as day by day my health was getting very weak and baby was on breast feeding only so he also became weak. Kabir understood my situation but couldn't do anything and left for his job. I wanted to go to my mother's home for rest after spending one and half month in Patan but mother-in-law didn't give me permission for going with my parents.

'Mom please I beg for your permission, I need a lot of rest. Please allow me to go.' I requested wholeheartedly.

I never felt that kind of pathetic situation, I never begged for anybody's permission to go out of home.

'Don't we give you rest?' asked she in anger.

'If you want to go, it is your choice but first arrange all the parcels of luggage which have been brought by your parents. You do your packing and also take care of baby, none of us is free to help you now.' said she in rough tone.

'But I have severe fever and it is the second month of cesarean. How can I take weight? How can I drag the heavy parcels?' I started crying but nobody cared for it.

But anyhow I wanted to get rid of that negative atmosphere. I took my baby upstairs, kept him on the bed and dragged the heavy parcels. I took whatever was required for the baby and arranged the reaming stuff back. I started my packing. I kept on playing with the baby, kept on shivering due to fever and continued packing. I was about to complete my packing. When they saw I was managing all without anybody's help, they came upstairs and asked,

'Do you need any help?'

'No thanks, it is done.' said I in a polite voice as I didn't want any fight while going from there.

'Let us see what your parents have brought for you and for us.' said my mother-in-law by dragging the parcels towards her.

They kept on seeing the cloths, toys, gold and other things and kept on criticizing for each thing. I felt very bad. Being the only earning member, my father spent two lacks and brought the expensive gifts. I felt so sorry for my parents that their things were not at all appreciated. In fact it was not even taken in consideration. I cursed the decision of getting married to Kabir; else I would have never come in touch with those females. I literally screwed my life by my own.

I was thinking all that and I got call from my mother,

'We are planning to finalize your sister's engagement, they are from Morbi itself and the boy is settled in Dubai. He is an IT manager.'

My mother discussed the matter in details regarding the guy and his family and status.

'Oh! Wow I know the guy. He was with me in commuting. He is a very nice guy but I know nothing about his family members? And did you clarify about Harsha's education and take permission for continuing her career even after her marriage, especially with the mother of a boy?' asked I to my mother.

'Yes we clarified everything, and they know everything about us - our lifestyle and they are forcing us to give Harsha's hand for their son.' said my mom.

'Oh that is nice, at least my sister will not be blamed for trapping a boy.' said I to my mom.

'I hope your mother-in-law is not listening all that.' asked my mom with very slow volume.

'No, she is in another room.' replied I in low voice.

'Hand over the phone to her; I will have a word with her regarding Harsha's engagement. I hope, she would permit you to come.' my mother asked.

She talked to her and also shared everything about the guy and his family.

'Oh, so your sister has also found a guy who lives alone?' asked my mother in-law in a satiric tone.

'No they have found my sister. They are the people who don't believe in caging their daughter-in-laws. They make their steps with the new world so they were in search of a working girl who knows time management for good and creative things, and don't waste her time in unnecessary and nonsense things which hurt others. So they have found my sister and my family for their educated son.' replied I in a taunting voice.

Finally, I came to Morbi with my father. My siblings welcomed the new baby with the shower of flowers. I entered inside and they took Nilkanth from me. It was an amazing feeling to go to your mother's home with your baby. I sat on the bed and started crying and speaking,

'I will never go back there, especially without Kabir.'

'Don't say anything, we know everything. Now we will not send you there without your husband, our daughter is not for all that.' said my mother tears in her eyes.

I stopped calling her and even sometimes stopped receiving her calls.

I felt very seek; my father took me to the laboratory for medical report. The report clarified that I had only 6% of haemoglobin which was very risky for the mother and the child. My mother kept on caring for me like anything; she took care of Nilkanth - (my son) by waking up for nights and nights. I got recovery within a week and enjoyed my sister's engagement. Kabir also came for attending the function. I stayed for one and half month at my mother's place and had all the training of baby caring.

Kabir came to receive me and we directly went to Bhavnagar. My mother-in-law wanted to me to come back to Patan. She didn't understand how difficult it was to do the packing again and again with the baby. We didn't follow her this time, and went directly to Bhavnagar. Now I was all alone to take care of the baby as well as the home. I was finding many difficulties to handle him alone with the house hold work.

After few days, I got a mail from my university. I was supposed to appear my 4th RPR of PhD. I was required to be present there for my presentation. I got extremely nervous as with the baby it was very difficult to prepare the presentation I couldn't appear for the previous presentation due to my pregnancy, as I was not allowed to travel the long route.

In the evening Kabir returned from office. I gave him this news. He asked me to start preparation anyhow and then promised me to take me there by hook or crook.

While discussion he said,

'Now, I want to give you a surprising news?'

'Surprising news? Now what is it?' asked I with surprise.

'Do you remember the interview which I gave before a month for abroad?'

'Yes.' I replied by narrowing down my eyebrows.

'I have been selected for that.'

'So?' asked I without giving any reactions.

'So, I am planning to join there.'

'What? Kabir, are you made? Have you thought about me and Nilkanth?'

'Of course I have thought about you and him, that is why I have taken this decision.'

'Then where will I go?' asked I

'You will come with me of course; I will not leave you alone here. I will take you with me but first I will have to go alone for three months. If I am comfortable with the place, weather and job, I will apply for your Visa and within three to four months you will get the dependent visa and I will come to receive you.' said he.

'Three to four months without you? And where will I stay?' asked I.

'It is your choice, where you want to go? Patan or Morbi?'

'I want to go to hell.' I got frustrated.

'But ou are already in the hell.' He gave me a tough look. After a while, he said, 'I want you to travel to heaven but for four months, ou will have to remain in hell again. I am sorry, I can't help it. But you have choice- you can go to your mother's house instead of Patan, I don't mind.' he said very clearly.

'Definitely I want to go to Morbi but I don't want to give opportunity to the society to criticize our family so I will have go to Patan ideally and for some days I will go to my mother's place also.' replied I.

'Ok, good decision.'

'By the way which country?'

'Lolongwe - Malawi.'

'An African country?'

'Yes.'

'And you said yes?'

'What is wrong with that?'

'I have heard about these countries, people are not safe there. I will not let you go there. Anytime firing starts there and people are robbed a lot. At least think about our little champ, what if something would happen to him? I have also heard that people don't go out after 6:00 pm. and also don't go on foot. I will not allow you to go there alone. You are well settled here, you have a government job, and we are also going to buy a flat soon. Do you want to leave all that? Why?' I asked various questions while feeding the baby.

'It is not only for money but for new experience, new adventures. You should not judge any place before going there or leading the life style of it. Of course we will have to play very safe there but that would be the part of our new adventure and experience. And you always wanted to go to abroad for your further education and career. Then what happened today?' asked Kabir.

'At least let Nilkanth grow up, and then we will think. It is not the right time for flying. I have been shifting since my pregnancy, now I want to have some relaxation from packing and all, I am tired. Isn't it too early to fly?' I asked.

'It is now or never. In fact this is the right time for flying as you are going to stay at home only due to baby. You are not going to work until Nilkanth goes to school. So you bring him up here or there, what makes difference? And as far as your packing is concerned, it would be your last packing as the contract is for two years. If we are alright with each other, me and the company – I can sign another contract of two years more. But now take the note of minimum two years.' clarified Kabir.

'Isn't it too early as the baby....?' I wanted to repeat the same issue and he interrupted, 'Don't take baby's name; nothing is too early or too late for good and progressive matters. Everything comes on right time for good. If we think a lot, we will never be able to do anything in life. Sometimes some decisions should be taken without thinking much.' finally he convinced me.

'Until the arrival of your visa, you finish your PHD work as much as you can.'

'Alright, I trust you blindly.' said I.

We discussed everything with our parents. None of our parents were ready to let us go to abroad and leave the country; especially they were worried about the child. My mother was very sad as her one daughter got engaged in Dubai and the another one was well settled in India, then also they planned to go to Lilongwe. She thought life might be better there or more miserable than India.

'But why do you want to go? For money?' asked my mother-in-law.

'For money and for new experience.' Kabir replied

Somehow he convinced everybody and put their minds at his for his right decision. Finally we started selling our things which were not required, some we sent to Patan which were needed there, like fridge, T.V and other appliances. We didn't sell the kitchen crockery by keeping that note in mind that we might come back to India after two years. Kabir finally resigned for his government job.

After few days, Kabir took me to the university for my Presentation. We went there by taking my three month's old little baby. I finished the RPR presentation before his leaving for the abroad.

My in-laws came to pick me up and we left for Patan. I cried a lot as I was very attached to my neighbours so did they. Kabir got the flight for Sharjah and changed the flight for Malawi and reached to an another continent. We reached Patan. We were welcomed nicely with my bhabhi. Again I was away from Kabir for three to four months. And I was again in the same place where I never wanted to come without Kabir. I was very scared and nervous as that time I was with my baby so I had a lot of responsibilities of him too. I decided to remain calm, and decided not to fall in any arguments whatever she says or even beats me. I thought it was just the matter of few months. I decided to keep calm at the utmost level.

Few days passed, I was missing my husband a lot. He used to call me every day. He was also missing me and the family of course. After few days, I got a mail from university again for the submission of my synopsis and presentation.

My mom-in-law didn't like if I used to talk in English with my professors as she used to feel very inferior. When I used to talk to my professor, she always looked through me to decrease my values.

'Nowadays, girls teach English language to their children but don't teach them any morals of life.' She taunted me for using English language for my professional matters.

I ignored it and requested to her, 'Mom, I will have to prepare a lot for my presentation and my synopsis, we will have to go the university for that. I need your help and support.'

'So do you want to continue your study still, even after child?' asked she.

'Please mom, I have been working for my PHD since four years. It is on the verge of completion. I want to finish it at least. I might not start a job for few years but I want to complete my education.' said I in a begging tone.

'The girls of today, nobody can convince them. Anyways it is your wish. If you want to do, you manage it with baby. We can spare you from some household work for few days but baby's responsibility is yours only. You do if you can handle both.' she said by drinking tea.

'I tried a lot for preparation but baby doesn't allow me to focus on work, please play with him for some time so I can focus on my work.' I literally begged like a beggar. I never felt that kind of impotency for my education.

But she knew it was very difficult to handle a baby along with study. She was sure I won't be able to do that. So she spared me from household work to show her support in front of everybody. But didn't even touch the baby for a while. Although she used to buy a lot of clothes and shoes for him to show everybody how intimate she was with her grandson. She didn't give me permission for going to my mother's place for my preparation. I was in a critical situation as I was not able to focus on my work due to Nilkanth as he was just four months old and he didn't like to sleep more than six hours a day.

'I thought after the child, she will leave everything and will stay at home only but she is not leaving anything. She is stretching herself too much and doing hard work for her career, anyways it is her choice.' said my mother-in-law to my sister-in-law on phone, fortunately I listened everything. I understood her intentions but I kept my courage high and started preparing by waking up nights and nights. I started feeling sick but didn't give up. I requested my mother-in-law to come with me to the university.

'You are the only one whom I trust and can leave Nilkanth with you when I am inside the class for my presentation. Else give me permission to go to my mom's place, she will definitely help me with this.' said I to provoke her to help me.

She didn't want my parents to take credit for helping me out for my career after marriage so she said, 'No I will come with you, else people will say Aditi's in-laws are not supportive, that is why she is still taking help of her parents. We will have to hire a car, the driver might take one thousand rupees and petrol charges will be extra but what to do….you girls…' she reminded me for those expenses but didn't give a single reminder to the money I earned during my pregnancy while working in the college. It was around three and half lacks but there was no value of my money earned by honesty and hard-work. But I didn't speak a single word as anyhow I wanted to complete my work in the absence of my husband.

'Dear, you want some money for fees or anything?' asked my father-in-law, the greatest person whom I adore and respect a lot by heart.

My mind can never be unoccupied from all those troubling and critical days. One side I was preparing for my presentation, other side; I was changing Nilkanth's pants, cleaning his potty. The date was just one day far for my presentation. On the previous night of presentation, I started packing my bag. I kept my papers, documents, wallet, pen drive, hard disk, and other required stuff for presentation and in the same bag I kept my son's cloths, diapers, drops, napkins, etc. I was juggling with numerous things at a same time. My head was spinning and I kept on working in the negative atmosphere. My mother-in-law's envy was at the top of the niddle as I was managing everything by my own. I couldn't control her inferior complex. I realized on that day that it was the toughest work on earth to take care of a baby single-handedly. That was the real exam of my life. I was missing Kabir a lot.

She came with me to the university and helped me at least for my work. I gave my baby to her. I saw him playing with his grand-mother at the campus. I was giving my presentation but was thinking of my son as he was just four months old and was on breast feeding only. I was worried, he would cry if he felt hungry. And before six months, we were not allowed to give him a single drop of water according to the doctor's suggestion so he was dependent only on mother's milk. Somehow I finished my presentation by popping out of the window again and again to see Nilkanth. My guide also appreciated me for juggling with all the things at a time.

It was not only my mother-in-law and my sister-in-law who jumped with the joy after the birth of my baby but many other women did the same as they thought now it was the end of my career. I started hating women. I never commented negatively on a house-wife but they had a lot of problems with my progress, my independence and freedom, especially with the self-respect and self-confidence which I owned.

I felt too hurt but overcame my tears and continued going ahead in my life and focused on my work.

I felt huge amount of relaxation after that presentation and we also attended a function. I was worried how I would get ready in the function as everyone would be busy. Who will take care of Nilkanth? But I got grips to the situation and I got ready faster than anybody else. But she didn't like my positive quality.

'Oh, you are ready?' asked one of the aunts at the function.

'Yes aunty.' replied I.

'And where is the baby? Is he ready?' asked she.

'Yes aunty, I got him ready first. He is with his grand-father.'

'Oh! Great. Your daughter-in-law is very smart and fast. She got ready for the function so soon, although she is a mother of a very little baby. We are still thinking what to wear and she is ready!' she appreciated me in front of my mother-in-law.

But she couldn't tolerate my praise and criticized my quality of getting ready fast and said, 'You are living alone, so you have got practice of handling everything single-handedly. It is not a big deal, my daughter is in joined family so she can't take the decision by her own, else she would have also got ready fast and by her own.'

Again she started comparing me with everyone, taunted me by giving the examples of nuclear family and joined family. She could never tolerate my appreciation. Sometimes I used to think and asked Kabir, 'Is she your real mother or step-mother? A mother always wants to see her children happy and progressive but she is not even happy to see you happy and independent. She also compares you with everyone and lets you down, it is too much.'

I just ignored the taunts and enjoyed the function, as it was the matter of one week only. I was counting the days to go to my mother's place. Now I was really wanted to go to abroad, I didn't mind if I was robed or killed by anybody over there or I was supposed to remain at home for the whole day, anything would be better than that kind of humiliation of each second. I was feeling suffocation and wanted to find an escape really. I realized 'Settling down in abroad' would be my escape. It could be the worst country on the planet but for me it could be a heaven.

I went to my mother's place. I took a lot of rest and satisfaction of life. I had my flight after a month. I again got a call from the university for next presentation and I was supposed to submit my pre-synopsis of my research. I went to the University for the further process with my mother with the fifth month old baby. I wanted to finish my official matters before I left for Lolongwe. I finished the official formalities and was asked to give my final viva online. I also submitted my thesis. I felt so relaxed after that.

Finally, Kabir came to India after three and half months. He came with my ticket. My parents wanted my in-laws to come to our place. My parents sent them warm invitation.

'We will definitely come.' said my father in law in a gentle tone.

'Actually we might not come but what would people say if we don't come to your place? They might think there would be something wrong between both the families.' she spoke negative as usual.

But my parents kept quite as we got used to with her taunts by the time. We were already expecting that kind of response from her.

We started preparation for the welcome of Kabir and his parents. They came and we welcomed them with the shower of flowers as they came first time to our place. We offered them various varieties of food, fresh fruits and also offered them various gifts. Finally I left my mother's place and went with them. I was feeling very emotional, tears were rolling down on my cheeks, my parents and siblings also became very emotional. We hugged each other and left for good.

It is said in chapter - 2, shloka -57

यः सर्वत्रानभिस्नेहस्तत्तत्प्राप्य शुभाशुभम्।
नाभिनन्दति न द्वेष्टि तस्य
प्रज्ञा प्रतिष्ठिता॥५७॥

Free from attachment at all times, he is unaffected by good or bad – neither rejoicing in it nor repulsing it, he is of a steady intellect.

Some situations in life make us detached from all positive and negative emotions. This detachment can lead us either into positive direction or into negative. My detached feelings might have directed me towards mental disorder if the path of escape might not have been selected.

CHAPTER 13

Next day, we got the flight for Lilongwe. It was very difficult to leave the motherland. I felt nostalgic when I was bidding bye to my in-laws at the Ahmadabad airport. I flew first time. It was a new journey of life with my little kid and husband. I was scared as well as excited for new adventures. I was also worried for the upbringing of Nilkanth single-handedly in a new atmosphere and crowd. Finally we landed to Lilongwe air-port at 11:30 at night. We finished the formalities at the airport; Kabir's company driver came to receive us with the car.I found Negroes everywhere. I held my baby tightly and kept on walking with fear in heart. I got into the car swiftly to hide my son from the sight of everyone around us. We reached to the flat given by the company. Kabir was also provided a car and other expenses by the company. We reached home around 12:30 at night. I made Nilkanth sleep in the room. It was a two bhk full furnished flat, although it was an old flat but full of facilities. A collection of crockery was also available. Everything was nice and new. We got fresh and slept. We were extremely tired. Kabir needed to go to the office next morning; it was not possible for him to keep a day off. So he left for the office at 6:30 in the morning. I was all alone at home with Nilkanth. I got my feet cold and was looking out from the thin line of the window by raising the curtains. I saw many black people sweeping the colony. I was observing them. I kept on holding my baby tightly for long as I was scared somebody would come, break the door for robbery and might snatch away him from me.

I was feeling very hungry but there was nothing to eat at home. I drank little milk kept in the fridge and found some biscuits to eat. I breast fed my baby but I was hungry. I couldn't even call Kabir as I did have neither internet connection nor local sim-card. I kept on waiting for Kabir till he came back from office. One of the ladies from neighbourhood came to invite me for lunch. Her husband was also working in the same company in which mine. She came around 3:00 o'clock. I went to her house for lunch with my baby. She offered me Dal-rice. I literally hogged the food due to my extreme hunger. For two-three days, we ordered tiffins for lunch and dinner. I was waiting for Kabir to get free time on Sunday. We went out to buy grocery and started making food at home. Slowly and gradually, I arranged the home properly. I found a nice group of ladies in the colony.We also started going out even at night for ice-cream. We made a very good group of friends. Slowly we came to know that the local public of Lilongwe was even better than Indian one. They were very happy, jolly and innocent people. They had a lot of respect and love for children their mothers. Everyday females came to sell vegetables and fruits in the colony, they became my good friends. I found a good hearted maid who became my friend. I just felt uncomfortable on the first day, and then I got used to with the place and weather. My little champ became the hero of the colony as he was the only little child in the colony so everyone used to play and talk to him while coming and going. I never found that I was not able to go out; nor I found any difficult situation for survival. I found a lot of freedom and space for myself.

'Our assumption was quite wrong about the people of here. They are so nice, helpful and innocent. And Asian people are also very nice here, they are extremely helpful and amiable to each other.' I shared my feelings with Kabir.

'That is why I asked you not to judge a place or people without visiting them.' said he

'Yes, you were absolutely right. I don't want to go back now, I am very happy here.' I said while changing cloths of Nilkanth.

I used to call my parents and my in-laws, and gave positive reviews about the place and the people.

'You must be happy; today's girls want that only, friends and freedom. But we have the value of family, so we are happier with the family.' taunted my mother- in-law even being across the seven seas.

She kept on doing it every day. Again a fight took place between me and my husband regarding this. I didn't complain for five months;when she crossed her limits, I couldn't control myself and said, 'Your mother doesn't spare me even here. Now what have I done?' asked I.

'Now what can I do? Due to all those quarrels, I took the decision to shift here. Now you will have to manage on phone or stop calling and receiving. I don't mind.' he uttered in little anger.

I was forced to keep distance with her, not only geographically but also mentally. I stopped sharing all the new things happening over there with us. I stopped sharing my new experiences with new places and people. We enjoyed lots of parties, visited new places. I used to share everything with her and also used to send photographs. But she always took all things in other way round so I stopped sharing anything with her. I decided to use just two words on phone, 'Yes' and 'No'. I had to do that to make her realize her blunders. I was not doing it by heart as I really considered her as my mother but sometimes her behaviour and animosity on phone forced me to behave harshly with her. I focused on my work. I started writing articles and books at home as I was not able to go out for job due to my little kid.

Six years passed. Our contract in Lilongwe got over for third time. We didn't sign the next one. We went to Canada for our job and stayed there for four years. After that, we worked in U.K for three years. I also started working in all those countries. I used to teach, used to write at freelance and became a professional speaker. My husband also kept on doing well in his work and further education. My son also became mature and independent. Things went well. We didn't select India for our profession for few years due to family issues. Of course we used to visit the motherland often for functions and festivals but didn't choose to settle down there for few years.

'I was a family oriented girl, always wanted to work and cherish with family but nobody understood me.' I expressed my grief to Kabir. 'We never get everything in life. Sometimes I think would I ever be able to make your mother happy even if I had stopped working and just had kept myself up to the house-hold work?' asked I to Kabir while doing my exercise.

He thought for a while and said, 'No, never. It is all up to natural tuning. Despite making extreme efforts, you both could not make place into each other's heart that shows it was not in your luck.' he said while drinking coffee.

'But even today, I love her and respect her.' I said by wiping my sweat.

'Then keep on doing it, but don't try to show it and also don't expect anything. That is the way of calm life. I also love her but don't show it or tell it, just perform your role honestly.' explained he.

'I think the distance of these many years between us might bring some changes in the situation and now she might understand me and accept me wholeheartedly.'

'Again you are making the mistakes of keeping expectations, better stop pushing your luck.' said he clearly.

'Leave about her, have you understood her yet?' asked he

'No.'

'Then? The distance of years you also faced but you are right at your end, and she might be at hers.'

'Then what about the bad words and intentions that she used for me?'

'Forget and forgive - the law of calm life.' he said.

'But I will always regret on one thing in my life?'

'What is it?' asked he.

'That I came in between you and your mother, I never ever intended that. I just wanted to be the part of the family, I never wanted to be the reason of split. I wanted my son to be bestowed love and blessings from his grand-parents. I always dreamed about a happy family around me. My child couldn't spend his childhood with his grand-parents, he couldn't play with them. Sometimes, I think; if there had be some another independent girl in your life, you would have faced the same problem if I think on the ground on a woman's insecurity for another woman.' I continued speaking in that direction.

He didn't speak for a while;then said, 'stop thinking much and focus on your article that you are writing now.' said he.

'She herself kept us away from her for so many years; else we would have definitely settle down in India.' I couldn't stop thinking and said.

'I do agree but that might be in our destiny. Well there is nothing wrong in that. If distance makes one happy and calm, it is better than everyday's quarrel.' clarified he.

'Hmmm. But, I curse myself for some reasons. I was portrayed what I was not. It can be a wonderful relation between a daughter-in-law and a mother-in-law if they gather understanding. No friendship can be better than this. I regret, I couldn't get love from the most important woman in my life, I considered her as my mother. Somewhere, I might be wrong or somewhere, my destiny didn't favour me to have that love and respect. Hope I get it in my next birth!' I continued speaking.

'By the way, why are you saving money for buying a flat in Lilongwe?' He interrupted by asking it.

'As the weather is very good over there and people are also nice. I enjoyed living there a lot.' I replied by looping my arms around my neck.

'But it was before ten years, why would you go there again?' asked my husband

'Might be for another escape.'

'Another escape? But from whom?'

'From my daughter-in-law, first I found an escape from my mother-in-law and progressed and lived my life the way I wanted to live. I might need it again after few years, or my daughter-in-law might need an escape from me for her progress or for her freedom. I may be broad minded and full of disciplined but she might not get adjusted with my discipline and my thoughts. She might not like to read books till late night. She might like to go for parties till late nights. She might not like to get up early in the morning, she might not be interested in regular exercise or worshiping the God. She might be the lover of bed-tea without brushing the teeth. I don't want to be the villain of her life, it would be her life and if my son is happy with all that, I wouldn't want to interfere. 'Leave your designation on time and give chance to others.' I think this is the motto of happy life in this century. We must go through all the stages of life on time described according to the Vedas. We have already gone through two stages - Brahmacharya and Grihastashram. we are in third stage-Vanaprasthashram and performing our duties nicely. Soon time would arrive for the fourth ashram- Sanyasashram. In this century, we might not able to leave materialistic aspects of life but at least we can continue enjoying them being in this materialistic world by keeping ourselves sanyasis who just try to unite their heart and mind to reach the crescendo of life and that is satisfaction. If he is satisfied, he will definitely get moksha. You get that satisfaction of life if you renounce some desires behind like - expectations, ego, attitude, fears, hopes, duties, responsibilities, moh, maya, etc. We just need to enjoy the life the way it comes without any interference and any expectations. We just need to keep on working without expecting fruits. That busy life for good works will keep us away from this materialistic world although we are the part of it and this contended heart will help us to connect with the Almighty God. In future, I don't want to be the victim nor want anybody else to be the victim of generation gap or difference of thoughts. Everyone has the right to live their life the way they want.' I gave a small philosophical lecture by getting impacted by The Bhagavad Gita and the Vedas.

'Oh ! My philosopher ! So you will send them to Lilongwe from beginning?' asked Kabir.

'Yes, on the second day of their marriage if they want or I might shift there to give them freedom.' said I with confidence.

'Don't you think you would create much distance from beginning?' asked he.

'No, my this distance will bring them near to me forever by heart not just for formality. The freedom that I would give them, will prevent them from having negative freedom.' I said with little confidence.

'Oh! Deep thinking my author, hope you succeed in your future plans.'

We laughed loudly while enjoying coffee.

'Buy the way, what about your article? Did you publish it in U.K newspaper?' asked my husband.

'No, I have sent it for the column of Times of India as it is for Indian society.'

'Do you want the people of small towns of India to read it?'

'Not only for the people of small towns. It is applicable for all those ones who possess narrow thinking for girls' education and work, especially after their marriage and for those ones who cage their daughter-in-laws and take away their freedom of thoughts by providing them a lot of gold and force them to consider that gold as real ornament but not their self-respect.'

'It has been selected and will be published in tomorrow's newspaper; I just had a word with editor and the publisher.'

'Oh great! Congratulations. By the way where is it? Let me read it.'

'Sure, here it is.' said I by handing over the print out of it.

Article :

A GIRL'S LIFE IS LIKE HIBISCUS

Dream is like a glitter which glints in every human-being's heart and mind. Today's parents, dominated by the dreams, start dreaming for their child since the child is spotted as a seed in the womb. They want their children to climb the ladder of success in their personal and professional life. Going with the positive flow, today's parents have put the gender discrimination aside. They also cultivate their girl child like a beautiful flower. They want her to be well-versed in each area. Like, education, Singing, dancing, cooking, technology, house-hold work, disciplines, etiquettes, etc. Parents assure themselves that their daughter is someone else's asset so they think if she is smart enough, she would be respected everywhere and will be able to live her happy independent life.

These cleverly cultivated girls similize the hibiscus flowers which are also abundant with admirable qualities. Hibiscus flowers are the showy blossoms that grow nearly in warm, tropical climes. In the same way, every daughter is nourished fresh and showy in the atmosphere of love and warm of her parents. Hibiscus flowers are available in various colors. Likewise, a girl also diversifies her bright and beautiful colors according to their age under the motivation of her parents. Hibiscus flowers are utilized in food and decoration; it is also tucked on the head behind the ear of any pretty girl to raise her beauty. In the same way, a girl is also decorated as a crown on her father's head and becomes his proud. Hibiscus is used in medicine; likewise, a mature girl also bestows relief in the tough time of family. Thus, all the parents up-bring their daughter like a flower makes her competent enough and sees plenty of dreams for her brighter future. They also want to find a great bride-groom and good family so that she could continue living her beautiful life and fulfilling her all dreams.

Now the burning questions arise.....

- *Does the same parents make all these efforts for their daughter-in-law?*
- *Do they allow her grab all these opportunities?*
- *Do they allow her fulfill her all dreams?*
- *Why do the same parents force their daughter-in-law stop her life?*
- *Why the demand of sacrifice from her?*
- *Isn't a daughter-in-law a daughter of somebody?*
- *If they spread the net of restrictions for their daughter-in-law, how can they forget that their daughter is also going to be somebody's daughter-in-law?*

Various so-called restrictions make each girl feel that marriage is the end of the life. Each girl mentally prepares herself for changes after marriage but negative beliefs and attitude which are just created by the society lead them towards the frustration. She might not have even thought that she would have to forget wearing her beautiful cloths just because she is married. Generally Indian educated/working girls face various these kinds of unaccepted restrictions. She encourages herself to fight with the wrong beliefs of the society and elders around her but slowly and gradually she mentally gets tired and considers this phase as the end of life and starts living the way she is forced. She blames her destiny and gradually enthusiasm and life inside her dies and she becomes the robot which is controlled by the remote control of social petty perceptions. In the same way, hibiscus dies in one day after its various usages. Thus the chapter of a girl's life also comes to an end after one phase of her life - The phase is her bachelor life.

Like hibiscus flower doesn't want water for its growth, it just wants cool and warm atmosphere. Likewise, a girl also doesn't want only wealth and materialistic aspects; she just wants her self-respect, motivation and love for living a happy life and for progressive career.

All most the girls do not escape from responsibilities but they just want a little freedom to maintain these responsibilities by heart. They beg to live their life as an independent female even after becoming a wife, daughter-in-law and mother. But her life is suppressed after her bachelor phase of life and they kill their all hopes and dreams. The death of life in a girl's living body resembles the hibiscus flower which also dies in a day after spreading happiness in the life of others.

Florists are giving their best efforts to enhance the age of hibiscus flower by providing required substances. We wish a girl's life; happiness and dreams would also prolong even after their one phase (Bachelor life) by the positive views of the society and people around her.

It is said in Bhagavad Geeta in chapter- 18, shloka-49

असक्तबुद्धिः सर्वत्र जितात्मा विगतस्पृहः।
नैर्ष्कम्यसिद्धिं परमां संन्यासेनाधिगच्छति।।४९।।

One whose intellect is unattached,
who has conquered himself, who is devoid
of all attachments, likes or yearning,
such a one attains supreme perfection in
selfless action through renunciation or sanyas.

It is difficult to renounce everything and take sanyas but some situations make us follow the path of distance. For that path one is required to conquer his mind and heart and the distance helps one to realize the importance of the person and things which were left. Sometimes, distance also helps to make a person calm as far as the relations are concerned.

CHAPTER 14

It is the law of life. If we want to succeed, nobody can help us excepting ourselves. The best relations of us might stand beside us but they also can't take stand or decision for us. They might take us to water but we are supposed to go ahead for drinking it. We are always motivated and encouraged by our well wishers but we ourselves need to pay the price of hard-work, honesty, sincerity and discipline for our success in any area. Thousand times we raise and fail while achieving our goals. We feel emotionally strong when we find people around us laughing with us when we are at the top ladder of our success and the same people also make us weak by laughing at us when we are at the bottom ladder of our success. The form of success might be anything – our job, education, marriage, social relationships, family terms, etc.

In our society, many ambitious girls suffer at the extreme level and struggle for continuing their career. Not only career minded girls but clever and smart girls also face problems of envy, especially when they turns to be a daughter-in-laws from daughters. She is forced to stop dreaming after marriage. There is nothing wrong to respect the elders or to look upon them; it is our moral duty but there is a vast difference between duty and slavery. At many places, the daughter-in-law is forced to go through mental slavery and forced to leave her dreams and ambitions without any reason. Already she takes a new birth after marriage which is full of responsibility. She accepts everything but she is broken mentally and become mentally paralyzed when she is not given her self-respect and freedom to fulfil her dreams. Young generation is always blamed for its behaviour and actions. The society discusses the matter of the generation gap which almost the time points out the wrong attitude of children towards their parents and elders. Are the juveniles always wrong?

A woman is always found an enemy of another woman in almost the cases. A woman faces huge amount of humiliation by a woman herself for the entire life and she repeats the history for another woman. But nobody tries to find out any solution or escape. They just keep on tolerating it. Sometimes a woman herself is responsible for her destroy and tyranny. Before women used to face tyranny on physical ground but now in this century they face it on mental ground. There is no escape for them since long.

Women almost the time play the role of sailors who sail in the same boat in the ocean which is full of salty water. Here the ocean of salty water is the metaphor of a woman's tendency of blaming others or complaining about the situations. Here are some common exemplifications of this salty water which spread various diseases in the mind of any normal woman:

'I couldn't continue my career after marriage as I had a lot of responsibilities.'

'I couldn't do anything after marriage as I was not permitted by my in-laws and we were in joined family.'

'I couldn't do anything as I got busy in the upbringing of children.'

Often we avail of these kinds of excuses for our failure. We also possess birth right of becoming a smart critic who criticize the successful women in a smart way. We love to blame the successful women to be lucky enough for their success rather than their rigorous efforts. We blindly give our assurance regarding their powerful background and upbringing for their success. Above all we criticize them for their lack of attention for their families and children.

That is strongly acceptable that situations play vital role in one's success but are these only situations? Sometimes it is difficult to under control the situation but efforts to change the individual can change the situation too.

Sometimes it is pretty good to have intrapersonal communication to get some answers hidden within.

'Can't I blame myself for few things to change my life and my situation?'

'Can't I ignore people's criticism and keep on moving with trust in myself?'

'Can't I change myself for my success?"

'Can't I find an escape from my situation for my self-respect and freedom?'

Nobody else can give the answers of these questions excepting ourselves.

We never wanted to fall apart from our family but situation made us take that decision. We made all reliable efforts to be with family but none of the effort waved a magic wand and we gave up the ghost. At last, we had to select the last escape of staying away from family for years for self-respect and independence. After thirteen years, we settled down in India. I and my husband both found an appropriate job there. I was very happy when we were welcomed with open arms by my mother-in-law. I found strong bonding in our relationship, far better than before. The distance among us changed everything and made us realize the importance of each other. My mother-in-law hugged me and kissed me on my forehead. She took me to the Music-school started by her especially for girls. My bhabhi also started her small tuition institute near by home. Now everybody used to talk about education, progress of an individual and making steps with the new and developing world. The atmosphere of home was full of positive vibrations.

I requested to my mother -in-law, 'Mom, let us stay together under one roof, please.'

'No dear, after a long time, we have found an escape from the golden cage, let it be continue, let us not get ourselves caged again.'

'Golden cage?' asked I by making tea for her.

'Yes, the gold which played the vital role of being the devil in disguise for many years and caged us for the entire life.'

'I didn't get you mom.'

'Here gold is the metaphor of the negative thoughts about daughter-in-laws, fake social rituals, bondage, fake beliefs. We women have faced a lot and also forced other women like you to continue the heritage of taking the bondage of that gold. We lost our self-respect by our own. We ruled one-another. Your distance made me understand how wrong I was. You were always right. I was not favoured by my elders to fulfill my ambitions but I must not have repeated the history, I must have supported my young generation to have their rights. I could have supported you; I regret for it now. Now it is time for me to find an escape from all these desires and duties. I want to enjoy my work for my self-esteem, self-satisfaction and for my freedom. I enjoy being at school. I feel so glad when I see those independent young girl students and teachers full of life and confidence. Let me enjoy my freedom, dear. Of course I will always be there for my children in their tough times but I want my space, too' said she holding my hand.

By listening to her words, first I booked the flat in Lilongwe by calling the dealer. I hugged her and touched her feet for blessings.

I was shocked to listen those words from her, it was unbelievable. My father-in-law gave me a smile full of satisfaction and patted me on my shoulder positively. I literally felt myself the daughter of that house. It was wonderful and incredible feelings. We used to meet our in-laws in week-ends and used to go out for dinner after hard work of the whole week. Now each member of our family became independent and busy in his and her own work and also started earning. But the get-to-gather of the family was the awesome time among all those works. Everyone used to have a lot of experiences of their workplace to share with one another. We never got bored of our life, work and relations. We were also allowed to wear whatever we wanted to wear. It was such an awesome feeling of freedom. I didn't even feel to go to my mother's place. I was so satisfied that my parents' dream came true of making their daughters really educated and independent.

I found my escape with the help of my courage and motivation of my husband. That doesn't mean that we need to go away from our relatives or loved ones but we are required to raise our voice against injustice for our freedom and self-respect.

Hope each woman gives her best to find her own escape for her dreams and ambitions.

It is said in Bhagavad Geeta in chapter- 6, shloka-7

जितात्मन: प्रशान्तस्य परमात्मा समाहित:।
शीतोष्णसुखदु:खेषु तथा मानापमानयो:॥७॥

The Supreme Lord Himself abides
in that emancipated one,
who remains steady and unperturbed
even whilst dwelling in heat and cold,
pleasure and pain, honour and dishonour.

God always helps those who remain steady in any situation of life. The situation may be good or bad but one needs to go through penance to achieve that status of mind. I with the help of escape, tried to achieve that status.

यदा यदा हि धर्मस्य ग्लानिर्भवति भारत।
अभ्युत्थानमधर्मस्य तदात्मानं सृजाम्यहम्।।७।।

Talking of His manifestation on earth, the Lord says:
Whenever *dharma* declines and *adharma* prevails,
I manifest Myself.

It has been said in Bhagavad Geeta in chapter -4, shloka -7 that Lord manifests himself on earth when adharma and injustice go beyond. He might not show his form that we see in the idols, he can arrive in any form, may be in the form of our friend, family member, guest, neighbour, teacher, classmate anyone. He won't solve the problems on our behalf but he would just show us the right path to do the right things. He pushes us to come out of the problems, like Shri Krishna did it by being the charioteer of Arjuna in Mahabharata war. Even in this century, He might be around us in any form as our friend or philosopher but He will just guide us, it is only we who will have to fight for ourselves for any situation of life.